# Information Technology Infrastructure and Its Management

# Information Technology Infrastructure and Its Management

(As Per New Syllabus Prescribed by U.P. Technical University, Lucknow)

**For IIIrd Semester B.Tech CS & IT Branch (ECS-304)**
**VIIIth Semester B.Tech IT Branch (TIT-802)**
**Includes Test Papers Modeled on the Latest UPTU Question Papers**

**SHAKUNTALA CHOUDHARY**
M.Tech, BE,
Faculty (Computer Science & Engg.)
Bansal Institute of Engg & Technology, Lucknow

**PRIYANKA SRIVASTAVA**
MBA From ICFAI University, B.Tech,
Faculty (Information Technology)
Bansal Institute of Engg & Technology, Lucknow

Khanna Book Publishing Co. (P) Ltd.
Delhi

Copyright © 2010 by **Khanna Book Publishing Co. (P) Ltd.**

This book is sold subject to the condition that it shall not, by way of trade or otherwise, be lent, resold, hired out, or otherwise circulated without the publisher's prior consent in any form of binding or cover other than that in which it is published and without a similar condition including this condition being imposed on the subsequent purchaser and without limiting the rights under copyright reserved above, no part of this publication may be reproduced, stored in or introduced into retrieval system, or transmitted any form or by any means (electronic, mechanical, photocopying, recording or otherwise), without the prior written permission of both the copyright owner and the above mentioned publisher of this book.

ISBN: 978-93-80016-39-9

**First Edition 2010**

**Reprint : 2014**

Published by:

**Khanna Book Publishing Co. (P) Ltd.**

1694-95, Nai Sarak, Delhi-110006 (India)
Phone: 011-23283211, 23256658
Mobile: +91-9312459590, 9810362434
Fax: 011-23256658
E-mail: contact@khannaedu.com
Website: www.khannaedu.com

*Cover Design & Layout by*
Limited Colors

*Printed in India*
Mehak Offset Printers, Delhi

**Dedicated**

**to**

My "**FATHER**"

Late Shri Ramji Lal Jhajhria

— *Shakuntala Choudhary*

**Dedicated**

**to**

My "**NANAJI**"

Late Shri Krishan Mohan Srivastava

— *Priyanka Srivastava*

# Preface

**IT Infrastructure Management:** Present day business operations are integral with the information technology that supports them. The business infrastructure should provide a secure, resilient and flexible environment that enables execution of processes, applications and enterprises in sync with technological innovation. IT Infrastructure Integration services aims at "Enabling Business Operations with High Performance Infrastructure Solutions" through a comprehensive set of services to support the design, development, installation and operations of complex networks.

A wide spectrum of IT Infrastructure services is provided through a continuous life cycle of "Analyze, Design, Implement, Stage and Manage".

**AUTHORS**

# Acknowledgement

It is with a great sense of satisfaction that we acknowledge the help and support rendered to us by many people in bringing this book in its current form.

I (Shakuntala Choudhary) especially thanks to my loving husband Surjeet Singh (MBA, IIM Lucknow), my mother, elder sister & Priyanka Srivastava for their kind support. Also express my gratitude to my Principle Prof. (Dr.) Virendra Singh for always encouraging me.

I (Priyanka Srivastava) especially thanks to one of my best friend, my mother Mrs Poonam Srivastava & Shakuntala Mam for giving me inspiration to write this book.

We would like to thank members of our family, friends & well wishers whose blessing, knowledge, advice and interaction have made this project a possible venture in our life.

We express our gratitude to our Chairman Sir, Director Sir & Dean Sir for providing us such a great facilities which have served as a guide during the development of the book.

Above all our very special thanks to the editorial staff of Khanna Book Publishing Co. (P) Ltd. for the cooperation, interest and assistance extended to us for this book.

**AUTHORS**

# Contents

CHAPTER 1

# Introduction of IT Infrastructure

## 1.1 INFORMATION TECHNOLOGY

**Information Technology (IT)**, as defined by the Information Technology Association of America (ITAA), is "the study, design, development, implementation, support or management of computer-based information systems, particularly software applications and computer hardware". IT deals with the use of electronic computers and computer software to convert, store, protect, process, transmit, and securely retrieve information.

When computer and communications technologies are combined, the result is information technology, or "InfoTech". *Information technology* is a general term that describes any technology that helps to produce, manipulate, store, communicate, and/or disseminate information.

**Information technology** is the use of computers and software to manage information. In some companies, this is referred to as **Management Information Services** (or MIS) or simply as Information Services (or IS). The information technology department of a large company would be responsible for storing information, protecting information, processing the information, transmitting the information as necessary, and later retrieving information as necessary.

## 1.2 COMPUTER HARDWARE

A personal computer is made up of multiple physical components of **computer hardware**, upon which can be installed an operating system and a multitude of software to perform the operator's desired functions.

### 1.2.1 Motherboard

The motherboard is the "brain" of the computer. Components directly attached to the motherboard include:

- The **central processing unit** (CPU) performs most of the calculations which enable a computer to function, and is sometimes referred to as the "brain" of the computer. It is usually cooled by a heat sink and fan.

- The **chipset** mediates communication between the CPU and the other components of the system, including main memory.
- **RAM** Stores all running processes (applications) and the current running OS. RAM Stands for Random Access Memory
- The **BIOS** includes boot firmware and power management. The **B**asic **I**nput **O**utput **S**ystem tasks are handled by operating system drivers.
- **Internal Buses** connect the CPU to various internal components and to expansion cards for graphics and sound.

### 1.2.2 Computer Monitor

A **monitor** or **display** (sometimes called a **visual display unit**) is a piece of electrical equipment which displays images generated by devices such as computers, without producing a permanent record. The monitor comprises the display device, circuitry, and an enclosure. The display device in modern monitors is typically a thin film transistor liquid crystal display (TFT-LCD), while older monitors use a cathode ray tube (CRT).

### 1.2.3 Central Processing Unit

A **central processing unit (CPU)** or **processor** is an electronic circuit that can execute computer programs.

#### *1.2.3.1 CPU Operation*

The fundamental operation of most CPUs, regardless of the physical form they take, is to execute a sequence of stored instructions called a program. The program is represented by a series of numbers that are kept in some kind of computer memory. There are four steps that nearly all CPUs use in their operation: **fetch**, **decode**, **execute**, and **write back**.

### 1.2.4 Random-Access Memory

**Random-access memory** (usually known by its acronym, **RAM**) is a form of computer data storage. Today, it takes the form of integrated circuits that allow stored data to be accessed in any order (i.e., at *random*). The word *random* thus refers to the fact that any piece of data can be returned in a constant time, regardless of its physical location and whether or not it is related to the previous piece of data

The word RAM is often associated with volatile types of memory where the information is lost after the power is switched off.

### 1.2.5 CD-ROM

**CD-ROM**, "compact disc read-only memory" is a pre-pressed compact disc that contains data accessible to, but not writable by, a computer.

### 1.2.6 Keyboard

In computing, a **keyboard** is an input device, partially modeled after the typewriter keyboard, which uses an arrangement of buttons or keys, to act as mechanical levers or electronic switches. A keyboard typically has characters engraved or printed on the keys and each press of a key typically corresponds to a single written symbol. However, to produce some symbols requires pressing and holding several keys simultaneously or in sequence. While most keyboard keys produce letters, numbers or signs (characters), other keys or simultaneous key presses can produce actions or computer commands

### 1.2.7 Mouse

In computing, a **mouse** is a pointing device that functions by detecting two-dimensional motion relative to its supporting surface. Physically, a mouse consists of an object held under one of the user's hands, with one or more buttons. It sometimes features other elements, such as "wheels", which allow the user to perform various system-dependent operations, or extra buttons or features can add more control or dimensional input. The mouse's motion typically translates into the motion of a pointer on a display, which allows for fine control of a Graphical User Interface.

## 1.3 COMPUTER SOFTWARE

**Computer software,** or just **software** is a general term used to describe the role that computer programs, procedures and documentation play in a computer system.

The term includes:

- Application software such as word processors which perform productive tasks for users.
- Firmware which is software programmed resident to electrically programmable memory devices on board main boards or other types of integrated hardware carriers.
- Middleware which controls and co-ordinates distributed systems.
- System software such as operating systems, which interface with hardware to provide the necessary services for application software.
- Software testing is a domain independent of development and programming. It consists of various methods to test and declare a software product fit before it can be launched for use by either an individual or a group. Many tests on functionality, performance and appearance are conducted by modern testers with various tools such as QTP, Load runner and Black box testing, to edit a checklist of requirements against the developed code.
- Testware which is an umbrella term or container term for all utilities and application software that serve in combination for testing a software package but not necessarily may optionally contribute to operational purposes. As such, testware is not a standing configuration but merely a working environment for application software or subsets thereof.

Software includes things such as websites, programs or video games, that are coded by programming languages like C or C++.

"Software" is sometimes used in a broader context to mean anything which is not hardware but which is *used* with hardware, such as film, tapes and records.

### 1.3.1 Types of Software

#### *1.3.1.1 System software*

System software helps run the computer hardware and computer system. It includes combination of the following:

- device drivers
- operating systems
- servers
- utilities
- windowing systems

The purpose of systems software is to unburden the applications programmer from the details of the particular computer complex being used, including such accessory devices as communications, printers, readers, displays and keyboards, and also to partition the computer's resources such as memory and processor time in a safe and stable manner.

#### *1.3.1.2 Application Software*

Application software allows end users to accomplish one or more specific (not directly computer development related) tasks. Typical applications include:

- industrial automation
- business software
- computer games
- telecommunications (i.e., the internet and everything that flows on it)
- databases
- educational software
- medical software
- military software
- spreadsheet
- photo-editing
- word processing

In computing, a **protocol** is a set of rules which is used by computers to communicate with each other across a network. A protocol is a convention or standard that controls or enables the connection, communication, and data transfer between computing endpoints. In its simplest form, a protocol can be defined as the rules governing the syntax, semantics, and synchronization of communication. Protocols may be implemented by hardware, software, or a combination of the two. At the lowest level, a protocol defines the behavior of a hardware connection.

## 1.4 COMPUTER NETWORK

A **computer network** is a group of interconnected computers. The network allows computers to communicate with each other and share resources and information. Networks may be classified according to a wide variety of characteristics.

### 1.4.1 What can a Network do For You?

#### *1.4.1.1 Introduction*

A computer network can be two computers connected:

Fig. 1.1

A computer network can also consist of, and is usually made for, more than two computers:

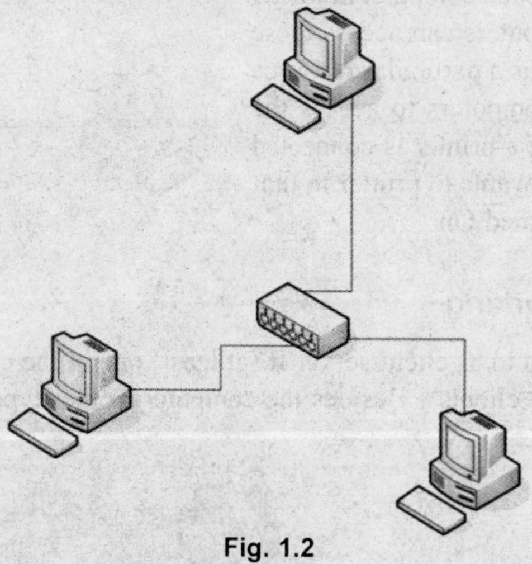

Fig. 1.2

### *1.4.1.2 Characteristics of a Computer Network*

The primary purpose of a computer network is to share resources:

- You can play a CD music from one computer while sitting on another computer
- You may have a computer with a CD writer or a backup system but the other computer doesn't have it; In this case, you can burn CDs or make backups on a computer that has one of these but using data from a computer that doesn't have a CD writer or a backup system
- You may have a computer that doesn't have a DVD player. In this case, you can place a movie DVD on the computer that has a DVD player, and then view the movie on a computer that lacks a DVD player
- You can connect a printer (or a scanner, or a fax machine) to one computer and let other computers of the network print (or scan, or fax) to that printer (or scanner, or fax machine)
- You can place a CD with pictures on one computer and let other computers access those pictures
- You can create files and store them in one computer, then access those files from the other computer(s) connected to it

## 1.4.2 Peer-to-Peer Networking

Based on their layout (not the physical but the imagined layout, also referred to as topology), there are two types of networks. A network is referred to as peer-to-peer if most computers are similar and run workstation operating systems:

It typically has a mix of Microsoft Windows 9X, Me, Windows XP Home Edition, or Windows XP Professional (you can also connect a Novell SUSE Linux as part of a Microsoft Windows-based network; the current release of the operating system is really easily to install and made part of the network).

In a peer-to-peer network, each computer holds its files and resources. Other computers can access these resources but a computer that has a particular resource must be turned on for other computers to access the resource it has. For example, if a printer is connected to computer A and computer B wants to printer to that printer, computer A must be turned On.

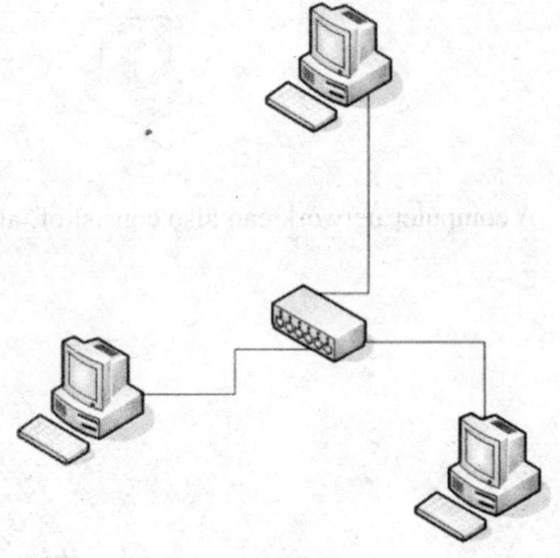

Fig. 1.3

### 1.4.3 Client/Server Networking

A computer network is referred to as client/server if (at least) one of the computers is used to "serve" other computers referred to as "clients". Besides the computers, other types of devices can be part of the network:

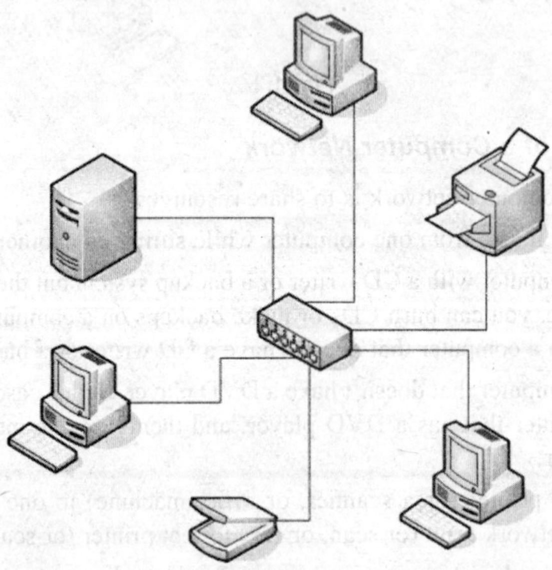

Fig. 1.4

In a client/server environment, each computer still holds (or can still hold) its (or some) resources and files. Other computers can also access the resources stored in a computer, as in a peer-to-peer scenario. One of the particularities of a client/server network is that the files and resources are centralized. This means that a computer, the server, can hold them and other computers can access them. Since the server is always On, the client machines can access the files and resources without caring whether a certain computer is On.

Another big advantage of a client/server network is that security is created, managed, and can highly get enforced. To access the network, a person, called a user must provide some credentials, including a username and a password. If the credentials are not valid, the user can be prevented from accessing the network.

The client/server type of network also provides many other advantages such as centralized backup, Intranet capability, Internet monitoring, etc.

### 1.4.4 Network Topology

#### *1.4.4.1 Diagram of Different Network Topologies*

**Network topology** is the physical interconnections of the elements (links, nodes, etc.) of a computer network. A local area network (LAN) is one example of a network that exhibits both a physical topology and a logical topology. Any given node in the LAN has one or more links to one or more other nodes in the network and the mapping of these links and nodes in a graph results in a geometrical shape that may be used to describe the physical topology of the network. Likewise, the mapping of the data flows between the nodes in the network determines the logical topology of the network. The physical and logical topologies may or may not be identical in any particular network.

Any particular network topology is determined only by the graphical mapping of the configuration of physical and/or logical connections between nodes. The study of network topology uses graph theory. Distances between nodes, physical interconnections, transmission rates, and/or signal types may differ in two networks and yet their topologies may be identical.

#### *1.4.4.2 Basic Topology Types*

The study of network topology recognizes four basic topologies:

- Bus topology
- Star topology
- Ring topology
- Tree topology

#### *1.4.4.3 Classification of Network Topologies*

There are also three basic categories of network topologies:

- Physical topologies
- Signal topologies
- Logical topologies

### 1.4.5 Physical Topologies

The mapping of the nodes of a network and the physical connections between them - i.e., the layout of wiring, cables, the locations of nodes, and the interconnections between the nodes and the cabling or wiring system.

#### *1.4.5.1 Classification of Physical Topologies*

**Point-to-point**

The simplest topology is a permanent link between two endpoints (the line in the illustration above). Switched point-to-point topologies are the basic model of conventional telephony. The value of a permanent point-to-point network is the value of guaranteed, or nearly so, communications between the two endpoints. The value of an on-demand point-to-point connection is proportional to the number of potential pairs of subscribers.

**Permanent (dedicated)**

Easiest to understand, of the variations of point-to-point topology, is a point-to-point communications channel that appears, to the user, to be permanently associated with the two endpoints. Children's "tin-can telephone" is one example, with a microphone to a single public address speaker is another. These are examples of *physical dedicated* channels.

Within many switched telecommunications systems, it is possible to establish a permanent circuit. One example might be a telephone in the lobby of a public building, which is programmed to ring only the number of a telephone dispatcher. "Nailing down" a switched connection saves the cost of running a physical circuit between the two points. The resources in such a connection can be released when no longer needed, for example, a television circuit from a parade route back to the studio.

**Switched**

Using circuit-switching or packet-switching technologies, a point-to-point circuit can be set up dynamically, and dropped when no longer needed. This is the basic mode of conventional telephony.

### 1.4.6 Bus

In local area networks where bus technology is used, each machine is connected to a single cable. Each computer or server is connected to the single bus cable through some kind of connector. A terminator is required at each end of the bus cable to prevent the signal from bouncing back and forth on the bus cable. A signal from the source travels in both directions to all machines connected on the bus cable until it finds the MAC address or IP address on the network that is the intended recipient. If the machine address does not match the intended address for the data, the machine ignores the data. Alternatively, if the data does match the machine address, the data is accepted. Since the bus topology consists of only one wire, it is rather inexpensive to implement when compared to other topologies. However, the low cost of implementing the technology is offset by the high cost of managing the network. Additionally, since only one cable is utilized, it can be the single point of failure. If the network cable breaks, the entire network will be down, since there is only one cable. Since there is one cable, the transfer speeds between the computers on the network is faster.

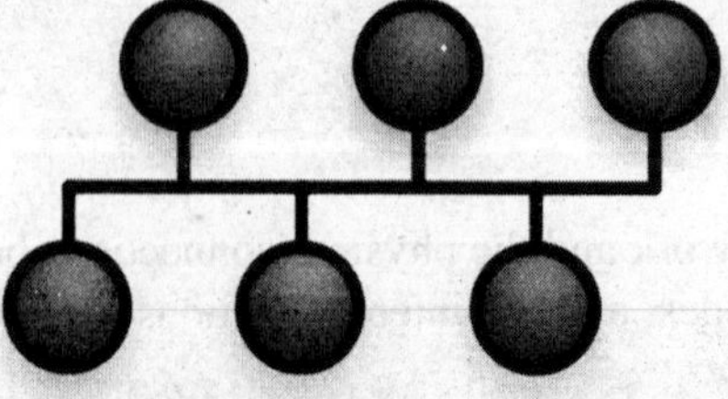

**Fig. 1.5:** Bus Network Topology

#### 1.4.6.1 Linear Bus

The type of network topology in which all of the nodes of the network are connected to a common transmission medium which has exactly two endpoints (this is the 'bus', which is also commonly referred to as the backbone, or trunk) — all data that is transmitted between nodes in the network is transmitted over this common transmission medium and is able to be received by all nodes in the network virtually simultaneously (disregarding propagation delays)

**NOTE:** The two endpoints of the common transmission medium are normally terminated with a device called a terminator that exhibits the characteristic impedance of the transmission medium and which dissipates or absorbs the energy that remains in the signal to prevent the signal from being reflected or propagated back onto the transmission medium in the opposite direction, which would cause interference with and degradation of the signals on the transmission medium.

#### 1.4.6.2 Distributed Bus

The type of network topology in which all of the nodes of the network are connected to a common transmission medium which has more than two endpoints that are created by adding branches to the main section of the transmission medium — the physical distributed bus topology functions in exactly the same fashion as the physical linear bus topology (i.e., all nodes share a common transmission medium).

***Notes:***

1. All of the endpoints of the common transmission medium are normally terminated with a device called a 'terminator'.
2. The physical linear bus topology is sometimes considered to be a special case of the physical distributed bus topology — i.e., a distributed bus with no branching segments.
3. The physical distributed bus topology is sometimes incorrectly referred to as a physical tree topology — however, although the physical distributed bus topology resembles the physical tree topology, it differs from the physical tree topology in that there is no central node to which any other nodes are connected, since this hierarchical functionality is replaced by the common bus.

### 1.4.7 Star

In local area networks where the star topology is used, each machine is connected to a central hub. In contrast to the bus topology, the star topology allows each machine on the network to have a point to point connection to the central hub. All of the traffic which transverses the network passes through the central hub. The hub acts as a signal booster or repeater which in turn allows the signal to travel greater distances. As a result of each machine connecting directly to the hub, the star topology is considered the easiest topology to design and implement. An advantage of the star topology is the simplicity of adding other machines. The primary disadvantage of the star topology is the hub is a single point of failure. If the hub were to fail the entire network would fail as a result of the hub being connected to every machine on the network.

***Notes:***

1. A point-to-point link (described above) is sometimes categorized as a special instance of the physical star topology — therefore, the simplest type of network that is based upon the physical star topology would consist of one node with a single point-to-point link to a second node, the choice of which node is the 'hub' and which node is the 'spoke' being arbitrary.

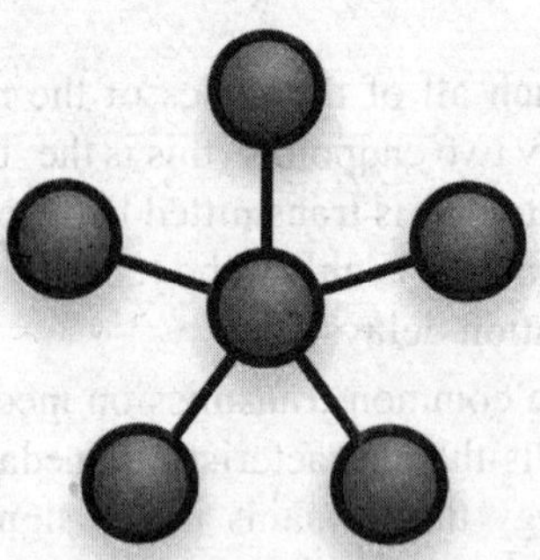

**Fig. 1.6:** Star network topology

2. After the special case of the point-to-point link, as in note 1.) above, the next simplest type of network that is based upon the physical star topology would consist of one central node — the 'hub' — with two separate point-to-point links to two peripheral nodes — the 'spokes'.
3. Although most networks that are based upon the physical star topology are commonly implemented using a special device such as a hub or switch as the central node (i.e., the 'hub' of the star), it is also possible to implement a network that is based upon the physical star topology using a computer or even a simple common connection point as the 'hub' or central node — however, since many illustrations of the physical star network topology depict the central node as one of these special devices, some confusion is possible, since this practice may lead to the misconception that a physical star network requires the central node to be one of these special devices, which is not true because a simple network consisting of three computers connected as in note 2.) above also has the topology of the physical star.
4. Star networks may also be described as either broadcast multi-access or nonbroadcast multi-access (NBMA), depending on whether the technology of the network either automatically propagates a signal at the hub to all spokes, or only addresses individual spokes with each communication.

#### *1.4.7.1 Extended Star*

A type of network topology in which a network that is based upon the physical star topology has one or more repeaters between the central node (the 'hub' of the star) and the peripheral or 'spoke' nodes, the repeaters being used to extend the maximum transmission distance of the point-to-point links between the central node and the peripheral nodes beyond that which is supported by the transmitter power of the central node or beyond that which is supported by the standard upon which the physical layer of the physical star network is based.

**NOTE:** If the repeaters in a network that is based upon the physical extended star topology are replaced with hubs or switches, then a hybrid network topology is created that is referred to as a physical hierarchical star topology, although some texts make no distinction between the two topologies.

#### *1.4.7.2 Distributed Star*

A type of network topology that is composed of individual networks that are based upon the physical star topology connected together in a linear fashion — i.e., 'daisy-chained' — with no central or top level connection point (e.g., two or more 'stacked' hubs, along with their associated star connected nodes or 'spokes').

### 1.4.8 Ring

In local area networks where the ring topology is used, each computer is connected to the network in a closed loop or ring. Each machine or computer has a unique address that is used for identification purposes. The signal passes through each machine or computer connected to the ring in one direction. Ring topologies typically utilize a token passing scheme, used to control access to the network. By utilizing this scheme, only one machine can transmit on the network at a time. The machines or computers connected to the ring act as signal boosters or repeaters which strengthen the signals that transverse the network. The primary disadvantage of ring topology is the failure of one machine will cause the entire network to fail.

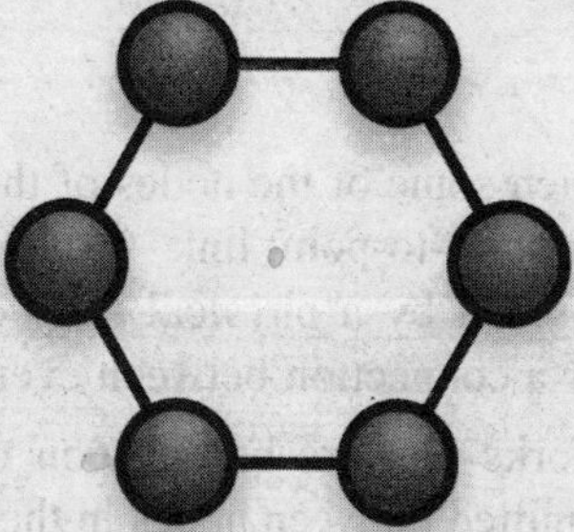

**Fig. 1.7:** Ring network topology

### 1.4.9 Mesh

The value of fully meshed networks is proportional to the exponent of the number of subscribers, assuming that communicating groups of any two endpoints, up to and including all the endpoints.

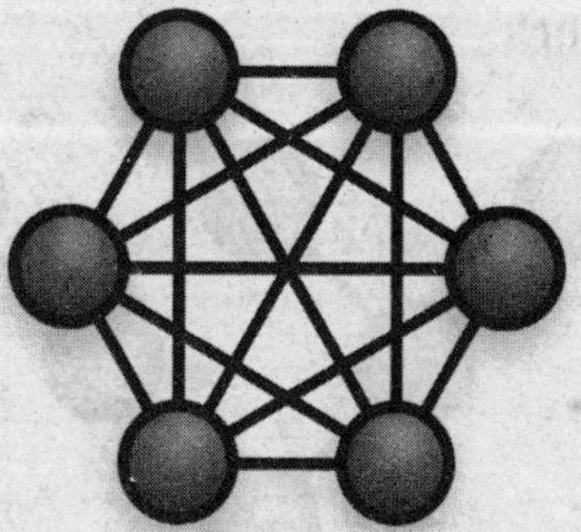

**Fig. 1.8:** Fully connected mesh topology

#### *1.4.9.1 Fully Connected*

The type of network topology in which each of the nodes of the network is connected to each of the other nodes in the network with a point-to-point link — this makes it possible for data to be simultaneously transmitted from any single node to all of the other nodes.

**NOTE:** The physical fully connected mesh topology is generally too costly and complex for practical networks, although the topology is used when there are only a small number of nodes to be interconnected.

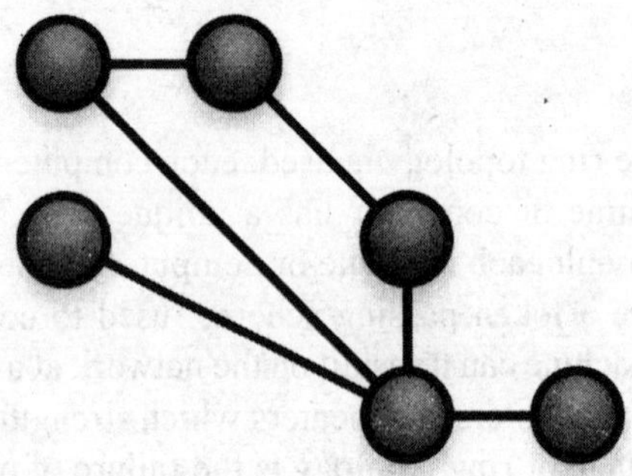

**Fig. 1.9:** Partially connected mesh topology

#### *1.4.9.2 Partially Connected*

The type of network topology in which some of the nodes of the network are connected to more than one other node in the network with a point-to-point link — this makes it possible to take advantage of some of the redundancy that is provided by a physical fully connected mesh topology without the expense and complexity required for a connection between every node in the network.

**NOTE:** In most practical networks that are based upon the physical partially connected mesh topology, all of the data that is transmitted between nodes in the network takes the shortest path (or an approximation of the shortest path) between nodes, except in the case of a failure or break in one of the links, in which case the data takes an alternate path to the destination. This requires that the nodes of the network possess some type of logical 'routing' algorithm to determine the correct path to use at any particular time.

### 1.4.10 Tree

Also known as a **hierarchical network**.

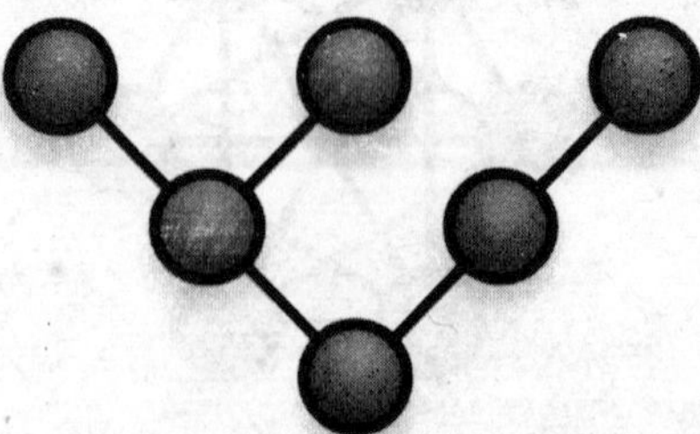

**Fig. 1.10:** Tree network topology

The type of network topology in which a central 'root' node (the top level of the hierarchy) is connected to one or more other nodes that are one level lower in the hierarchy (i.e., the second level) with a point-to-point link between each of the second level nodes and the top level central 'root' node, while each of the second level nodes that are connected to the top level central 'root' node will also have one or more other nodes that are one level lower in the hierarchy (i.e., the third level) connected to it, also with a point-to-point link, the top level central 'root' node being the only node that has no other node above it in the hierarchy (The hierarchy of the tree is symmetrical.) Each node in the network having a specific fixed number, of nodes connected to it at the next lower level in the hierarchy, the number, being referred to as the 'branching factor' of the hierarchical tree.

1. A network that is based upon the physical hierarchical topology must have at least three levels in the hierarchy of the tree, since a network with a central 'root' node and only one hierarchical level below it would exhibit the physical topology of a star.
2. A network that is based upon the physical hierarchical topology and with a branching factor of 1 would be classified as a physical linear topology.
3. The branching factor, f, is independent of the total number of nodes in the network and, therefore, if the nodes in the network require ports for connection to other nodes the total number of ports per node may be kept low even though the total number of nodes is large — this makes the effect of the cost of adding ports to each node totally dependent upon the branching factor and may therefore be kept as low as required without any effect upon the total number of nodes that are possible.
4. The total number of point-to-point links in a network that is based upon the physical hierarchical topology will be one less than the total number of nodes in the network.
5. If the nodes in a network that is based upon the physical hierarchical topology are required to perform any processing upon the data that is transmitted between nodes in the network, the nodes that are at higher levels in the hierarchy will be required to perform more processing operations on behalf of other nodes than the nodes that are lower in the hierarchy. Such a type of network topology is very useful and highly recommended.

### 1.4.11 Network Classification

The following list presents categories used for classifying networks.

#### *1.4.11.1 Connection Method*

Computer networks can also be classified according to the hardware and software technology that is used to interconnect the individual devices in the network, such as Optical fiber, Ethernet, Wireless LAN, HomePNA, Power line communication or G.hn. Ethernet uses physical wiring to connect devices. Frequently deployed devices include hubs, switches, bridges and/or routers.

Wireless LAN technology is designed to connect devices without wiring. These devices use radio waves or infrared signals as a transmission medium.

#### *1.4.11.2 Wired Technologies*

**Twisted-Pair Wire**: This is the most widely used medium for telecommunication. Twisted-pair wires are ordinary telephone wires which consist of two insulated copper wires twisted into pairs and are used for both voice and data transmission. The use of two wires twisted together helps to reduce crosstalk and electromagnetic induction. The transmission speed range from 2 million bits per second to 100 million bits per second.

**Coaxial Cable**: These cables are widely used for cable television systems, office buildings, and other worksites for local area networks. The cables consist of copper or aluminum wire wrapped with insulating layer typically of a flexible material with a high dielectric constant, all of which are surrounded by a conductive layer. The layers of insulation help minimize interference and distortion. Transmission speed range from 200 million to more than 500 million bits per second.

**Fiber Optics**: These cables consist of one or more thin filaments of glass fiber wrapped in a protective layer. It transmits light which can travel over long distance and higher bandwidths. Fiber-optic cables are not affected by electromagnetic radiation. Transmission speed could go up to as high as trillions of bits per second. The speed of fiber optics is hundreds of times faster than coaxial cables and thousands of times faster than twisted-pair wire.

#### *1.4.11.3 Wireless Technologies*

**Terrestrial Microwave:** Terrestrial microwaves use Earth-based transmitter and receiver. The equipment look similar to satellite dishes. Terrestrial microwaves use low-gigahertz range, which limits all communications to line-of-sight. Path between relay stations spaced approx. 30 miles apart. Microwave antennas are usually placed on top of buildings, towers, hills, and mountain peaks.

**Communications Satellites:** The satellites use microwave radio as their telecommunications medium which are not deflected by the Earth's atmosphere. The satellites are stationed in space, typically 22,000 miles above the equator. These Earth-orbiting systems are capable of receiving and relaying voice, data, and TV signals.

**Cellular and PCS Systems:** Use several radio communications technologies. The systems are divided to different geographic area. Each area has low-power transmitter or radio relay antenna device to relay calls from one area to the next area.

**Wireless LANs:** Wireless local area network use a high-frequency radio technology similar to digital cellular and a low-frequency radio technology. Wireless LANS use spread spectrum technology to enable communication between multiple devices in a limited area. Example of open-standard wireless radio-wave technology is IEEE 802.11b.

**Bluetooth:** A short range wireless technology. Operate at approx. 1Mbps with range from 10 to 100 meters. Bluetooth is an open wireless protocol for data exchange over short distances.

**The Wireless Web:** The wireless web refers to the use of the World Wide Web through equipments like cellular phones, pagers, PDAs, and other portable communications devices. The wireless web service offers anytime/anywhere connection.

### 1.4.12 Types of Networks

#### *1.4.12.1 Personal Area Network*

A personal area network (PAN) is a computer network used for communication among computer devices close to one person. Some examples of devices that are used in a PAN are printers, fax machines, telephones, PDAs and scanners. The reach of a PAN is typically about 20-30 feet (approximately 6-9 meters), but this is expected to increase with technology improvements.

#### *1.4.12.2 Local Area Network*

A local area network (LAN) is a computer network covering a small physical area, like a home, office, or small group of buildings, such as a school, or an airport.

#### *1.4.12.3 Metropolitan Area Network*

A metropolitan area network (MAN) is a network that connects two or more local area networks or campus area networks together but does not extend beyond the boundaries of the immediate town/city. Routers, switches and hubs are connected to create a metropolitan area network.

#### *1.4.12.4 Wide Area Network*

A wide area network (WAN) is a computer network that covers a broad area (i.e. any network whose communications links cross metropolitan, regional, or national boundaries). Less formally, a WAN is a network that uses routers and public communications links Contrast with personal area networks (PANs), local area networks (LANs), campus area networks (CANs), or metropolitan area networks (MANs), which are usually limited to a room, building, campus or specific metropolitan area (e.g., a city) respectively. The largest and most well-known example of a WAN is the Internet. A WAN is a data communications network that covers a relatively broad geographic area (i.e. one city to another and one country to another country) and that often uses transmission facilities provided by common carriers, such as telephone companies. WAN technologies generally function at the lower three layers of the OSI reference model: the physical layer, the data link layer, and the network layer.

### 1.4.13 Internetwork

An Internetwork is the connection of two or more distinct computer networks or network segments via a common routing technology. The result is called an internetwork (often shortened to internet). Two or more networks or network segments connected using devices that operate at layer 3 (the 'network' layer) of the OSI Basic Reference Model, such as a router. Any interconnection among or between public, private, commercial, industrial, or governmental networks may also be defined as an internet work.

In modern practice, interconnected networks use the Internet Protocol. There are at least three variants of internet works, depending on who administers and who participates in them:

- Intranet
- Extranet
- Internet

Intranets and extranets may or may not have connections to the Internet. If connected to the Internet, the intranet or extranet is normally protected from being accessed from the Internet without proper authorization. The Internet is not considered to be a part of the intranet or extranet, although it may serve as a portal for access to portions of an extranet.

#### *1.4.13.1 Intranet*

An intranet is a set of networks, using the Internet Protocol and IP-based tools such as web browsers and file transfer applications, that is under the control of a single administrative entity. That administrative entity closes the intranet to all but specific, authorized users. Most commonly, an intranet is the internal network of an organization. A large intranet will typically have at least one web server to provide users with organizational information.

#### *1.4.13.2 Extranet*

An extranet is a network or internetwork that is limited in scope to a single organization or entity but which also has limited connections to the networks of one or more other usually, but not necessarily, trusted organizations or entities (e.g., a company's customers may be given access to some part of its intranet creating in this way an extranet, while at the same time the customers may not be considered 'trusted' from a security standpoint). Technically, an extranet may also be categorized as a CAN, MAN, WAN, or other type of network, although, by definition, an extranet cannot consist of a single LAN; it must have at least one connection with an external network.

#### *1.4.13.3 Internet*

The Internet consists of a worldwide interconnection of governmental, academic, public, and private networks based upon the networking technologies of the Internet Protocol Suite. It is the successor of the Advanced Research Projects Agency Network (ARPANET) developed by DARPA of the U.S. Department of Defense. The Internet is also the communications backbone underlying the World Wide Web (WWW).

## 1.5 INTERNET

The **Internet** is a global system of interconnected computer networks that use the standardized Internet Protocol Suite (TCP/IP), serving billions of users worldwide. It is a *network of networks* that consists of millions of private and public, academic, business, and government networks of local to global scope that are linked by copper wires, fiber-optic cables, wireless connections, and other technologies. The Internet carries a vast array of information resources and services, most notably the inter-linked hypertext documents of the World Wide Web (WWW) and the infrastructure to support electronic mail. In addition it supports popular services such as online chat, file transfer and file sharing, gaming, commerce, social networking, publishing, video on demand, and teleconferencing and telecommunications. Voice over Internet Protocol (VoIP) applications allow person-to-person communication via voice and video.

The origins of the Internet reach back to the 1960s when the United States funded research projects of its military agencies to build robust, fault-tolerant and distributed computer networks. This research and a period of civilian funding of a new U.S. backbone by the National Science Foundation spawned worldwide participation in the development of new networking technologies and led to the commercialization of an international network in the mid 1990s, and resulted in the following popularization of countless applications in virtually every aspect of modern human life. As of 2009, an estimated quarter of Earth's population uses the services of the Internet.

### 1.5.1 History

#### *1.5.1.1 Creation*

The USSR's launch of Sputnik spurred the United States to create the Advanced Research Projects

Agency, known as ARPA, in February 1958 to regain a technological lead. ARPA created the Information Processing Technology Office (IPTO) to further the research of the Semi Automatic Ground Environment (SAGE) program, which had networked country-wide radar systems together for the first time. J. C. R. Licklider was selected to head the IPTO. Licklider moved from the Psycho-Acoustic Laboratory at Harvard University to MIT in 1950, after becoming interested in information technology. At MIT, he served on a committee that established Lincoln Laboratory and worked on the SAGE project. In 1957 he became a Vice President at BBN, where he bought the first production PDP-1 computer and conducted the first public demonstration of time-sharing.

At the IPTO, Licklider got Lawrence Roberts to start a project to make a network, and Roberts based the technology on the work of Paul Baran, who had written an exhaustive study for the U.S. Air Force that recommended packet switching (as opposed to circuit switching) to make a network highly robust and survivable. After much work, the first two nodes of what would become the ARPANET were interconnected between UCLA and SRI International (SRI) in Menlo Park, California, on October 29, 1969. The ARPANET was one of the "eve" networks of today's Internet. Following on from the demonstration that packet switching worked on the ARPANET, the British Post Office, Telenet, DATAPAC and TRANSPAC collaborated to create the first international packet-switched network service. In the UK, this was referred to as the International Packet Switched Service (IPSS), in 1978. The collection of X.25-based networks grew from Europe and the US to cover Canada, Hong Kong and Australia by 1981. The X.25 packet switching standard was developed in the CCITT (now called ITU-T) around 1976.

X.25 was independent of the TCP/IP protocols that arose from the experimental work of DARPA on the ARPANET, Packet Radio Net and Packet Satellite Net during the same time period. Vinton Cerf and Robert Kahn developed the first description of the TCP protocols during 1973 and published a paper on the subject in May 1974. Use of the term "Internet" to describe a single global TCP/IP network originated in December 1974 with the publication of RFC 675, the first full specification of TCP that was written by Vinton Cerf, Yogen Dalal and Carl Sunshine, then at Stanford University. During the next nine years, work proceeded to refine the protocols and to implement them on a wide range of operating systems. The first TCP/IP-based wide-area network was operational by January 1, 1983 when all hosts on the ARPANET were switched over from the older NCP protocols. In 1985, the United States' National Science Foundation (NSF) commissioned the construction of the NSFNET, a university 56 kilobit/second network backbone using computers called "fuzzballs" by their inventor, David L. Mills. The following year, NSF sponsored the conversion to a higher-speed 1.5 megabit/second network. A key decision to use the DARPA TCP/IP protocols was made by Dennis Jennings, then in charge of the Supercomputer program at NSF.

The opening of the network to commercial interests began in 1988. The US Federal Networking Council approved the interconnection of the NSFNET to the commercial MCI Mail system in that year and the link was made in the summer of 1989. Other commercial electronic e-mail services were soon connected, including OnTyme, Telemail and Compuserve. In that same year, three commercial Internet service providers (ISPs) were created: UUNET, PSINet and CERFNET. Important, separate networks that offered gateways into, then later merged with, the Internet include Usenet and BITNET. Various other commercial and educational networks, such as Telenet, Tymnet, Compuserve and JANET were interconnected with the growing Internet. Telenet (later called Sprintnet) was a large privately funded national computer network with free dial-up access in cities throughout the U.S. that had been in operation since the 1970s. This network was eventually interconnected with the others in the 1980s as the TCP/IP protocol became increasingly popular. The ability of TCP/IP to work over virtually any pre-existing communication networks allowed for a great ease of growth, although the rapid growth of the Internet was due primarily to the availability of an array of standardized commercial routers from many companies, the availability of commercial Ethernet equipment for local-area networking, and the widespread implementation and rigorous standardization of TCP/IP on UNIX and virtually every other common operating system.

The **World Wide Web** is a system of interlinked hypertext documents accessed via the Internet. With a web browser, one can view Web pages that may contain text, images, videos, and other multimedia and navigate between them using hyperlinks. Using concepts from earlier hypertext systems, English physicist Tim Berners-Lee, now the Director of the World Wide Web Consortium, wrote a proposal in March 1989 for what would eventually become the World Wide Web. He was later joined by Belgian computer scientist Robert Cailliau while both were working at CERN in Geneva, Switzerland. In 1990, they proposed using "HyperText to link and access information of various kinds as a web of nodes in which the user can browse at will", and released that web in December.

Connected by the existing Internet, other websites were created, around the world, adding international standards for domain names and the HTML. Since then, Berners-Lee has played an active role in guiding the development of Web standards (such as the markup languages in which Web pages are composed), and in recent years has advocated his vision of a Semantic Web. The World Wide Web enabled the spread of information over the Internet through an easy-to-use and flexible format. It thus played an important role in popularizing use of the Internet. Although the two terms are sometimes conflated in popular use, *World Wide Web* is not synonymous with *Internet*. The Web is an application built on top of the Internet.

**HTML**, which stands for **Hyper Text Markup Language**, is the predominant markup language for web pages. It provides a means to create structured documents by denoting structural semantics for text such as headings, paragraphs, lists etc as well as for links, quotes, and other items. It allows images and objects to be embedded and can be used to create interactive forms. It is written in the form of HTML elements consisting of "tags" surrounded by angle brackets within the web page content. It can include or can load scripts in languages such as JavaScript, which affect the behavior of HTML processors like Web browsers, and Cascading Style Sheets (CSS) to define the appearance and layout of text and other material. The W3C, maintainer of both HTML and CSS standards, encourages the use of CSS over explicit presentational markup.

### 1.5.2 HTML Markup

HTML markup consists of several key components, including *elements* (and their *attributes*), character-based *data types*, and *character references* and *entity references*. Another important component is the *document type declaration*, which specifies the Document Type Definition. As of HTML 5, no Document Type Definition will need to be specified, and will only determine the layout mode.

```
<html>
  <head>
    <title>Hello HTML</title>
```

```
</head>
<body>
  <p>Hello World!</p>
</body>
</html>
```

**Hypertext Transfer Protocol** (**HTTP**) is an application-level protocol for distributed, collaborative, hypermedia information systems. Its use for retrieving inter-linked resources led to the establishment of the World Wide Web.

HTTP development was coordinated by the World Wide Web Consortium and the Internet Engineering Task Force (IETF), culminating in the publication of a series of Requests for Comments (RFCs), most notably RFC 2616 (June 1999), which defines HTTP/1.1, the version of HTTP in common use.

Support for pre-standard HTTP/1.1 based on the then developing RFC 2068 was rapidly adopted by the major browser developers in early 1996. By March 1996, pre-standard HTTP/1.1 was supported in Netscape 2.0, Netscape Navigator Gold 2.01, Mosaic 2.7, Lynx 2.5, and in Internet Explorer 3.0. End user adoption of the new browsers was rapid. In March 1996, one web hosting company reported that over 40% of browsers in use on the Internet were HTTP 1.1 compliant. That same web hosting company reported that by June 1996, 65% of all browsers accessing their servers were HTTP 1.1 Compliant. The HTTP 1.1 standard as defined in RFC 2068 was officially released in January 1997. Improvements and updates to the The HTTP/1.1 standard were released under RFC 2616 in June 1999.

HTTP is a request/response standard of a client and a server. A client is the end-user, the server is the web site. The client making an HTTP request — using a web browser, spider, or other end-user tool — is referred to as the *user agent*. The responding server — which stores or creates *resources* such as HTML files and images — is called the *origin server*. In between the user agent and origin server may be several intermediaries, such as proxies, gateways, and tunnels. HTTP is not constrained to using TCP/IP and its supporting layers, although this is its most popular application on the Internet. Indeed HTTP can be "implemented on top of any other protocol on the Internet, or on other networks." HTTP only presumes a reliable transport; any protocol that provides such guarantees can be used."

Typically, an HTTP client initiates a request. It establishes a Transmission Control Protocol (TCP) connection to a particular port on a host (port 80 by default; see List of TCP and UDP port numbers). An HTTP server listening on that port waits for the client to send a request message. Upon receiving the request, the server sends back a status line, such as "HTTP/1.1 200 OK", and a message of its own, the body of which is perhaps the requested resource, an error message, or some other information.

Resources to be accessed by HTTP are identified using Uniform Resource Identifiers (URIs) — or, more specifically, Uniform Resource Locators (URLs) — using the http: or https URI schemes.

## 1.6 COMPUTING RESOURCES

A **resource**, or **system resource**, is any physical or virtual component of limited availability within a computer system. Every device connected to a computer system is a resource. Every internal system component is a resource. Virtual system resources include files, network connections and memory areas.

### 1.6.1 Major Resource Types

- CPU time
- Random access memory and virtual memory
- Hard disk space
- Network throughput
- Electrical power
- External Devices

#### 1.6.1.1 Central Processing Unit

A **Central Processing Unit** (**CPU**) or **processor** is an electronic circuit that can execute computer programs, which are actually sets of instructions. This term has been in use in the computer industry at least since the early 1960s.. The form, design and implementation of CPUs have changed dramatically since the earliest examples, but their fundamental operation remains much the same.

Early CPUs were custom-designed as a part of a larger, sometimes one-of-a-kind, computer. However, this costly method of designing custom CPUs for a particular application has largely given way to the development of mass-produced processors that are made for one or many purposes. This standardization trend generally began in the era of discrete transistor mainframes and minicomputers and has rapidly accelerated with the popularization of the integrated circuit (IC). The IC has allowed increasingly complex CPUs to be designed and manufactured to tolerances on the order of nanometers. Both the miniaturization and standardization of CPUs have increased the presence of these digital devices in modern life far beyond the limited application of dedicated computing machines. Modern microprocessors appear in everything from automobiles to cell phones and children's toys.

#### 1.6.1.2 Virtual Memory

**Virtual memory** is a computer system technique which gives an application program the impression that it has contiguous working memory (an address space), while in fact it may be physically fragmented and may even overflow on to disk storage. Systems that use this technique make programming of large applications easier and use real physical memory (e.g. RAM) more efficiently than those without virtual memory. Virtual memory differs significantly from memory virtualization in that virtual memory allows resources to be virtualized as memory for a specific system, as opposed to a large pool of memory being virtualized as smaller pools for many different systems.

#### 1.6.1.3 Random-Access Memory

**Random-access memory** (usually known by its acronym, **RAM**) is a form of computer data storage. Today, it takes the form of integrated circuits that allow stored data to be accessed in any order (i.e., at *random*). The word *random* thus refers to the fact that any piece of data can be returned in a constant time, regardless of its physical location and whether or not it is related to the previous piece of data.

By contrast, storage devices such as tapes, magnetic discs and optical discs rely on the physical movement of the recording medium or a reading head. In these devices, the movement takes longer than data transfer, and the retrieval time varies based on the physical location of the next item.

The word RAM is often associated with volatile types of memory (such as DRAM memory modules), where the information is lost after the power is switched off. Many other types of memory are RAM, too, including most types of ROM and flash memory called *NOR-Flash*.

#### 1.6.1.4 Hard Disk Drive

A **hard disk drive** often shortened as hard disk hard drive or HDD) is a non-volatile storage device that stores digitally encoded data on rapidly rotating platters with magnetic surfaces. Strictly speaking, "drive" refers to a device distinct from its medium, such as a tape drive and its tape, or a floppy disk drive and its floppy disk. Early HDDs had removable media; however, an HDD today is typically a sealed unit (except for a filtered vent hole to equalize air pressure) with fixed media.

#### 1.6.1.5 Computer Networking

**Computer networking** is the engineering discipline concerned with communication between computer systems or devices. Networking, routers, routing protocols, and networking over the public Internet have their specifications defined in documents called RFCs. Computer networking is sometimes considered a sub-discipline of telecommunications, computer science, information technology and/or computer engineering. Computer networks rely heavily upon the theoretical and practical application of these scientific and engineering disciplines. There are three types of networks: 1. Internet. 2. Intranet. 3. Extranet. A computer network is any set of computers or devices connected to each other with the ability to exchange data. Examples of different networks are:

- Local area network (LAN), which is usually a small network constrained to a small geographic area.
- Wide area network (WAN) that is usually a larger network that covers a large geographic area.
- Wireless LANs and WANs (WLAN & WWAN) are the wireless equivalent of the LAN and WAN.

All networks are interconnected to allow communication with a variety of different kinds of media, including twisted-pair copper wire cable, coaxial cable, optical fiber, power lines and various wireless technologies. The devices can be separated by a few meters (e.g. via Bluetooth) or nearly unlimited distances (e.g. via the interconnections of the Internet).

#### 1.6.1.6 Power management

**Power management** is a feature of some electrical appliances, especially copiers, computers and computer peripherals such as monitors and printers, that turns off the power or switches the system to a low-power state when inactive. One power management standard for computers is ACPI, which supersedes APM. All recent (consumer) computers have ACPI support.

### 1.6.2 Motivations

Power management for computer systems are desired for many reasons, particularly:

- Prolong battery life for portable and embedded systems.
- Reduce cooling requirements.
- Reduce noise.
- Reduce operating costs for energy and cooling.

Lower power consumption also means lower heat dissipation, which increases system stability, and less energy use, which saves money and reduces the impact on the environment.

### 1.6.3 Peripheral

A **peripheral** is a device attached to a host computer behind the chipset whose primary functionality is dependent upon the host, and can therefore be considered as expanding the hosts capabilities, while not forming part of the system's core architecture.

#### *1.6.3.1 Common Peripherals*

- Storage
- Input — Input device
- Output — Output device
  - — Display device
  - — Graphical output device
  - — Computer display

## 1.7 IT INFRASTRUCTURE

Present day business operations are integral with the information technology that supports them. The business infrastructure should provide a secure, resilient and flexible environment that enables execution of processes, applications and enterprises in sync with technological innovation. IT Infrastructure Integration services aims at **"Enabling Business Operations with High Performance Infrastructure Solutions"** through a comprehensive set of services to support the design, development, installation and operations of complex networks.

A wide spectrum of IT Infrastructure services is provided through a continuous life cycle of "Analyze, Design, Implement, Stage and Manage".

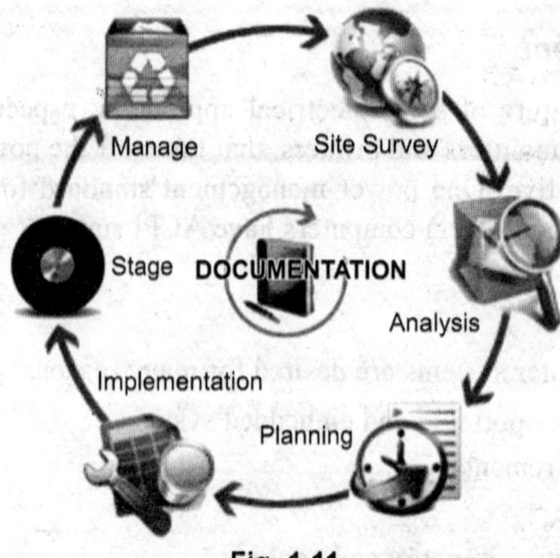


Fig. 1.11

The network portion includes a review of the following major categories:

- Current Network Infrastructure and Current Projects
- Planned Changes to existing Network Infrastructure
- Router/Switch/Hub Configurations (concerns and configuration process)
- Traffic Patterns (LAN and WAN, peak and off-peak)
- Bottlenecks (use monitoring tools to isolate bottlenecks/congestion)
- Utilization (look at router ports and interconnected switch/hubs)
- Response Times (LAN Services)
- Identify Collisions and Errors

The server portion includes a review of the following major categories:

- Hardware (processor, memory, disk space, file system)
- Windows Services (operating system, Service packs, DNS)
- Applications (SQL, remote administration software, e-mail, backup, anti-virus)
- Performance and capacity management (processor and memory utilization, drive shares)
- Operational processes and procedures (system management tools and processes)
- Current server architecture (Active Directory, Domain Structure)

**IT Infrastructure** consists of ***Client ware***, ***Middleware***, ***Server ware***, ***Manage ware***, and ***Platforms***, as illustrated in figure 1.12.

In the figure 1.12, ***Clientware*** refers to software that runs on ***clients***, including the following sub-categories:

- **Office** (e.g., word processors and spreadsheets)
- **Internet** (e.g., web browsers and e-mail clients)
- **Graphics** ( e.g., bitmap and vector)
- **Publishing**

**Serverware** — software running on **servers** — refers to the following sub-categories:

- **Basic** (e.g., file server and print server)
- **Internet** (e.g., web server and application server)
- **Database** (e.g., SQL server and XML server)
- **Content**

**Middleware** provides the **glue** that connects **clients** and **servers**. Its sub-categories include: .

- Formats & Protocols
- Directory & Security
- Application Partitioning
- Application Integration
- Web Services

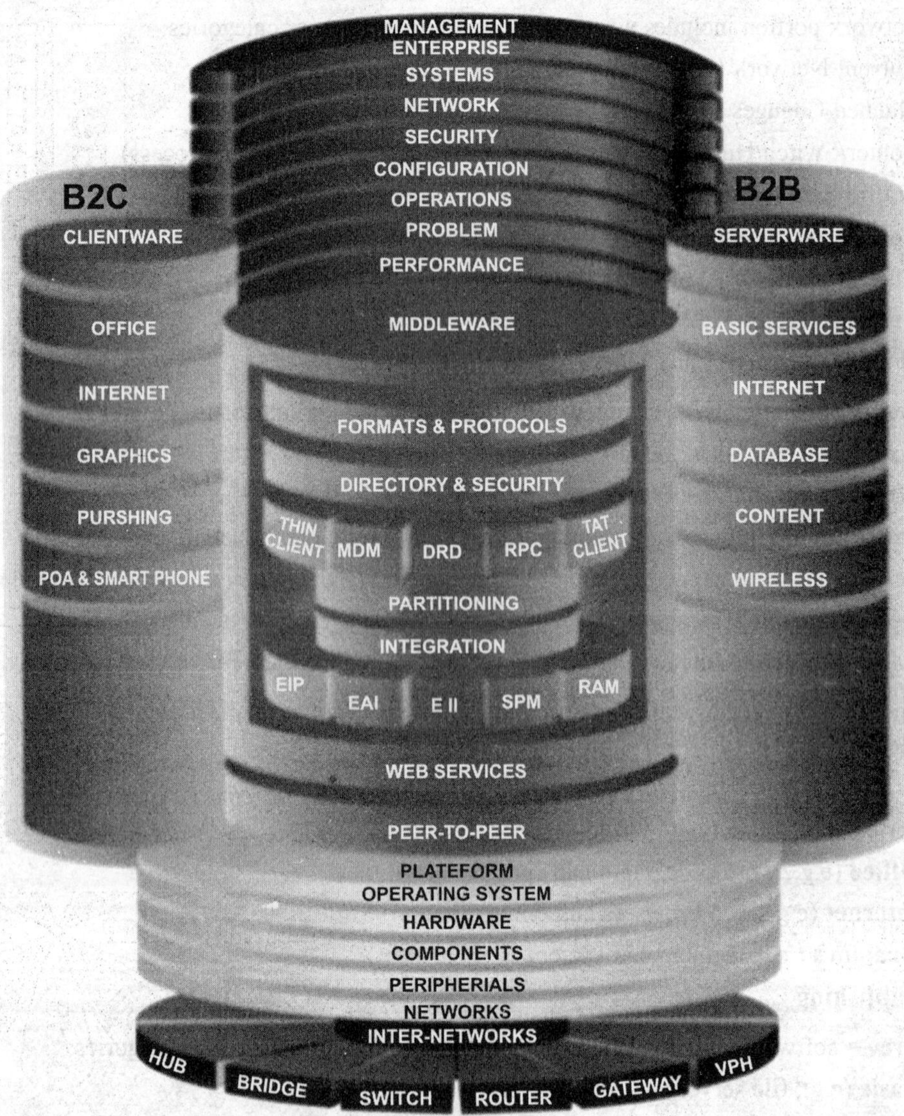


**Fig. 1.12:** IT Infrastructure Roadmap

**Platforms** provide the base foundation for computing and communication — consisting of:

- Operating Systems
- Hardware
- Components
- Peripherals
- Networks

## 1.8 INFRASTRUCTURE MANAGEMENT

Infrastructure management (IM) is the management of essential operation components, such as policies, processes, equipment, data, human resources, and external contacts, for overall effectiveness. Infrastructure management products are available from a number of vendors including, as divided into categories of system management and network management & storage management, and vendors including HP, IBM, MICROSOFT.

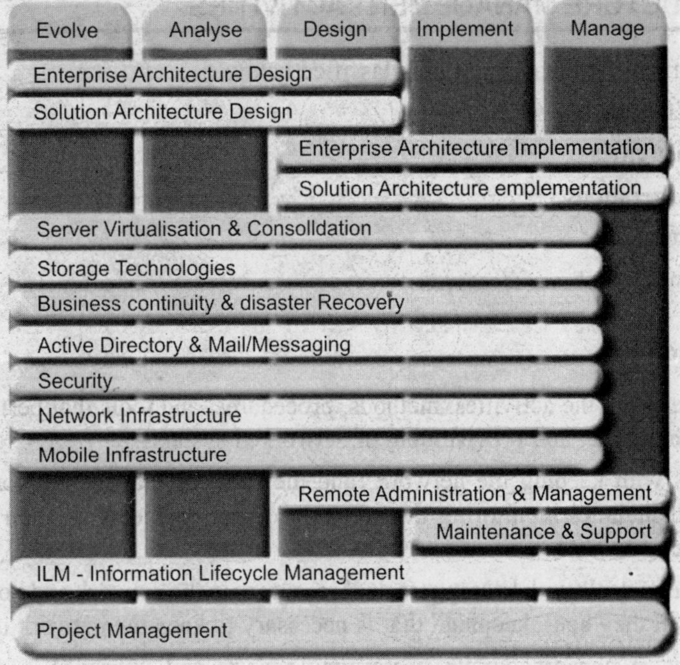


**Fig. 1.13:** Shows Infrastructure Management

Among other purposes, infrastructure management seeks to:

- Reduce duplication of effort
- Ensure adherence to standards
- Enhance the flow of information throughout an information system
- Promote adaptability necessary for a changeable environment
- Ensure interoperability among organizational and external entities
- Maintain effective policies and practices
- Reduce the total cost of IT operations.
- Focus limited IT resources on core business activities.
- Rationalize IT staffing costs
- Optimize IT asset utilization

- Facilitate service delivery
- Improve uptime & system availability.

Although all business activities depend upon the infrastructure, planning and projects to ensure its effective management are typically undervalued to the detriment of the organization. According to IDC, a prominent research firm, investments in infrastructure management have the largest single impact on an organization's revenue.

## 1.9 INFRASTRUCTURE MANAGEMENT ACTIVITIES

Activities of Infrastructure Management are classified below:

- Network activities
- Technical activities
- Computer Operations
- Customer service
- System management

### 1.9.1 Network Activity

**Network activity** refers to the activities, methods, procedures, and tools that pertain to the operation, administration, maintenance, and provisioning of networked systems.

Operation deals with keeping the network (and the services that the network provides) up and running smoothly. It includes monitoring the network to spot problems as soon as possible, ideally before users are affected.

- Administration deals with keeping track of resources in the network and how they are assigned. It includes all the "housekeeping" that is necessary to keep the network under control.
- Maintenance is concerned with performing repairs and upgrades — for example, when equipment must be replaced, when a router needs a patch for an operating system image, when a new switch is added to a network. Maintenance also involves corrective and preventive measures to make the managed network run "better", such as adjusting device configuration parameters.
- Provisioning is concerned with configuring resources in the network to support a given service. For example, this might include setting up the network so that a new customer can receive voice service.

A common way of characterizing network management functions is FCAPS Fault, Configuration, Accounting, Performance and Security.

Functions that are performed as part of network management accordingly include controlling, planning, allocating, deploying, coordinating, and monitoring the resources of a network, network planning, frequency allocation, predetermined traffic routing to support load balancing, cryptographic key distribution authorization, configuration management, fault management, security management, performance management, bandwidth management, Route analytics and accounting management.

Data for network management is collected through several mechanisms, including agents installed on infrastructure, synthetic monitoring that simulates transactions, logs of activity, sniffers and real user monitoring. In the past network management mainly consisted of monitoring whether devices were up or down; today performance management has become a crucial part of the IT team's role which brings about a host of challenges — especially for global organizations.

## 1.9.2 Database Administration

**Database administration** is the function of managing and maintaining database management systems (DBMS) software. Mainstream DBMS software such as Oracle, IBM DB2 and Microsoft SQL Server need ongoing management. As such, corporations that use DBMS software often hire specialized IT (Information Technology) personnel called Database Administrators or DBAs.

### *1.9.2.1 DBA Responsibilities*

- Installation, configuration and upgrading of Database server software and related products.
- Evaluate Database features and Database related products.
- Establish and maintain sound backup and recovery policies and procedures.
- Take care of the Database design and implementation.
- Implement and maintain database security (create and maintain users and roles, assign privileges).
- Database tuning and performance monitoring.
- Application tuning and performance monitoring.
- Setup and maintain documentation and standards.
- Plan growth and changes (capacity planning).
- Work as part of a team and provide 7×24 support when required.
- Do general technical trouble shooting and give consultation to development teams.
- Interface with Oracle / Microsoft Corporation for technical support

### *1.9.2.2 Types of Database Administration*

There are three types of DBAs:

1. Systems DBAs (sometimes also referred to as Physical DBAs, Operations DBAs or Production Support DBAs)
2. Development DBAs
3. Application DBAs

Depending on the DBA type, their functions usually vary. Below is a brief description of what different types of DBAs do:

1. Systems DBAs usually focus on the physical aspects of database administration such as DBMS installation, configuration, patching, upgrades, backups, restores, refreshes, performance optimization, maintenance and disaster recovery.

2. Development DBAs usually focus on the logical and development aspects of database administration such as data model design and maintenance, DDL (data definition language) generation, SQL writing and tuning, coding stored procedures, collaborating with developers to help choose the most appropriate DBMS feature/functionality and other pre-production activities.
3. Application DBAs are usually found in organizations that have purchased 3rd party application software such as ERP (enterprise resource planning) and CRM (customer relationship management) systems. Examples of such application software includes Oracle Applications, Siebel and PeopleSoft (both now part of Oracle Corp.) and SAP. Application DBAs straddle the fence between the DBMS and the application software and are responsible for ensuring that the application is fully optimized for the database and vice versa. They usually manage all the application components that interact with the database and carry out activities such as application installation and patching, application upgrades, database cloning, building and running data cleanup routines, data load process management, etc.

### 1.9.3 System Administration

**System administration** — Activities performed by a system administrator (or "admin", "sysadmin", "site admin") such as monitoring security configuration, managing allocation of user names and passwords, monitoring disk space and other resource use, performing backups, and setting up new hardware and software.

***Administration* means management of computer infrastructures in a way to minimize human-computer interaction.**

In other words, system administrators should manage, order, build, install, configure, and maintain (your) computers so that you will have to use them less, or not at all. The definition applies to itself in so far as system administrators will seek to minimize their own human-computer interaction.

The act of system administration is somewhat like *medical care*. A medical practitioner should keep you healthy, and, if she or he succeeds in doing so, you should never need to see your doctor. Best system administration means you should never need to work with computers.

And, just like medical practitioners, system administrators are to keep confidential any information to which they have access.

#### *1.9.3.1 Duties of a System Administrator*

A system administrator's responsibilities might include:

- Analyzing system logs and identifying potential issues with computer systems.
- Introducing and integrating new technologies into existing data center environments.
- Performing routine audits of systems and software.
- Performing backups.
- Applying operating system updates, patches, and configuration changes.
- Installing and configuring new hardware and software.
- Adding, removing, or updating user account information, resetting passwords, etc.

- Answering technical queries.
- Responsibility for security.
- Responsibility for documenting the configuration of the system.
- Troubleshooting any reported problems.
- System performance tuning.
- Ensuring that the network infrastructure is up and running.

In larger organizations, some tasks listed above may be divided among different system administrators or members of different organizational groups. For example, a dedicated individual(s) may apply all system upgrades, a Quality Assurance (QA) team may perform testing and validation, and one or more technical writers may be responsible for all technical documentation written for a company.

In smaller organizations, the system administrator can also perform any number of duties elsewhere associated with other fields:

- Technical support
- Database administrator (DBA)
- Network administrator/analyst/specialist
- Application analyst
- Security administrator
- Programmer

### 1.9.4 Computer Operation

These include all the operations done on the computer systems.

#### *1.9.4.1 Customer Service*

**Customer service** is the provision of service to customers before, during and after a purchase.

According to Jamier L. Scott. (2002), "Customer service is a series of activities designed to enhance the level of customer satisfaction – that is, the feeling that a product or service has met the customer expectation."

Its importance varies by product, industry and customer; defective or broken merchandise can be exchanged, often only with a receipt and within a specified time frame. Retail stores will often have a desk or counter devoted to dealing with returns, exchanges and complaints, or will perform related functions at the point of sale.

Customer service may be provided by a person (e.g., sales and service representative), or by automated means called self-service. Examples of self service are Internet sites. The experience a customer has of a product also affect the total service experience, but this is more of a product direct feature than what is included in the definition of customer service.

Customer service is normally an integral part of a company's customer value proposition. In their book *Rules to Break and Laws to Follow*, Don Peppers and Martha Rogers, Ph.D. write that "customers have memories. They will remember you, whether you remember them or not." Further, "customer trust can be destroyed at once by a major service problem, or it can be undermined one day at a time, with a thousand small demonstrations of incompetence."

From the point of view of an overall sales process engineering effort, customer service plays an important role in an organization's ability to generate income and revenue. From that perspective, customer service should be included as part of an overall approach to systematic improvement.

How poor customer support can affect your business:

- Your customer feels ignored when their complaints go unresolved.
- Your customer loses trust in your company when you don't answer them.
- Dissatisfied customers share complaints with other potential customers.
- You lose both existing and prospective customers.

These functions include:

1. **Support:** Support services include resolution of billing queries, order taking, activation of accounts, registration of new customers and recording complaints.
2. **Marketing:** Marketing tasks carried out through a contact center include sending outbound emails, telemarketing, surveys and poling, responding to inbound emails and management of marketing campaigns.
3. **Sales:** Sales tasks include inbound sales, outbound sales, web chat, web call-back and co-browsing.
4. **Technical Support:** Customers require different technical support services such as data verification, application support, address updates and problem resolution through the technical help desk.
5. **Customer Analytics:** Customer analytics includes profitability analytics, quality auditing, reporting and complaint analysis.

### 1.9.5 Systems Management

**Systems management** refers to enterprise-wide administration of distributed computer systems. Systems management is strongly influenced by network management initiatives in telecommunications. System management may involve one or more of the following tasks:

- Hardware inventories.
- Server availability monitoring and metrics.
- Software inventory and installation.
- Anti-virus and anti-malware management.
- User's activities monitoring.
- Capacity monitoring.
- Security management.
- Storage management.
- Network capacity and utilization monitoring.

## 1.10 INFORMATION INFRASTRUCTURE DESIGN IN IT

### 1.10.1 Information Infrastructure

Information Infrastructure is the collection of communication networks and the software associated with it. It refers to the networks and the software, which supports interaction among people and organizations. Information infrastructure refers to the currently available networks and the prospective facilities that they will make available. It includes the Internet, the telecommunication networks and the embedded systems as also the computers.

Internet that is regarded as the network of networks is the information infrastructure of today. It is a collection of interconnected computer networks that transmit data in the form of packets using the Internet Protocol. Each of the networks carries information and services like mail and file transfer. World wide web, a collection of documents and other resources, is a service offered by the Internet.

Information infrastructure design is concerned with issues like privacy, security, translation, right to information and most of all the software and hardware compatibilities. Let us look at each of them.

- **Privacy**: Privacy of information is related to the collection of personal information. Many a times we are asked to furnish our personal details on the web. It might be in case of an online transaction or in the process of a registration. Such information collected over the web has to be kept private and confidential. People should feel safe while letting out such information. For this purpose, it is important to include information privacy in the design of information infrastructure.
- **Information Security**: Securing information is about protecting it from unauthorized access, disclosure or modification. An unauthorized access to information should not result in destruction of that information. Information security deals with confidentiality, availability and integrity.
  1. **Confidentiality**: It is preventing the information from being disclosed through unauthorized access.
  2. **Availability**: Computing systems that store information and the communication channels that enable access to it, must function properly. The information in an information system should be available for the users at any time.
  3. **Integrity**: In information security, integrity means that the information cannot be modified without authorization.
- **Rights surrounding Information**: Citizens have a right to obtain information. They are allowed to access copies of certain official documents. Law allows us as citizens of a country to access information. Information rights pertain to possession of the rights to copy or modify the acquired information. People who create content are its logical owners. So anyone other than the author cannot modify it. One is not permitted to steal content of another author. Rights to translation of content are as prescribed by law. To organize information in an information infrastructure, it is necessary to manage the rights to information.

- **Compatibility issues**: While accessing information over the web, different users access it in different ways. The software and hardware they use is different. The type of communication network over which they access information may be different. Here arise the compatibility issues. Looking at the pace with which new types of software and hardware are being built, backward compatibility of newer versions with the older ones is a serious concern.

National Information Infrastructure is associated with Information Infrastructure. It relates to the integrated communication system of the US. It takes into account the high-speed public and private broadband and narrowband networks. It also includes the satellite, wireless and terrestrial communications. It is inclusive of all the information that flows over the infrastructure.

### 1.10.2 Free Information Infrastructure

Free Information Infrastructure is a term used in Europe and it resembles the National Information Infrastructure. The use of the word 'free' in the term in intended to focus on freedom and the internet which is freely accessible. It comprises of no software patents. It sometimes refers to open source software. It is about free access, open standards, network neutrality and less control by state.

### 1.10.3 Global information Infrastructure

Global Information Infrastructure is an upcoming communication framework that is meant to connect the computer and telecommunication networks all over the world. Currently the Internet is considered as the Global Information Infrastructure.

Information infrastructure in IT is actually a vast subject. It deals with the creation, design and organization of information. It focuses on an information infrastructure that caters to the security and access needs of information. In the words of William Pollard, "Information is a source of learning. But unless it is organized, processed, and available to the right people in a format for decision making, it is a burden, not a benefit."

## 1.11 CUSTOMER REQUIREMENTS

Statements of fact and assumptions that define the expectations of the system in terms of mission objectives, environment, constraints, and measures of effectiveness and suitability. The customers are those that perform the eight primary functions of systems engineering, with special emphasis on the operator as the key customer. Operational requirements will define the basic need and, at a minimum, answer the questions posed in the following listing:

**Operational distribution or deployment:** Where will the system be used?

**Mission profile or scenario:** How will the system accomplish its mission objective?

**Performance and related parameters:** What are the critical system parameters to accomplish the mission?

**Utilization environments:** How are the various system components to be used?

**Effectiveness requirements:** How effective or efficient must the system be in performing its mission?

**Operational life cycle:** How long will the system be in use by the user?

**Environment:** What environments will the system be expected to operate in an effective manner?

**Methods for Identification of Customers requirements**

- Exploratory research
- In-depth interview
- Focus group

### 1.11.1 Exploratory Research

Exploratory research provides insights into and comprehension of an issue or situation. It should draw definitive conclusions only with extreme caution. **Exploratory research** is a type of research conducted because a problem has not been clearly defined. Exploratory research helps determine the best research design, data collection method and selection of subjects. Given its fundamental nature, exploratory research often concludes that a perceived problem does not actually exist.

There are three types of objective in a marketing research project.

- Exploratory Research
- Descriptive research
- Causal research

***Exploratory Research:*** 'The objective of exploratory research is to gather preliminary information that will help define problems and suggest hypotheses.'

***Descriptive Research:*** 'The objective of descriptive research is to describe things, such as the market potential for a product or the demographics and attitudes of consumers who buy the product.'

***Causal Research:*** 'The objective of causal Research is to test hypotheses about cause-and-effect relationships

### 1.11.2 In-depth Interview

An **in-depth interview** is a qualitative research technique that allows person to person discussion. It can lead to increased insight into people's thoughts, feelings, and behavior on important issues. This type of interview is often unstructured and therefore permits the interviewer to encourage an informant (respondent) to talk at length about the topic of interest.

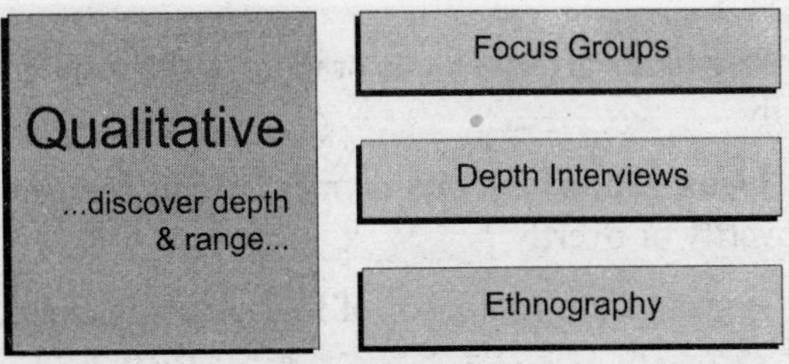


**Fig. 1.14**

The in-depth interview uses a flexible interview approach. It aims to ask questions to explain the reasons underlying a problem or practice in a target group. You can use the technique to gather ideas, to gather information, and to develop materials for drug use interventions.

**Table 1.1:** Summary of Key Steps in Conducting In-depth Interview

| | |
|---|---|
| **Step 1:** | Plan how you will conduct the in-depth interviews. |
| **Step 2:** | Decide who your respondents will be. |
| **Step 3:** | Prepare interview guide for each category of informants. |
| **Step 4:** | Select your interviewers. |
| **Step 5:** | Train the interviewers. |
| **Step 6:** | Conduct the actual interviews. |
| **Step 7:** | Analyse the data. |
| **Step 8:** | Write a report and recommend intervention(s). |

### 1.11.3 Focus Group

A **focus group** is a form of qualitative research in which a group of people are asked about their attitude towards a product, service, concept, advertisement, idea, or packaging. Questions are asked in an interactive group setting where participants are free to talk with other group members.

The first focus groups were created at the Bureau of Applied Social Research by associate director, sociologist Robert K. Merton. The term itself was coined by psychologist and marketing expert Ernest Dichter.

#### *1.11.3.1 Types of Focus Groups*

Variants of focus groups include:

- **Two-way focus group** — one focus group watches another focus group and discusses the observed interactions and conclusion
- **Dual moderator focus group** — one moderator ensures the session progresses smoothly, while another ensures that all the topics are covered
- **Dueling moderator focus group** — two moderators deliberately take opposite sides on the issue under discussion
- **Respondent moderator focus group** — one or more of the respondents are asked to act as the moderator temporarily
- **Client participant focus groups** — one or more client representatives participate in the discussion, either covertly or overtly
- **Mini focus groups** — groups are composed of four or five members rather than 6 to 12
- **Teleconference focus groups** — telephone network is used
- **Online focus groups** — computers connected via the internet are used

Focus groups are a powerful means to evaluate services or test new ideas. Basically, focus groups are interviews, but of 6-10 people at the same time in the same group. One can get a great deal of information during a focus group session.

#### 1.11.3.2 Preparing for the Session

1. **Identify the major objective of the meeting.**
2. **Carefully develop five to six questions (see below).**
3. **Plan your session (see below).**
4. **Call potential members to invite them to the meeting.** Send them a follow-up invitation with a proposed agenda, session time and list of questions the group will discuss. Plan to provide a copy of the report from the session to each member and let them know you will do this.
5. **About three days before the session, call each member to remind them to attend.**

#### 1.11.3.3 Developing Questions

1. **Develop five to six questions** — Session should last one to 1.5 hours — in this time, one can ask at most five or six questions.
2. **Always first ask yourself what problem or need will be addressed by the information** gathered during the session, e.g., examine if a new service or idea will work, further understand how a program is failing, etc.
3. **Focus groups are basically multiple interviews.** Therefore, many of the same guidelines for conducting focus groups are similar to conducting interviews (see the Basics of Conducting Interviews).

#### 1.11.3.4 Planning the Session

1. **Scheduling:** Plan meetings to be one to 1.5 hours long. Over lunch seems to be a very good time for other to find time to attend.
2. **Setting and Refreshments:** Hold sessions in a conference room, or other setting with adequate air flow and lighting. Configure chairs so that all members can see each other. Provide name tags for members, as well. Provide refreshments, especially box lunches if the session is held over lunch.
3. **Ground Rules:** It's critical that all members participate as much as possible, yet the session move along while generating useful information. Because the session is often a one-time occurrence, it's useful to have a few, short ground rules that sustain participation, yet do so with focus. Consider the following three ground rules: a) keep focused, b) maintain momentum and c) get closure on questions.
4. **Agenda:** Consider the following agenda: welcome, review of agenda, review of goal of the meeting, review of ground rules, introductions, questions and answers, wrap up.
5. **Membership:** Focus groups are usually conducted with 6-10 members who have some similar nature, e.g., similar age group, status in a program, etc. Select members who are likely to be participative and reflective. Attempt to select members who don't know each other.
6. **Plan to record the session with either an audio or audio-video recorder.** Don't count on your memory. If this isn't practical, involve a co-facilitator who is there to take notes.

#### *1.11.3.5 Facilitating the Session*

1. **Major goal of facilitation is collecting useful information to meet goal of meeting.**
2. **Introduce yourself and the co-facilitator, if used.**
3. **Explain the means to record the session.**
4. **Carry out the agenda** — (See "agenda" above).
5. **Carefully word each question** before that question is addressed by the group. Allow the group a few minutes for each member to carefully record their answers. Then, facilitate discussion around the answers to each question, one at a time.
6. **After each question is answered, carefully reflect back a summary of what you heard (the note taker may do this).**
7. **Ensure even participation.** If one or two people are dominating the meeting, then call on others. Consider using a round- table approach, including going in one direction around the table, giving each person a minute to answer the question. If the domination persists, note it to the group and ask for ideas about how the participation can be increased.
8. **Closing the session** — Tell members that they will receive a copy of the report generated from their answers, thank them for coming, and adjourn the meeting.

#### *1.11.3.6 Immediately After Session*

1. **Verify if the tape recorder, if used, worked throughout the session.**
2. **Make any notes on your written notes**, e.g., to clarify any scratching, ensure pages are numbered, fill out any notes that don't make senses, etc
3. **Write down any observations made during the session.** For example, where did the session occur and when, what was the nature of participation in the group? Were there any surprises during the session?

## 1.12 IT SYSTEMS MANAGEMENT

The general area of Information Technology (IT) that concerns and managing computer resources, especially network resources.

Systems management is strongly influenced by network initiatives in telecommunications. System management may involve one or more of the following tasks:

- Hardware inventories.
- Server availability monitoring and metrics.
- Software inventory and installation.
- Anti-virus and anti-malware management.
- User's activities monitoring.
- Capacity monitoring.
- Security management.
- Storage management.
- Network capacity and utilization monitoring.

**Fault Management**

- Troubleshootin, error logging and data recovery

**Configuration Management**

- Hardware and software inventory
- Provising, software depolyment and package management

**Accounting Management**

- Billing and statistics gathering

**Performance Management**

- Software metering, event and metric monitoring

**Security Management**

- Idemtity management
- Policy management

## 1.13 INFORMATION TECHNOLOGY INFRASTRUCTURE LIBRARY

The **Information Technology Infrastructure Library (ITIL)** also known as **Infrastructure Management Service (IMS)** is a set of concepts and policies for managing (IT) infrastructure, development and operations

ITIL gives a detailed description of a number of important IT practices with comprehensive checklists, tasks and procedures that any IT organization can tailor to its needs

(ITIL) A method of organising the system and network management departments of large organisations. ITIL defines the (work) processes involved and the interfaces between them.

### 1.13.1 History

In the 1980s, the UK Government's developed a set of recommendations, in response to the growing dependence on IT, and the recognition that without standard practices, government agencies and private sector contracts were independently creating their own IT management practices.

In the 1980s, the UK Government's developed a set of recommendations, in response to the growing dependence on IT, and the recognition that without standard practices, government agencies and private sector contracts were independently creating their own IT management practices.

The **IT Infrastructure Library** originated as a collection of books each covering a specific practice within IT Service Management. ITIL was built around a process-model based view of controlling and managing operations often credited to and his cycle.

After the initial publication in 1989, the number of books quickly grew within ITIL v1 to over 30 volumes.

In 2000/2001, to make ITIL more accessible (and affordable), ITIL v2 consolidated the publications into 8 logical 'sets' that grouped related process guidelines to match different aspects of IT management, applications, and services. However, the main focus was known as the Service Management sets (Service Support and Service Delivery) which were by far the most widely used, circulated, and understood of ITIL v2 publications.

In May 2007, this organization issued the version 3 of ITIL (also known as the ITIL Refresh Project) consisting of 26 processes and functions, now grouped under only 5 volumes, arranged around the concept of Service lifecycle structure.

In 2009, the OGC officially announced that ITIL v2 would be withdrawn and launched a major consultation as per how to proceed.

### 1.13.2 ITIL Methodology

The Information Technology Infrastructure Library (ITIL) is a collection of best practices that aim to improve and then maintain a certain level of computing services quality in the information technology sector. ITIL covers organizational structure and skill requirements for an IT organization via a comprehensive set of procedures with which an organization can manage its IT operations. These procedures do not rely on a particular vendor's technology and apply to all aspects of IT infrastructure.

ITIL consists of a collection of 7 books. The sets are sub-divided into disciplines, each of which is focused on a specific subject.

**Service Delivery:** Covers the processes required for the planning and delivery of quality IT services, and looks at the longer-term processes associated with improving the quality of IT services delivered.

*IT Financial Management*

*Capacity Management*

*Availability Management*

*IT Continuity Management*

*Service Level Management*

**Service Support:** Describes the processes associated with the day-to-day support and maintenance activities involved in the provision of IT services.

*Change Management*

*Release Management*

*Problem Management*

*Incident Management*

*Configuration Management*

*Service Desk*

**Planning to Implement Service Management:** Examines the issues and tasks involved in planning, implementing, and improving service management processes within an organization; also addresses the issues associated with addressing cultural and organizational change, the development of a vision and strategy, and the most appropriate method of approach.

**Security Management:** Details the process of planning and managing a defined level of security for information and IT services, including all aspects of security incidents. Also includes the assessment and management of risks and vulnerabilities and the implementation of cost-justifiable countermeasures.

**Information and Communications Technology (ICT) Infrastructure Management:** Covers all aspects of ICT infrastructure management from identification of business requirements through the procurement process, to the testing, installation, deployment, and ongoing operation and optimization of ICT components and IT services.

*Network service Management*

*Operations Management*

*Management of local processors*

*Computer installation and acceptance*

*Systems Management*

**The Business Perspective**: Provides advice and guidance to help IT personnel understand how they can contribute to business objectives and how their roles and services can be better aligned and exploited to maximize contribution.

**Application Management:** Describes how to manage applications from the initial business need through all stages in the application lifecycle, up to and including retirement. Places emphasis on ensuring that IT projects and strategies are tightly aligned with those of the business through the application lifecycle, to ensure that business obtains the best value from its investment.

From the beginning, the ITIL framework has been publicly available (however, it is copyright protected). This means that any organization can use the framework described by the OGC in its numerous books. Because of this, ITIL guidance has been used by a wide range of organizations including government, energy, public utilities, retail, finance, and manufacturing. Very large organizations, very small organizations and everything in between have implemented ITIL processes.

### 1.13.3 Overview of the ITIL v3 library

Five key volumes comprise the ITIL v3, published in May 2007:

1. **Service Strategy**
2. **Service Design**
3. **Service Transition**
4. **Service Operation**
5. **Continual Service Improvement**

#### *1.13.3.1 Service Strategy*

As the center and origin point of the ITIL Service Lifecycle, the Service Strategy volume provides guidance on clarification and prioritization of service provider investments in services. More generally, Service Strategy focuses on helping IT organizations improve and develop over the long term. In both cases, Service Strategy relies largely upon a market-driven approach. Key topics covered include service value definition, business case development, service assets, market analysis, and service provider types. Processes covered include service portfolio management, demand management, and IT financial management.

#### 1.13.3.2 Service Design

The ITIL Service Design volume provides good practice guidance on the design of IT services, processes, and other aspects of the service management effort. Significantly, design within ITIL is understood to encompass all elements relevant to technology service delivery, rather than focusing solely on design of the technology itself. As such, Service Design addresses how a planned service solution interacts with the larger business and technical environments, service management systems required to support the service, processes which interacts with the service, technology, and required to support the service, and the supply chain required to support the planned service. Within ITIL, design work for an IT service is aggregated into a single Service Design Package (SDP). Service Design Packages, along with other information about services, are managed within the service catalog. Processes covered in this volume include , availability management, capacity management, IT service continuity management, information security management, supplier management, and service catalog management.

#### 1.13.3.3 Service Transition

Service transition relates to the delivery of services required by the business into live/operational use, and often encompasses the "project" side of IT rather than "BAU" (Business As Usual). This area also covers topics such as managing changes to the "BAU" environment. Topics include Service Asset and Configuration Management, Transition Planning and Support, Release and deployment management, change management, knowledge management, as well as the key roles of staff engaging in Service Transition.

#### 1.13.3.4 Service Operation

Best practice for achieving the delivery of agreed levels of services both to end-users and the customers (where "customers" refer to those individuals who pay for the service and negotiate the SLAs). Service Operations is the part of the  where the services and value is actually directly delivered. Also the monitoring of problems and balance between service reliability and cost etc are considered. Topics include balancing conflicting goals (e.g. reliability vs cost etc), Event management, , , request fulfillment, access management, . The functions include technical management,application management , operations management and Service Desk as well as, responsibilities for staff engaging in Service Operation.

#### 1.13.3.5 Continual Service Improvement (CSI)

Aligning and realigning IT services to changing business needs (because standstill implies decline).

The goal of Continual Service Improvement is to align and realign IT Services to changing business needs by identifying and implementing improvements to the IT services that support the Business Processes. The perspective of CSI on improvement is the business perspective of service quality, even though CSI aims to improve process effectiveness, and cost effectiveness of the IT processes through the whole lifecycle. To manage improvement, CSI should clearly define what should be controlled and measured.

CSI needs to be treated just like any other service practice. There needs to be upfront planning, training and awareness, ongoing scheduling, roles created, ownership assigned,and activities identified to be successful. CSI must be planned and scheduled as process with defined activities, inputs, outputs, roles and reporting.

### 1.13.4 Overview of the ITIL 2 library

The eight ITIL version 2 books and their disciplines are:

The IT Service Management sets

1. **Service Delivery**
2. **Service Support**

Other operational guidance

3. **ICT Infrastructure Management**
4. **Security Management**
5. **The Business Prespective**
6. **Application Management**
7. **Software Asset Management**
8. **Planning to Implement Service Management**
9. **ITIL small-scale Implementation**

#### *1.13.4.1 Service Delivery*

The Service Delivery discipline is primarily concerned with proactive services the ICT must deliver to provide adequate support to business users. It focuses on the business as the *customer* of the ICT services. The discipline consists of the following processes, explained in subsections below:

Service Level Management

Capacity Management

IT Service Continuity Management

Availability Management

Financial Management

#### *1.13.4.2 Service Support*

The Service Support ITIL discipline is focused on the *User* of the ICT services and is primarily concerned with ensuring that they have access to the appropriate services to support the business functions.

To a business, customers and users are the entry point to the process model. They get involved in service support by:

Asking for changes

Needing communication, updates

Having difficulties, queries.

Real process delivery

The is the single contact point for customers problems. If there is a direct solution, it tries to resolve the problem. If not, it creates an . *Incidents* initiate a chain of processes: Incident Management, Problem Management, Change Management, Release Management and Configuration Management (see following sections for details). This chain of processes is tracked using the Configuration Management Database (CMDB), which records each process, and creates output documents for traceability (Quality Management).

#### *1.13.4.3 Service Desk / Service Request Management*

Tasks include handling incidents and requests, and providing an interface for other ITSM processes.

Single Point of Contact (SPOC) and not necessarily the First Point of Contact (FPOC)

There is a single point of entry and exit

Easier for Customers

Data Integrity

Communication channel is streamlined

The primary *functions* of the Service Desk are:

**Incident Control:** life cycle management of all Service Requests

**Communication:** keeping the customer informed of progress and advising on workarounds

The Service Desk function is known under various names.

: main emphasis on professionally handling large call volumes of telephone-based transactions

: manage, co-ordinate and resolve incidents as quickly as possible

Service Desk not only handles incidents, problems and questions but also provides an interface for other activities such as change requests, maintenance contracts, software licenses, service level management, configuration management, availability management, Financial Management and IT Services Continuity Management

The three *types* of structure that can be considered are:

**Local Service Desk:** to meet local business needs - is practical only until multiple locations requiring support services are involved.

**Central Service Desk:** for organizations having multiple locations - reduces operational costs and improves usage of available resources.

**Virtual Service Desk:** for organizations having multi-country locations - can be situated and accessed from anywhere in the world due to advances in network performance and telecommunications, reducing operational costs and improving usage of available resources.

### 1.13.5 ICT Infrastructure Management

ICT Infrastructure Management recommend best practice for requirements analysis, planning, design, deployment and ongoing operations management and technical support of an ICT Infrastructure. ("ICT" is an acronym for "Information and Communication Technology".)

The Infrastructure Management processes describe those processes within ITIL that directly relate to the ICT equipment and software that is involved in providing ICT services to customers.

- **ICT Design and Planning**
- **ICT Deployment**
- **ICT Operations**
- **ICT Technical Support**

These disciplines are less well understood than those of Service Management and therefore often some of their content is believed to be covered 'by implication' in Service Management disciplines.

### *1.13.5.1 ICT Design and Planning*

ICT Design and Planning provides a framework and approach for the Strategic and Technical Design and Planning of ICT infrastructures. It includes the necessary combination of Business (and overall IS) strategy, with technical design and architecture. ICT Design and Planning drives both the Procurement of new ICT solutions through the production of Statements of Requirement ("SOR") and Invitations to ("ITT") and is responsible for the initiation and management of ICT Programmes for strategic business change. Key Outputs from Design and Planning are:

- ICT Strategies, Policies and Plans
- The ICT Overall Architecture & Management Architecture
- Feasibility Studies, ITTs and SORs
- Business Cases

### *1.13.5.2 ICT Deployment Management*

ICT Deployment provides a framework for the successful management of design, build, test and roll-out (deploy) projects within an overall ICT . It includes many disciplines in common with , but has a broader focus to include the necessary integration of Release Management and both functional and non functional testing.

### *1.13.5.3 ICT Operations Management*

ICT Operations Management provides the day-to-day technical supervision of the ICT infrastructure. Often confused with the role of Incident Management from Service Support, Operations is more technical and is concerned not solely with Incidents reported by users, but with Events generated by or recorded by the Infrastructure. ICT Operations may often work closely alongside Incident Management and the Service Desk, which are not-necessarily technical, to provide an 'Operations Bridge'. Operations, however should primarily work from documented processes and procedures and should be concerned with a number of specific sub-processes, such as: Output Management, Job Scheduling, Backup and Restore, Network Monitoring/Management, System Monitoring/Management, Database Monitoring/ Management Storage Monitoring/Management. Operations are responsible for:

- A stable, secure ICT infrastructure
- A current, up to date Operational Documentation Library ("ODL")
- A log of all operational Events

- Maintenance of operational monitoring and management tools.
- Operational Scripts
- Operational Procedures

#### *1.13.5.4 ICT Technical Support*

ICT Technical Support is the specialist technical function for infrastructure within ICT. Primarily as a support to other processes, both in Infrastructure Management and Service Management, Technical Support provides a number of specialist functions: Research and Evaluation, Market Intelligence (particularly for Design and Planning and Capacity Management), Proof of Concept and Pilot engineering, specialist technical expertise (particularly to Operations and Problem Management), creation of documentation (perhaps for the Operational Documentation Library or Known Error Database).

### 1.13.6 Security Management

The ITIL-process Security Management describes the structured fitting of information security in the management organization. ITIL Security Management is based on the code of practice for information security management also known as ISO/IEC 17799.

A basic concept of the Security Management is the information security. The primary goal of information security is to guarantee safety of the information. Safety is to be protected against risks. Security is the means to be safe against risks. When protecting information it is the value of the information that has to be protected. These values are stipulated by the confidentiality, integrity and availability. Inferred aspects are privacy, anonymity and verifiability.

The current move towards ISO/IEC 27001 may require some revision to the ITIL Security Management best practices which are often claimed to be rich in content for physical security but weak in areas such as software/application security and logical security in the ICT infrastructure.

### 1.13.7 The Business Perspective

The Business Perspective is the name given to the collection of best practices that is suggested to address some of the issues often encountered in understanding and improving IT service provision, as a part of the entire business requirement for high IS quality management. These issues are:

**Business Continuity Management** describes the responsibilities and opportunities available to the business manager to improve what is, in most organizations one of the key contributing services to business efficiency and effectiveness.

**Surviving Change.** IT infrastructure changes can impact the manner in which business is conducted or the continuity of business operations. It is important that business managers take notice of these changes and ensure that steps are taken to safeguard the business from adverse side effects.

**Transformation of business practice through radical change** helps to control IT and to integrate it with the business.

**Partnerships and outsourcing.** This volume is related to the topics of IT Governance and IT Portfolio Management.

### 1.13.8 Application Management

ITIL Application Management set encompasses a set of best practices proposed to improve the overall quality of IT software development and support through the life-cycle of software development projects, with particular attention to gathering and defining requirements that meet business objectives.

### 1.13.9 Software Asset Management

Software Asset Management (SAM) is the practice of integrating people, processes and technology to allow software licenses and usage to be systematically tracked, evaluated and managed. The goal of SAM is to reduce IT expenditures, human resource overhead and risks inherent in owning and managing software assets.

SAM practices include:

- Maintaining software license compliance
- Tracking inventory and software asset use
- Maintaining standard policies and procedures surrounding definition, deployment, configuration, use, and retirement of software assets and the Definitive Software Library.

SAM represents the software component of IT asset management. This includes hardware asset management because effective hardware inventory controls are critical to efforts to control software. This means overseeing software and hardware that comprise an organization's computers and network.

### 1.13.10 Planning to Implement Service Management

The ITIL discipline — Planning To Implement Service Management attempts to provide practitioners with a framework for the alignment of business needs and IT provision requirements. The processes and approaches incorporated within the guidelines suggest the development of a Continuous Service Improvement Programme (CSIP) as the basis for implementing other ITIL disciplines as projects within a controlled programme of work. Planning To Implement Service Management is mainly focused on the Service Management processes, but is also generically applicable to other ITIL disciplines.

- create vision
- analyze organization
- set goals
- implement IT service management

### 1.13.11 Small-Scale Implementation

ITIL **Small-Scale Implementation** provides an approach to ITIL framework implementation for smaller IT units or departments. It is primarily an auxiliary work that covers many of the same best practice guidelines as *Planning To Implement Service Management, Service Support, and Service Delivery* but provides additional guidance on the combination of roles and responsibilities, and avoiding conflict between ITIL priorities.

CHAPTER 2

# Service Delivery Process

**Introduction:** As accountants and business advisors, approach the task of planning for the future of your business as a comprehensive process, rather than a series of independent transactions.

The philosophy is to help you develop the most appropriate strategies by:

- Focusing on the business asset as the essential element of your plan;
- Describing in a straightforward manner the menu of estate planning vehicles and tools available, including trusts;
- Reviewing current and projected cash flows of the business to ensure that recommended strategies are affordable and practical;
- Considering strategies for the business that make sense in the context of personal and family issues; and
- Providing year-round advice in response to changes in your business, goals or family circumstances, or to changes in the tax laws — all of which may necessitate revisions to your current estate plan (e.g., wills, trusts, and charitable plans).

And then committed to developing a comprehensive plan that balances the needs of owners/ managers, their families and their businesses.

## 2.1 SERVICE DELIVERY PROCESS

Service Level Management involves negotiating, defining, managing and improving the quality of IT services at an acceptable cost to the business. To optimize this process, IT needs to strike the right balance between business expectations and what it can actually deliver. Service Level Management often involves organizational and cultural change, since the IT organization needs to move from "systems" to "services" based thinking. From an ITIL perspective, effective Service Level Management results in a sound working relationship between IT and the business. Service Level Management is a means to building partnerships and working collaboratively towards common goals.

Service delivery process is focused on three major design criteria:

- Low transaction costs

- High flexibility of interaction
- Regular coordination

Generally there are three types of Service delivery process Phases as shown below in diagram.

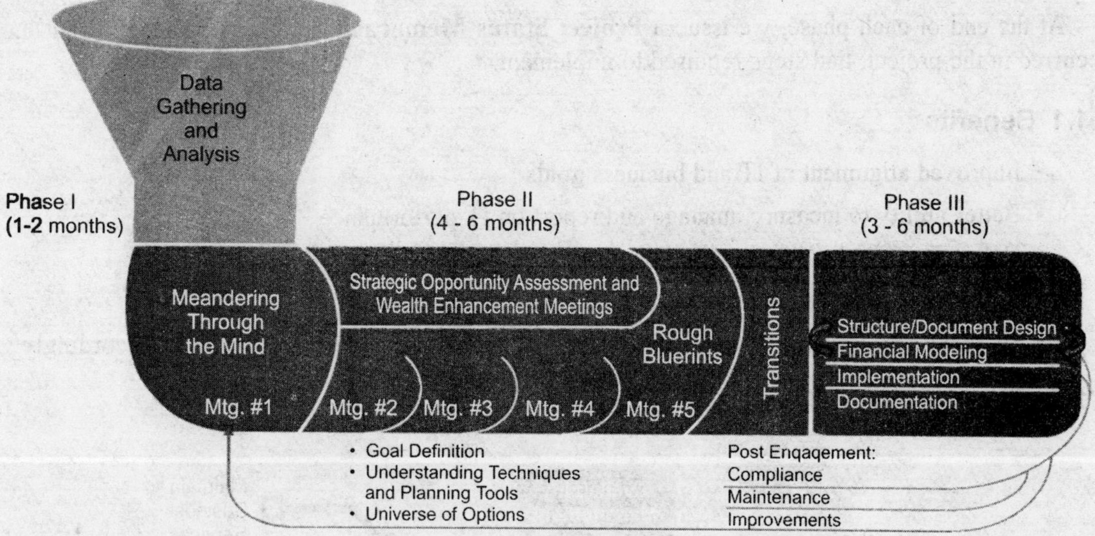


**Fig. 2.1:** Shows the Phases of Service delivery process

**Phase I: Data Gathering and Analysis**

**Data gathering and analysis** includes all information related to the numeric and fact-based information peculiar to the client. Examples of quantitative data include income tax returns, financial statements, wills, trust documents, etc.

Deliverable:

Summary of existing plan ,

"Soft Spots", urgent items to address, and

Projected Liabilities — current and date of death,

**Phase II: Meandering Through The Mind**

**Meandering Through the mind** is the process of identifying the subjective goals of the client. It relates to philosophy, fears, family relationships, establishing goals, and conflict avoidance issues. It is important to look beyond the "numbers" — wealth planning is designed to improve the lives of families and achieve goals: preserve family harmony; maintain control; minimize taxes.

The ultimate goal of **Phase II** is to educate the client on the extensive techniques and strategies, that he or she may use in his or her estate plan, and define how these techniques will achieve the ultimate goals of the client.

In **Phase II, meetings 2–5**, we discuss dozens of possible techniques and strategies of benefit to your family. We schedule these meetings every 4 to 6 weeks.

In Phase II, we utilize **Universe of Options**. This sophisticated software tool comprehensively illustrates the strategies we discuss. We present "concepts" slides that explain fundamental estate planning concepts. The training allows selection of the strategies that will create a **Rough Blueprint:** the client's proposed estate structure. Detailed narrative reports, explaining the structures, concepts, and techniques, can also be provided.

At the end of each phase, we issue a **Project Status Memorandum**. This documents what has occurred in the project, and steps required to implement.

### 2.1.1 Benefits

- Improved alignment of IT and business goals
- Better ability to measure, manage and report on IT performance
- Helps create and maintain a customer-centric focus for IT activities
- Supports continuous improvement of Quality of Service (QoS)
- Helps IT spot trends that could lead to service degradation, and adapt services Accordingly

### 2.1.2 The Service Delivery Map

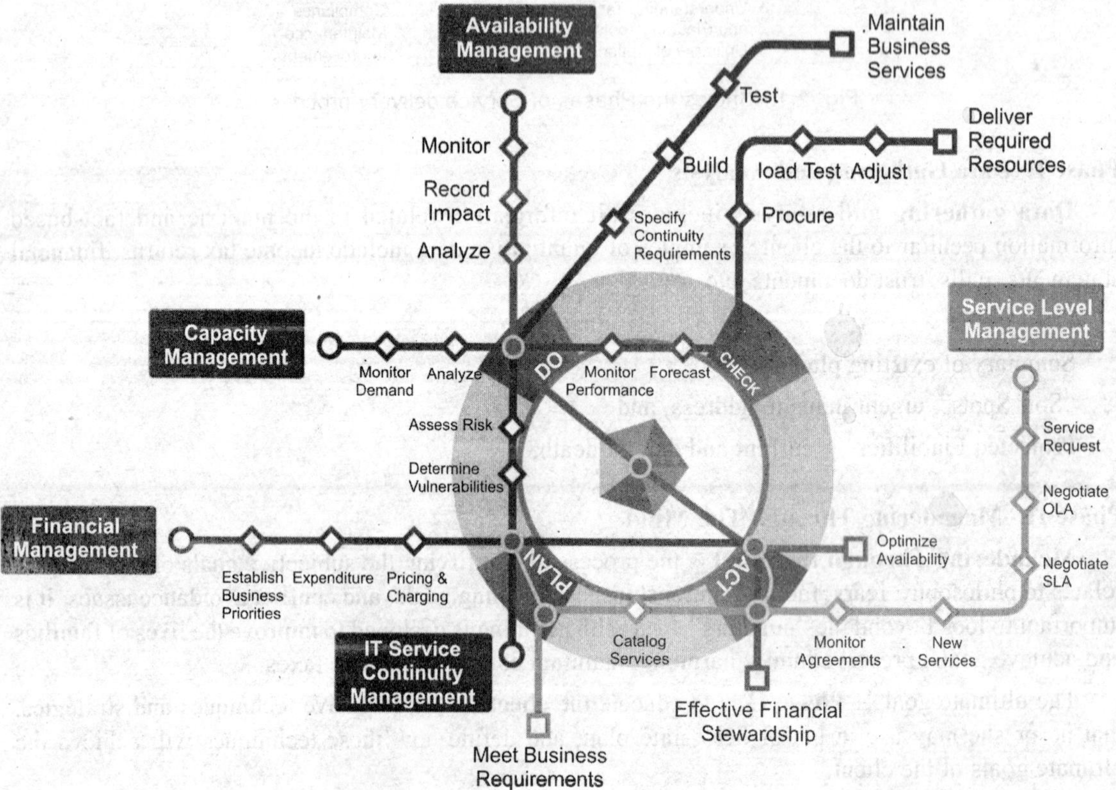


**Fig. 2.2:** Shows the Service Delivery Map

## 2.2 SERVICE LEVEL MANAGEMENT

**Introduction:** Service Level Management (SLM) is probably the most important set of processes within the ITIL framework. SLM processes provide a framework by which services are defined, levels of service required to support business processes are agreed upon, Service Level Agreements (SLAs) and Operational Level Agreements (OLAs) are developed to satisfy the agreements, and costs of service are developed.

SLAs define the bounds within which each service is provided. SLAs also transfer the accountability for the definition of levels of service from IT to the business. If done right, they also offer the business units choices.

For example, when we were children, most of us had some type of food that our mother served us that we didn't like. For some it was broccoli, for others it was squash or carrots or another vegetable. When we wrinkled our nose as she put it on our plate, she would probably say something like, "Eat it. It's good for you".

Later in life we discovered restaurants. There was a menu of items from which we could choose. In many companies, business units feel the same way we did as children. They do not know the discussions behind the development of the IT budget and the services rendered. As a result it is the "IT Budget". Implementing SLAs transforms the "IT Budget" into a series of business budgets to purchase IT services. As a result, the business units have choices, usually driven by economics. They may not like the end result, but they control the levels of service rendered within the constraints of the business unit budget.

Therefore executing these processes permits IT staff to more accurately and cost effectively provision identified levels of service to the business. The processes ensure business and IT understand their roles and responsibilities. The processes empower the business units.

### 2.2.1 What Is Service Level Management?

Service level management is the process by which an organization identifies and agrees on the level of IT service needed to support the business and defines a mechanism to monitor the identified service levels to see that they are being achieved. Within the service level management process, organizations typically use service level agreements (SLAs) to define specifically what a service is, to define the level at which it must be provided, and to gain agreement with all parties on the desired result.

Service Level Management involves negotiating, defining, managing and improving the quality of IT services at an acceptable cost to the business. The journey occurs in an environment of rapidly changing business requirements, increasing demands and unrelenting cost pressure. To optimize this journey, the IT organization needs to strike the right balance between business expectations and what IT can actually deliver. To that end, the journey of Service Level Management is an exercise in managing simple IT economics, understanding customer perceptions and building business relationships. This exercise often involves organizational and cultural change, since the IT organization needs to move from "systems" to "services" based thinking. A major benefit of Service Level Management is that it enables overall IT service performance to be measured, managed and reported on. From an ITIL perspective, effective Service Level Management results in a sound working relationship between IT and the business. Along this critical journey, IT and the business forge Service Level Agreements (SLAs) or contracts. These agreements document IT services that are designed to meet Service Level

Requirements (SLRs) and agreed service targets, and should never force either IT or the business do something that is not in its best interest. Service Level Management should be a means to building partnerships and working collaboratively towards common goals. Many organizations, unfortunately, use service contracts to convey service delivery in terms that are not relevant or meaningful to the business, which often increases conflict. IT must realize that Service Level Management is a journey for both IT and its customers — one of partnership and collaboration that helps IT and the business forge a stronger relationship based on common organizational business goals and objectives. In Service Level Management, ITIL places great emphasis on a Service Catalog, which is comprised of IT services to which a user can subscribe, along with standard service levels and associated costs. A Service Catalog is one of the most important elements of Service Level Management, since it helps IT present itself as a true service provider rather than a technology department. To be truly effective, a Service Catalog presents service levels and costs for each service, and provides a description of the services in the customers' own language. The Service Catalog should reflect business processes rather than technology platforms, and must shield the user from complexities, utilizing automated work-flow to complete service activations and fulfillment procedures.

## 2.2.2 ITIL Service Level Management

Service Level Management (SLM) is one of five components in the ITIL Service Delivery area. It is arguably the most important set of processes within the ITIL framework. SLM processes provide a framework by which services are defined, service levels required to support business processes are agreed upon, Service Level Agreements (SLAs) and Operational Level Agreements (OLAs) are developed to satisfy the agreements, and costs of services are developed.

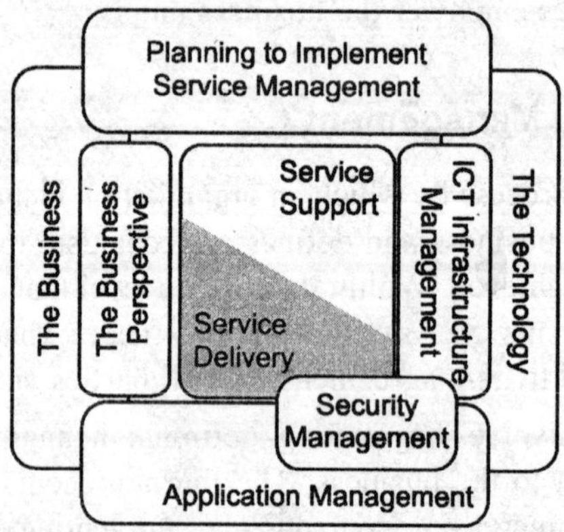


Fig. 2.3: Service Level Management

Executing Service Level Management processes permits IT staff to more accurately and cost effectively provision identified levels of service to the business. The processes ensure business and IT understand their roles and responsibilities and empower the business units.

In the end, business units are justifying to senior management the levels of service needed to support business processes, not IT. And the built-in continuous improvement processes ensure that when business needs change, supporting IT services change with them.

Service Level Management activities include:

- Identifying business requirements by working with business units.
- Establishing the scope of services, timeliness, hours of operation, recovery aspects, and service performance.
- Translating business requirements into IT requirements.
- Developing and maintaining a service catalog, including costs for different tiers of service performance.
- Performing gap analysis between business requirements and available services.
- Determining the costs related to services such that service goals satisfy business needs at a price the business can afford.
- Drafting, negotiating and refining SLAs with the business units, ensuring business requirements are met and agreement from all parties involved.
- Implementing SLAs.
- Measuring SLA performance, reporting results and adjusting as necessary.

#### 2.2.2.1 Why should I Implement Service Level Management?

Immediate benefits to implementing SLM processes include:

- Enabling a better understanding between business units and IT.
- Setting more accurate service quality expectations and effectively measuring, monitoring and reporting service quality.
- Clearly delineating roles and responsibilities.
- Providing the necessary flexibility for business to react quickly to market conditions.
- Creating more accurate infrastructure sizing based on clearly defining service levels.
- Avoiding or mitigating the costs of excess or insufficient capacity.
- Providing discipline in supporting internal or external sourcing of IT services.

Service Level Management teams have close ties to business processes and customer management, Financial Management for IT Services, and Capacity Management. Capacity Management provides performance data to the SLM team for SLA sizing. Service Level Management passes information about service gaps and interruptions back to Capacity Management for capacity assessment and implementation of required changes.

#### 2.2.2.2 Why Service Level Management First?

Service Level Management processes are tightly integrated with business processes and customer management, financial management for IT services, and capacity management (CP). By implementing SLM first, the agreements are already in place and goals already set so integration with these other areas during future implementations is facilitated, reducing the time for them to become fully operational.

The immediate benefits SLM will bring to the organization are:

- Enabling IT to understand the individual business units' service needs and the individual business units to understand the IT services provided. With better understanding, service quality expectations can be more accurately set and service quality more effectively measured, monitored and reported.
- Business and IT clearly understand their roles and responsibilities, the details of the services to be provided and the associated costs. Thus the value that IT brings to the business processes is clearly understood.
- Providing the necessary flexibility for business to react quickly and compete in an ever-changing marketplace.
- Requiring that levels of service are clearly defined, creating more accurate infrastructure sizing. This ensures the appropriate amount of capacity is available, thus avoiding or mitigating the costs of unnecessary excess capacity and/or service performance problems due to insufficient capacity.
- Supporting of internal or external sourcing of IT services through disciplines. Without disciplines in place, the organization may be in a poor position to manage external sourcing vendors and control sourcing costs.

### 2.2.3 The Service Level Management Process

Service Level Management is responsible for ensuring that the appropriate IT services are in place to satisfy planned business needs and that those services are economically viable and effectively used. The desired goal for capacity management is to provide a service that is proactive rather than reactive in nature.

The high level steps in the SLM process are:

- **Identifying business requirements** — the process establishes a dialogue between the individual business units and IT to determine needs for IT services and the bounds of service performance. Requirements will cover the scope of services, timeliness, hours of operation, recovery aspects, and service performance. This step is usually time consuming due to comprehension of the individual business process needs and translating them into IT service requirements.
- **Develop and maintain a service catalog** — process by which all IT services are identified and categorized. Individual components of the IT services and the work required to support them are understood and documented. Where multiple classes of performance are offered for a service, the performance tiers are identified and documented. Costs of each service are identified and documented. Service level bounds for each service are identified and documented. The information is gathered and published in a single document for use by customers (those paying for the services) and users (those using the services). The service catalog will be the starting point in developing Service Level Agreements (SLAs). Most of this work is performed at process implementation time. Maintenance activities occur only when IT services or their related costs change.
- **Perform gap analysis** — process for determining gaps between business requirements and available services. Results of this process could be the establishment of a new IT service or the modification of an existing service.

- **Sizing and costing** — working with capacity, finance, availability, and continuity management, determine the costs related to services needed to satisfy business demand. This is an iterative process with the goal being to determine service goals that satisfy business needs at a price the business can afford.
- **Definition and negotiations** — this process covers the work of drafting and refining SLAs, ensuring they meet business requirements and gaining agreement from all parties involved. In parallel, work to define Operational Level Agreements (OLAs) is performed in conjunction with all the service providers supporting the IT service. The service providers can be from internal or external organizations.
- **Implement the SLA** — once all parties have agreed, the SLA is published, a start date determined and the affected operational teams notified.
- Measure SLA performance and report results.
- **Refine** — assess the effectiveness of the service, locate where gaps or changes have occurred and execute the SLA definition process to adjust the SLA.

#### *2.2.3.1 Which other ITIL Processes Interface with SLM?*

Service Level Management processes are tightly integrated with business processes and customer management, financial management for IT Services, and capacity management. The interface to capacity management is probably the most important. CM collects and condenses IT infrastructure performance data before passing it to SLM. The data is used for Service Level Agreement sizing and to measure the effectiveness of in-place SLAs. SLM passes information about service gaps and interruptions back to CM so that capacity positions can be assessed and any approved changes implemented to meet the SLA requirements.

#### *2.2.3.2 Staffing Considerations*

**The service level manager must be an expert in relationship management.**

This person needs to be a people person, able to communicate well and build relationships with business as well as technical staff. The manager needs to understand business processes and have a solid understanding on all facets of IT technology. Over time this person will probably interface with every leader in the organization. The manager will need strong negotiation skills to be able to initiate and close the SLA work.

**This person must understand the business of IT and the associated costs.**

The manager must be able to translate business process needs into components of IT services and must be able to influence corrective actions when service anomalies occur or historical trends signal potential service problems. Reporting Good candidates for these positions have experience in management reports, especially in condensing highly technical information into simple dashboards and senior management status reports.

**Process Champion**

This is the person auditing the process on an annual basis and responsible for making the appropriate process changes as dictated by changes in the work-flow. This is usually not a full time position and could be filled outside the SLM team.

### 2.2.4 Steps to Implement Service Level Management

All successful projects start with a project plan. Implementing Service Level Management is no different. A project manager with a record of success in implementing large, complex projects should be assigned. Additional staff, as required by the company's project management process, should be assigned at the same time. Support staff will be needed to document the progress. Since this implementation is a pilot, the support staff should be sufficient to quickly handle any anomalies during the execution of the project plan and should be the ones to make adjustments to the general implementation procedures to smooth the way for future process implementations.

#### *2.2.4.1 Step 1: Gather the Data*

The first step is to identify an SLM Manager. In most shops this should be a "full time" position, the actual work involved may only be part time in smaller shops. This person should not be part of an operational team as day-to-day challenges and occasional crises tend to distract from SLM staff from maintaining a strategic view.

**Perform a current state assessment.** This is frequently done with the assistance of a consultant or facilitator, however Office of Government Commerce (OGC) does provide a self-assessment checklist that can be used to narrow the focus of the assessment work. The project team should survey the entire IT organization and discover where and to what extent SLM work is being performed today.

A tools and software inventory should also be performed. In most organizations, different tools are used by different departments to perform monitoring, capacity planning, performance management, and chargeback work. Data from these tools can be used to support the SLM processes. Experience shows that in many cases, SLM can leverage capacity management tools leaving minimal requirements for reporting.

Once the assessment and inventories have been completed, the next step is to perform a gap analysis. The gap analysis will show areas that need process improvements or new work to be performed and where efforts are duplicated. Staffing needs and/or skills and training requirements will be identified. The project team will identify any tools needs and any duplication. The results of the gap analysis is essential to build the project plan; define the work that needs to be accomplished; identify any tools that need to be acquired along with the staffing requirements and costs Now that the gap analysis has revealed the changes required to migrate to the new organization, the project plan can be developed and a cost analysis completed. Staffing, tools and equipment needs will be translated into costs and included in the cost analysis.

#### *2.2.4.2 Step 2: Build the Plan*

Sufficient information will be available to tailor an implementation plan to attain vision after completing the gap analysis. The plan will be responsible for establishing the three major components of capacity management — people, processes and tools. The plan will also determine the costs necessary to sustain the organization, build a preliminary budget and compare it to the current expenditures for similar function — possibly spread across the organization.

**The components of the implementation plan are:**

Determine where the Service Level Manager is located in the IT organization. The ideal placement is as a direct report to the CIO, IT Director or within the service management group. It should be noted that a number of organizations opt to place it in the operations area. This may not be a good choice as applications and user areas may believe Service Level Management may make biased decisions in favor of operations. In addition, SLM can get bogged down with day-to-day details and lose its focus when attached to an operational area.

Sufficient time must be allowed to develop the process documents. The documents should have a description of all the data inputs, information outputs and work processes. A flow chart of the work flow should also be included. Much thought needs to occur to ensure all interfaces and work are identified. In addition, the project plan needs to develop a process and identify a team to handle any process gaps during or immediately following implementation.

The plan, which will vary depending on management's decision to staff internally or externally, must include tasks to identify and train people performing the work. In addition, the plan should allocate sufficient time for Human Resources to review and adopt job descriptions.

Sufficient time must also be built into the plan to train not only the SLM team but any other IT team that interfaces with SLM. Many organizations have chosen to train all IT staff on SLM processes since in many ways SLAs and OLAs involve everyone in the IT organization. Some organizations choose to train their business managers on SLM processes since they will be involved in SLA negotiations at some point.

Any work regarding acquisition, consolidation and/or implementation of capacity and performance tools will be included in the plan. If tools are to be acquired, the project manager needs to allow sufficient time in the plan for corporate acquisition policies and procedures to be followed.

The project manager needs to develop and discuss the plan and its processes with the organization. Many organizations use their internal corporate communications team to accomplish this task. Due to demands on their talents, the project manager should schedule the work with corporate communications well in advance so project goals can be achieved.

The project should include members of the finance team so a comprehensive implementation and ongoing operations budget can be developed. In addition, these project team members will assist in identifying current expenditures throughout the organization that performs capacity management functions. All the financial information is then fed into the Total Cost of Ownership (TCO) document and submitted to management with the proposed project plan.

Project reports should be determined and agreed upon. Many organizations employ the use of a dashboard report, using traffic lights (Green, Yellow, Red) to signify project status.

Once the project plan and the budget have been completed, the project manager and the project sponsor present the plan for approval.

#### *2.2.4.3 Step 3: Execute the Plan*

**Assign the Staff**

The SLM staff should be assigned immediately. By participating from the onset, the staff is very familiar with all facets of the processes, business and technology data.

**Document and publish the Processes**

Since this is a pilot, defining and writing the processes is more work than a "normal" ITIL implementation. Interim interfaces to existing IT units have to be identified as well as those needed for end-state so work can be accomplished with a minimum of interruption while the rest of the organization rolls out.

It is necessary to document the work-flow: inputs, outputs, work accomplished, steps to accomplish, who does the work, who receives the work, and outside assistance needed to execute the processes. It may be advantageous to employ the services of a professional writer to do the bulk of the work with management and technical staff creating an outline to minimize disruption of day-to-day activities. Doing so ensures the processes are documented consistently, in the same format and in the same language (tone and wording).

**Acquire and Implement the Tools**

Historical infrastructure performance data and reporting tools are as important as the people in SLM. The accurate reporting of service performance is critical to the team's success. Without the right detailed data it is difficult for the staff to efficiently or effectively execute processes and procedures. Ideally a single tool will provide all the functions mentioned below. However economics may dictate that a number of existing products must be used and integrated. The service level manager must review the portfolio carefully to ensure that data from all tools is based upon the same collection interval and that data can be easily moved among tools. Manual input of data from one tool into another can be a productivity drain and subject to errors. Therefore it is advised to have automated methods of integrating the tools. Temporary means may be utilized until the capacity management team is implemented and more sophisticated tools become available.

**Inventory IT Services and Build a Service Catalog**

If a chargeback system is already in place, services may have already been identified and defined, so work here would be minimal. Otherwise IT work needs to be identified and broken into services. Chargeback will become a process once financial management is implemented. This means services must be defined in ways that meet financial management's requirements where utilization data can be obtained and associated to a particular service. Examples of services are Daytime Batch, Web Services, Application Maintenance, and Network Services.

In building services, one must account for support services that the customer or user does not see. Therefore each service should account for overhead components such as operating system maintenance, security, change control, management oversight, and backup/recovery.

The catalog should identify each service, describe the functions provided and the terms of service (e.g., hours of operation, customer support options), any service tiers, and the unit costs of the service. The service owner should be identified along with contact information. Identify the support included with the service such as database definition and/or indexing, job scheduling or application tuning support.

**Identify, Develop, Negotiate and Implement SLAs and OLAs**

The first step should be to canvass the users and customers to determine their feelings toward the existing IT services. In accomplishing this task, the team will identify a list of business units for which SLAs need to be developed and a feeling of customer satisfaction for existing services. In conjunction with this work, the team needs to gather any historical performance data. This data will be used as a baseline to draft the initial SLAs.

The second step will be to work with the individual business units to identify their IT requirements and translate them into components of IT services. This is probably one of the most difficult and labor intensive tasks. Keep a good customer focus.

In most cases your business partners will welcome you when you want to understand their business processes and determine their service needs. They are as proud of what they do as you are of your work. However in some cases the business is not sure of it requirements and in others, there is no desire to quantify or cap services. When those situations are encountered, it is vital that senior leadership intervene and lend its support.

Once the data has been gathered and the business requirements translated into components of service, the team must start to craft the SLAs and underpinning OLAs. These documents should be written at a basic level so everyone can understand. Each should only be a page or two in length and include:

- An introduction that identifies:
  - — The parties involved
  - — Start, end and review dates
  - — Scope of the agreement
  - — Description of the services provided
  - — Roles and responsibilities of each of the parties
- Hours of operation
- Service availability
- Service reliability
- Support
- Throughput, transaction times and/or response times
- Change turnaround targets
- Security requirements and consideration
- Service continuity
- Costs of the service and how they are charged
- Service reporting
- Service incentives and penalties

OLAs are generally processed first since they impact the terms of the SLAs. Once the OLAs have been finalized and agreed upon, the SLA drafts are shared with the customer for review and approval. Refinements usually occur during this process before all parties agree and sign the documents.

**Gap Analysis**

As a result of the previous work, the team may identify required services not currently provided by IT. It those cases, the team will use the SLM processes to assess the needs, identify and cost justify solutions and implement them upon approval.

In addition, the team may encounter contradictions that will need to be resolved through the SLM processes.

**Define Metrics to Measure Success**

As with all ITIL processes, there needs to be a way to measure the success and ongoing performance of the different IT units. Metrics need to be meaningful and measurable. They should be tied to business value rather than technical measures. Metrics should be fewer in number, succinct, and to the point, while still providing management with good representation of the unit's effectiveness. Remember that each ITIL process will have at least one metric, which will be rolled up into an overall IT report. It is necessary to keep metrics at a manageable level as executives and managers do not have the time or desire to read through many pages of metrics reports. In SLM, most metrics will be related to service quality.

**Build the Training Materials and Execute the Training Plan**

As stated previously, sufficient time must be built into the plan to train not only the SLM team but any other team that interfaces with service level management. To accomplish this, it will be necessary to develop training materials based upon the processes previously drafted. Generally the use of a presentation tool such as Microsoft PowerPoint or Adobe Acrobat is desirable since it permits self study or group presentations.

From previous experience, self study seems to work well in a busy IT environment. However managers must ensure that each member of their staff has sufficient time to read and comprehend the information. Some organizations have opted to develop online training facilities, permitting staff to go through the material in a computer-based interactive environment.

To ensure comprehension, testing should be performed. Passing the test should be made mandatory. Some organizations offer financial incentives, others tie success to future compensation and include them in staff Major Job Objectives.

Once again, it cannot be stressed enough that you increase your chances for success and fewer miss-steps by spending more time testing. In most cases, the work-flows will be substantially different than the work performed today; therefore it is necessary for each staff member to understand the work for which he or she is accountable and the value of the work to the organization.

**Implement Reporting and Exception Processes and Procedures**

Quality of service cannot be determined without some type of reporting. Two types of reporting need to be put into place. High level reporting is used to keep senior management informed of service quality. These reports are generally in the form of a "dashboard", using the colors red, yellow, and green to represent service quality. It is important that each service has two measures—current status and trend.

In this way management can understand what current status is and where it is trending. For example, a service with a yellow current status indicator and a green trend indicator may need less attention than a service with a green current status indicator and a yellow or red trend indicator. The SLM team and those staff assisting with corrective actions need more detailed reporting to identify problematic service areas and to track results of actions taken.

### *2.2.4.4 Step 4: Initiate the ongoing work of SLM*

Once the SLAs have been signed and implementations scheduled, reporting needs to be put in place.

The reporting process should be automated with some intelligence built in to alert the SLM team when service performance starts to under perform or fails to meet agreed upon performance targets. In addition, proactive trending intelligence should be put in place to alert the SLM staff when trends show that performance is approaching the agreed upon limits. Doing so permits the team to take corrective actions in time to prevent service outages or poor service performance.

Review meetings should be scheduled on a regular basis to cover results. These meetings are normally held monthly or quarterly and should take no more than one hour. To maintain interest, the data presented should be concise and only address performance issues and corrective actions. Do not read down a list of metrics and cite results.

The continuous improvement process will be engaged as the review dates specified in the individual SLAs are reached. In addition, unforeseen business events could cause early review of affected services. The service level manager needs to be aware of business plans and events so work to adjust SLAs where needed can be completed and put in place prior to the actual event.

#### *2.2.4.5 Step 5: Perform Post Implementation Review*

At the end of the implementation project, the project manager should quickly put together a "lessons learned" document that identifies any process changes that would facilitate future process migrations. Any implementation process changes should be made at this time.

Perform a post implementation audit 6-12 months after completion. Determine if the new processes are being adhered to and if the new organization is delivering the expected business benefit. Some of the questions that should be asked are:

- Did we accomplish what we set out to do?
- Are the metrics measuring the team's performance valid?
- Is the team communicating successfully with the organization in accordance with the SLM processes?
- Are the interfaces working smoothly?
- Did we meet expectations on benefit delivered to the business?
- Have IT services improved overall?
- Are we capturing the correct data?
- Are the processes accepted and observed by staff, both internal and external to SLM?

**Success Factors**

- Management needs to be very supportive of training, implementation and execution efforts. Managers at all levels need to be ITIL cheerleaders.
- Business units must be willing to work within the new processes.
- Business units must support Service Level Agreements.
- The right people must be in the right positions to do the work.
- Patience is needed to allow the teams sufficient time to become proficient in the new processes and for old behaviors to die.

- Processes and pre-defined teams need to be in place and ready for dealing with gaps once implementation is completed. These teams will be used until all ITIL implementations have been completed. The business work must continue in spite of the changes so when gaps occur it is essential that the gaps can be addressed before service problems occur.
- Compensation policies should be adjusted to reinforce ITIL practices and drive the appropriate behaviors. Common goals should be in place for all ITIL processes, especially financial and quality.

**Potential Inhibitors**

- Unrealistic expectations by management can erode confidence in the processes. One must remember that a large number of companies have successfully implemented ITIL frameworks and best practices, many considering the new organization a competitive advantage. To succeed, they ensured management expectations were set realistically.
- Some management may view this unit as purely overhead and superfluous, making it difficult to sustain the team and its value to the organization.

  Substantial resistance to developing SLAs and OLAs can erode the effectiveness of the unit as a whole. If senior management fails to support the processes, the unit will fail.
- A lack of patience could result in partial or cancelled implementation. It takes staff, and those who interface with the organization, time to become familiar with new work-flows. It is essential to allow sufficient time for gaps and issues to be addressed and processes to mature..
- Not enforcing adherence to processes may result in falling back to old behaviors. Two processes are more confusing and probably more detrimental than a single bad process. Surprisingly, a significant amount of work is accomplished through the influence of social networks. Managers must resist the temptation and let the processes work. It may not seem like it at the time but when all implementations are completed and the staff is familiar with the new processes, work will flow through the system much faster. For example one company saw the time needed to install a software change reduce from 45 days to 2 days due to ITIL process improvements.

## 2.2.5 The Service Level Management Process Service

### *2.2.5.1 Service Request*

The first step on the Service Level Management journey is the Service Request station. Traditionally, IT has scrambled to meet each new request for new IT services. In these situations, every new service request is treated as important, since they haven't been prioritized, and IT often lacks the means to reliably assess whether resources are available to meet the demand. An effective Service Level Management journey starts with IT and the business prioritizing services and establishing the appropriate service levels the business requires. Technology can play a key role here, by centralizing and coordinating all service requests, and utilizing portfolio management techniques to prioritize service requests according to agreed business criteria. The Service Request station is especially critical since it involves uniting IT and the business and is the foundation upon which agreements are made. At this station, it is essential that IT doesn't get bogged down in technical details, but works collaboratively with all stakeholders to discuss business needs and requirements. Only when it has achieved this primary goal can the Service Level Management journey continue to the process of translating the requirements into technical specifications and supporting activities.

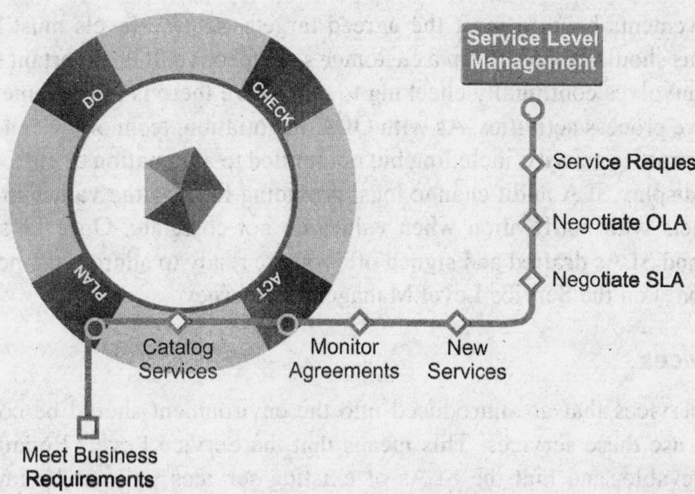


**Fig. 2.4:** Shows The Service Level Management Process Services

### *2.2.5.2 Negotiate OLAs*

Once services have been identified and prioritized, the process of negotiating agreements between internal IT departments (via Operational Level Agreements or OLAs) and external providers (via Underpinning Contracts) begins. Here, IT begins an internal process of detailing agreements about the delivery of specific elements of an IT service. Every IT service will be underpinned by OLAs, and IT needs to establish a process whereby each element of IT supporting the overall IT service is not only documented, but can be measured, monitored and improved according to how it supports the overall 7IT service. Defining, drafting and negotiating OLAs is necessary in order to document the relationship and expectations between the different IT teams; and, when performed effectively, can help break down "IT silos" and communication barriers. Creating and using OLAs is an iterative process. Business requirements and technology are constantly changing, which may alter any IT capabilities. For these reasons, the process of working with OLAs involves continuously matching IT capabilities to changing business requirements, and periodically reassessing existing OLAs. This requires discussion and agreement between IT departments. Technology can help by establishing automatic links between OLAs and Underpinning Contracts, with automatic alerts sent to the Service Level Manager when values do not match.

### *2,2.5.3 Negotiate SLAs*

An SLA is a formal agreement between the customer(s) and the IT service provider specifying service levels and the terms under which a service or a package of services is provided to the customer. Remember, SLAs are used for internal customers. If IT and the customer don't work collaboratively, true service quality improvements will not happen. Both parties must agree on the goals. This is achieved by setting up meetings with the customer to negotiate the structure of the SLAs, and the levels of service to be provided. The objective is to match the customer's expectation with what can be achieved, negotiating a "win-win" situation for both parties. Here begins the drafting and definition of SLAs to mirror the formal agreements from the negotiation meeting. This is the basis of an SLA or contract.

Since service achievements have to meet the agreed targets, service levels must be monitored with appropriate tools. This should be done from a customer's perspective. It is important to note that Service Level Management involves continually checking to make sure there is improvement, which is why it is made up of iterative process activities. As with OLA negotiation, technology can also help optimize the SLA negotiation process activity, including but not limited to automation of customizable templates, ability to track and display SLA audit change logs, providing links to the values in related OLAs and underpinning contracts with notification when values do not correlate. Once IT services have been defined, and OLAs and SLAs drafted and signed off, you are ready to address the next process activity (i.e., the next "station") on the Service Level Management journey.

### 2.2.5.4 New Services

At this point, new services that are introduced into the environment should be communicated to all customers who may use these services. This means that the Service Level Requirements (SLRs) of the service are achievable, and that the SLAs of existing services will not be impacted because of poor planning. These new services and their associated requirements are now documented in contract form.

### 2.2.5.5 Monitor Agreements

As we move to the Monitor Agreements station, we are armed with documented service requirements, service level targets and negotiated agreements. To optimize service quality, you need to capture the monitoring and auditing of SLAs in meaningful reports on a periodic basis. These reports should highlight key metrics that indicate areas of improvement and gaps between capabilities and agreed service levels. At this stage of the journey, it is important to identify what metrics are meaningful to the business, establish goals for a sound baseline ,review the results against that baseline and be able to coach and measure staff on their performance in achieving service levels — taking corrective action to avoid service degradations and service level breaches. Technology can support monitoring of service levels and should be able to integrate with system management software to automatically alert Service Level Managers when SLAs are about to be breached.

### 2.2.5.6 Catalog Services

A Service Catalog identifies and documents all IT services. It specifies key IT service features, options and service levels and is a non-technical document using common terms of reference. Ultimately the Service Catalog can become a master SLA, describing every IT service, SLA and supporting OLAs in the customers own language. The Service Catalog is a vital communications tool, helping IT establish itself as a true service provider that better manages customer demand and expectations. Technology and process automation can help greatly here, by enabling the IT organization to quickly build and present an online catalog of business-facing IT services. These IT services are presented in terms understandable by the business, and ideally provide work-flow to ensure the services are quickly provisioned, together with automated monitoring of the underlying service levels. On the administrative side, security technology can ensure that controls are in place to allow only authorized personnel to view, create and alter the Service Catalog, SLAs, OLAs and Underpinning Contracts. Integration with Change Management is also supported by technology through the automatic ability to track and display detailed audit logs that record changes to the Service Catalog.

### 2.2.5.7 Meet Business Requirements

As we approach the end of the Service Level Management process journey optimization and automation of many process activities will have helped build a service-centric culture and closer relationship with the business. As with all ITIL processes, Service Level Management is a journey of continuous improvement, with the focus here on continuously reviewing the business validity of Underpinning Contracts, OLAs and SLAs against the Service Catalog. Regular meetings to ensure that service contracts are still current and relevant to the organization are the foundation of continuous service improvement and reflect the goal of Service Level Management to meet business objectives. This is an ongoing continuous service improvement process; as new changes are introduced to the environment, there is a cycle of defining, agreeing and negotiating, and a check and balance to ensure alignment with the business. To ensure meeting business requirements, both business and IT stakeholders should participate in service review meetings, discussing trends on service performance, assigning ownership for incidents causing defects, and working together to remediate defects and continuously measure the impact of changes. A formal plan is then documented and put in place to carry out this remediation, the Service Improvement Plan (SIP).

### 2.2.5.8 Optimizing the Service Level Management Journey

To be truly optimized, Service Level Management needs to integrate with other Service Delivery processes and many Service Support processes, too. For example, Configuration Items (CI) define the relationships between CI, people and processes that make up the IT services offered through the Service Catalog, and which form the foundation for SLA, OLA and Underpinning Contract development, negotiation and monitoring. With such an all — encompassing, critical process, process automation is vital, and should deliver the following capabilities:

- Monitoring of service levels and notification of service level thresholds and breaches that provide automatic alerts based on the SLA, business rules and escalation procedures
- The ability to build and measure OLAs and aggregate to SLAs and contracts
- A controlled and secure means of access
- Web-enabled client access offering integration with other applications and the Configuration Management Database (CMDB)
- Integration across both Service Support and Service Delivery processes
- Ability to build and present an online actionable and fully integrated Service Catalog

### 2.2.5.9 Avoiding Service Level Management Problems

The following recommendations will help you avoid Service Level Management Problems:

- Never ignore the integration points to all of the other ITIL processes. As each process is being designed, it is important to recognize that there are key touch points between all of the processes. It is vital to understand that there is a certain level of integration (inputs become outputs) that naturally takes place among these ITSM activities.
- Do not define IT services without collaborating with the business (the customer). Avoid defining and setting service targets without customer input because they must be well understood and agreed upon by both parties in order to avoid any confusion.

- Do not forget that SLAs should be used as a basis for financial allocation/chargeback; this helps to demonstrate the value the business is receiving for money spent on IT.
- Without an appointed Service Level Manager, there is no one to ensure compliance and no one is held accountable for the end-to-end Service Level Management process.
- Automation of service level monitoring and breach notification enhances the Service Level

Management process and can also support integration among Service Level Management activities; just be sure to design the process before attempting to automate it.

### 2.2.6 Three Simple Rules for Service Level Management

**Rule 1:** A service is not a server An IT service is a collection of IT capabilities and resources that support a business process. A server is just part of what makes a service work.

**Rule 2:** Monitor things the business cares about When monitoring SLAs, make sure to measure and monitor what the business really cares about. If you don't, you risk missing the big point.

**Rule 3:** Get agreement on SLAs Agreement is what makes SLAs work. Agreement happens within the business and within IT

#### *2.2.6.1 The S, L, and A of Service Level Agreement*

**S—Service**

A service, within the context of an SLA, is collection of IT capabilities that combine to make a business process possible. The service is used by the end user in the business to support the user's job or the objectives of the organization. It is not a specific IT thing, rather it is a collection of IT resources that make a business process possible.

For example, email is a service that is offered to the business to support various communications functions. It makes business communications possible in the modern world and underpins a majority of business transactions. The service is comprised of hardware, software, networking, end-points, training, and support, all of which helps allow the business to effectively communicate internally and externally. Many of the components that comprise the service — like network infrastructure — are shared across multiple services. However, the individual components are not a service in themselves. Rather, each is just one of many parts that comprise the service.

When defining a service it is critical to understand and define the service in the context of the business process it is supporting. By defining a service from the business-use perspective, the SLA will be more relevant and will help ensure that the service provided supports the current and future needs of the business.

**L — Level**

The level in an SLA defines the specifics or performance criteria of how a service is delivered and should behave. The details of level are very important because they define how to measure and manage the service and ensure that the service delivered is actually facilitating the business. Continuing with the email example, a level for email can include the size of an email inbox or the maximum time for delivering a message. When defining levels, it is critical to consider the needs of the business user. If these needs are not considered, organizations risk misalleging the service with the business need. Quality discussions with business users will help in defining meaningful level requirements. IT organizations tend to define level in terms of things that can be easily measured, such as server uptime or application response time. While system availability is a concern to business users, IT-centric metrics are only part of what makes a service meaningful to the business. IT organizations need to challenge themselves to identify the elements of level that are the essence of what makes a service meaningful to the business.

**A — Agreement**

The agreement in an SLA happens when business users and IT concur that the service and the level at which it is provided meet a business need. With agreement, IT organizations can make definitive decisions on architecture, support models. and deployment. Agreement allows business users to assess and plan for the timing, volume, and effectiveness of their processes. Most importantly, agreement makes the IT services relevant and aligned to the needs of the business. As mentioned previously, organizations are rapidly evolving from a world based on physical processes to one based on virtual processes. If the business is going to have confidence in implementing these changes to the virtual business processes, agreement on service and the way it supports the business will be key. Agreement gives the business confidence that the service will support the business and key processes, with controls in place to ensure that their new virtual factories will be stable, quality-driven resources for the long term.

## 2.3 FINANCIAL MANAGEMENT

### 2.3.1 Introduction

Where Service Level Management (SLM) defines and manages the services, Financial Management determines the costs of services and provides financial accounting support to ensure expenditures fall within approved plans and that funds are well spent. The role of Financial Management varies depending upon the view of IT within the corporation. Different best practices are suggested for each role. Some companies view IT as an expense center, some as a profit center, and some as a cost recovery center. However in all cases, Financial Management supports the "business" of IT.

#### *2.3.1.1 What is it?*

Financial Management for IT is one of five components in the ITIL Service Delivery area. It determines the costs of services and provides financial accounting support to ensure expenditures fall within approved plans and that funds are well-spent.

The role of Financial Management varies depending upon the view of IT within the company. Some companies view IT as an expense center, some as a profit center, and some as a cost-recovery center. However, in all cases, Financial Management supports the "business" of IT.

Financial Management activities include:

- Providing oversight of all IT expenditures
- Ensuring funds are available for planned events

- Providing detailed financial information for proposed initiatives
- Influencing the use of IT assets to maximize the return on IT investments through chargeback systems
- Tracking current expenditures against the budget

#### *2.3.1.2 Why should I implement Financial Management?*

Financial Management processes allow you to:

- Plan and predict IT expenditures required to maintain or improve services
- Ensure expenditures fall within approved plan guidelines and that money is well-spent
- Assist senior management in understanding the ongoing total cost of a proposed IT initiative
- Promote a better understanding of the costs associated with providing specific services
- Foster an environment of control to ensure IT services are effectively and efficiently used

Financial Management has close ties to **Service Level Management**, **Capacity Management**, and **Configuration Management** areas, as well as the Corporate Finance Department.

#### *2.3.1.3 Why Financial Management for IT?*

Financial Management processes are tightly integrated with Service Level Management, Capacity Management, Configuration Management and the Corporate Finance Department.

The values of this process:

- Provide a budget planning process for the business of IT that dovetails with the corporate budgeting cycle to plan and predict future expenditures required to maintain and improve services. Business plans, both short and long term, provide the input needed to work closely with Capacity Management and SLMs to develop the IT budget.
- IT accounting ensures expenditures fall within approved plan guidelines and that the money is well spent.
- Cost benefit analyses projects assist senior management in understanding the ongoing total cost of ownership of a proposed IT initiative. As a result, the business can make more informed decisions when prioritizing future work.
- Chargeback promotes a better understanding of the costs of providing services to a particular business unit. It fosters an environment of controls to ensure IT services are more effectively and efficiently used. Chargeback places responsibility for service consumption with the business unit. Effective costing disciplines can also influence changes in consumption patterns to better utilize IT infrastructure assets. For example, a lower rate for batch jobs run overnight can influence business units to perform work during hours when idle computing capacity is available, releasing capacity during peak hours, thus delaying expensive capacity upgrades.

## 2.3.2 The Financial Management Process

Financial Management (FM) is responsible for the oversight of all IT expenditures; ensuring funds are available for planned events. The team assists in the IT decision-making process by providing detailed financial information supporting proposed initiatives. FM processes, through the use of chargeback systems, influence the use of IT assets to maximize the return on IT investments. The component processes of Financial Management are:

### *2.3.2.1 Budget*

The budgeting process identifies all IT expenses for a specified period of time to ensure the appropriate funding is available to sustain operations. Budgeting normally takes into account costs of providing current services, known project requirements and planned business growth. Budgets are usually built annually with estimates covering the costs of the current and subsequent accounting periods. Some organizations build budgets for the subsequent three years to permit improved financial planning decisions. The budgeting process provides insight into how expenses change year-to-year. In addition, the process helps management better understand the impacts to new applications, cost-of-living increases and technology unit price improvements. For most shops budgeting is a balancing act, maximizing services within the constraints of available capital, available expense monies, Service Level Agreements (SLA) and external market forces such as vendor service rates. At a minimum, budget categories should contain hardware, software, staffing, telecommunications and external services (e.g., disaster recovery) costs. Account for support costs outside the actual cost of the unit or application when planning future hardware and software purchases. Identify costs when adding new hardware for the following:

- Installation
- Cabling
- Operating System Software
- Capacity-based software upgrades
- Facilities (e.g., floor space, power, cooling)
- Administration
- Maintenance
- Consumables (e.g., tapes, CDs, paper)
- Backup/recovery

In addition, identify costs when adding software applications to the budget:

- Installation
- Hardware capacity
- Software upgrades
- Database maintenance
- Administration
- Testing
- Quality Assurance
- Consumables (e.g., tapes, CDs, paper forms)
- Business data backup/recovery

The value of the budgeting process is the business justification and prioritizing of IT services required to support business operations. Through the use of the process, senior management will understand the components of cost and thus make informed decisions on where to direct IT investments that best satisfy the needs of the organization as a whole.

#### 2.3.2.2 Accounting

The goal of IT accounting is to provide accurate and timely financial information regarding IT expenditures - current and proposed. IT and business management can then make sound decisions over priorities in supplying IT services to the business and gain an improved comprehension of IT cost components. Components of IT accounting work include:

- **Tracking current** — expenditures against a budget or financial plan
- **Coordinating IT** — accounting data with corporate accounting departments
- Analyzing proposed investments to identify true costs to implement and operate
- Providing senior management with sufficient data to understand the short and long term aspects of IT initiatives and weigh financial risks associated with them
- **Supporting the charging for IT services**.

This work is performed from an IT perspective, revealing true costs of IT services and is not meant to address more complex corporate accounting issues such as tax accounting. Caution must be exercised in developing these capabilities so the cost of performing the work does not exceed the benefit.

Therefore the level of detail and reporting will vary depending upon the size and complexity of the organization. There are several different IT accounting methodologies that can be employed by an organization:

- **Accounting** — simple gathering and reporting of IT expense information, usually aligning it to IT services to promote cost awareness within the organization. This methodology creates an awareness of IT expenses and how they are affected by changes in business volumes and priorities. However it does not promote effective use of resources. If individual business units are not held accountable for consumed resources, it is difficult for the IT organization to provide cost effective services.
- **Cost Recovery** — a methodology in which costs are apportioned by service and recovery from organizational units in a fair and equitable manner. This methodology is considered best practice as it forces discipline in the organization's use of IT services. Similar discipline is employed within the organization to control cost-effective use of travel and office supplies.
- **Profit center** — a methodology employed mostly by IT service providers. A profit is generated by selling IT services. Charging and service delivery must be competitive with the marketplace to maintain the customer base. Profits are used to improve services and grow the business. This methodology can be effective in controlling vendors as financial incentives can substantially reduce profits if service quality declines. Some companies embrace this methodology internally as a measure against external services and — similar to service providers — use the profits from the services to provide the funding needed to sustain and grow IT services.

There are two major components to the accounting process.

**1. Cost Accounting**

Best practices dictate that some level of IT accounting detail take place. There are a variety of ways to perform this function, depending upon size and complexity of the organization. Some organizations employ a simple approach and account for IT costs as a whole without any definition of how the resources are consumed. A better practice is to identify costs based upon what each customer consumes. Doing so provides some customer accountability for what is consumed. Some organizations go into more detail and account for costs based upon business applications. Examples of this method would be costs for running General Ledger or Call Center Applications. Another more effective method is to account for costs based upon business processes. Examples of this method would be IT costs per online sale or customer inquiry. The more detailed and business oriented methods provide the greater value, albeit at a greater cost. Caution must be exercised however to ensure the costs of the accounting do not far exceed the benefit to the organization. The cornerstone of cost accounting is the cost model. This document reveals all the IT costs associated with the desired level of detail. The model generally covers a fixed period of time, usually concurrent with the organization's fiscal year. The gathered cost detail should be much more than just today's costs. Since business volumes are rarely static, it is also necessary to estimate what they will be at the end of the accounting period. We do this since the actual costs to the customer over the accounting period will be a blend of today's costs and costs for every day in the future up to the end of the accounting period. There are two types of costs that are gathered.

- Capital costs are dollars spent now and affect the organization's cash flow, yet do not affect the financial plan in the same manner. These costs are generally related to the acquisition of hardware, major application software such as SAP or CRM, and facilities. Capital expenditures are depreciated, a financial method of spreading the cost of an asset over its useful life. Most organizations already employ a depreciation methodology used by IT accounting. Depreciation methods used in the USA are mostly determined by FASB and IRS guidelines. The budget or financial plan accounts for the amount of depreciation incurred during the term of the budget/plan. Therefore capital and expenses must be kept separate and not confused when building the financial plans.
- Operational costs are the day-to-day expenditures to sustain IT operations. Operational costs will include:
  - — Hardware and software maintenance
  - — Telecommunications — data and voice
  - — Personnel
  - — Consumables — tapes, CDs, paper, forms, office supplies
  - — Facilities — floor space rent or allocation, power, cooling, uninterruptible power, physical security
  - — External services — such as disaster recovery, consultants, vendors
  - — Transfer — costs such as corporate overhead, HR costs, Finance, Security

The spreadsheet is the primary tool of IT accounting. Financial data is gathered from across the organization to identify IT costs and associated business metrics. Costs must be determined to be fixed or variable. For example, the base costs for an 800 phone service will be fixed as the contract would need to be renegotiated to change the rate. The vendor would charge any additional minutes of service on a per-minute or tiered charge; therefore that portion of the cost would be variable since it depends on business usage. Once costs are gathered, it is necessary to break them down by unit of use if a more detailed accounting approach is chosen. When breaking the costs down by customer, application or business process, it is first necessary to understand how services and infrastructure components are consumed. "Cost centers" are set up to hold the individual cost components. Cost centers have "direct" and "indirect" or "overhead" costs associated with them. A cost center could be assigned to a customer, an application or a business process. Direct costs are those expenses directly attributable to a particular cost center. Examples of direct costs are dedicated servers, departmental desktops, staffing dedicated to supporting a particular application, or a business process. Indirect costs are generally those shared by all and allocated to the various costs centers in an equitable manner. Examples of indirect costs are facilities, senior IT management and support staff, telephone switchboards or PBX. The allocation methodology is important to the process. It is critical that it be easy to understand and consistent across the cost centers. It should also be employed in the chargeback process. In doing so, the customer will understand the charging and if it is fair and reasonable, accept it. If a variety of allocation methods are employed and/or they are not easily understood, suspicions arise and IT is not looked upon favorably. Probably the most popular allocation method is by percent consumption. Those costs directly attributable to a cost center are usually easy to identify. The remaining costs, usually called "overhead," are applied across the cost centers in an equitable fashion. In this case, they are allocated on a percentage of the whole basis. For example, if a cost center consumes 30 percent of the total direct costs across all cost centers, then it will also attract 30 percent of the unallocated overhead costs. The FM staff collects the information, segregates it by cost center, prepares the spreadsheet, and distributes the results. Business units will understand the actual IT costs to support each cost center, be it a group of users, application(s) or business processes. Where services prove to not be cost effective, IT and the business can work together to develop more cost effective alternatives. The data can be saved in a historical database and trends analyzed with results used for building future IT investment plans.

### 2.3.3 Steps to Implement Financial Management

All successful projects start with a project plan. Implementing IT Financial Management is no different. A project manager with a record of success in implementing large, complex projects should be assigned. Additional staff as required by the company's project management process should be assigned at the same time. Support staff will be needed to document the progress. Since this implementation is the pilot, the support staff should be sufficient to quickly handle any anomalies during the execution of the project plan and should be the ones to make adjustments to the general implementation procedures to smooth the way for future process implementations.

#### *2.3.3.1 Step 1: Gather the Data*

The first step is to identify a finance manager. In most shops this should be a "full time" position and probably already performed in some form by corporate finance. Separating this function permits one to focus on the peculiarities of finance as it pertains to IT. Substantial IT knowledge is desired to ensure proper oversight of IT expenditures. Perform a current state assessment. This is frequently done with the assistance of a consultant or facilitator, however OGC does provide a self-assessment checklist that can be used to narrow the focus of the assessment work. The project team should survey the entire IT organization and discover where and to what extent FM work is being performed today. A tools and software inventory should also be performed. In most organizations, spreadsheet and accounting programs are already being used, however facilities to relate IT consumption by users to expenditures may not be in place. As a result, data from the Capacity Management organization may be available to FM to support the FM processes, otherwise commercial usage chargeback packages may be required. Once the assessment and inventories have been completed, the next step is to perform a gap analysis. The gap analysis will show the areas that need process improvements or new work to be performed and where efforts are duplicated. Staffing needs and/or skills and training requirements will be identified. The project team will identify tool needs and duplication. The result of the gap analysis is essential to build the project plan, define the work that needs to be accomplished, identify tools that need to be acquired, and understand the staffing requirements and costs. Now that the gap analysis has revealed the changes required to migrate to the new organization, the project plan can be developed and a cost analysis completed. Staffing, tools and equipment needs will be translated into costs and included in the cost analysis.

#### 2.3.3.2 Step 2: Build the Plan

Once the gap analysis has been completed, sufficient information will be available to tailor an implementation plan to attain the vision. The plan will be responsible for establishing the three major components of Financial Management — people, processes and tools. The plan will also determine the costs necessary to sustain the organization, build a preliminary budget and compare it to the current expenditures for similar function — possibly spread across the organization. The components of the implementation plan are: Determine where the finance manager is located in the IT organization. The ideal placement is as a direct report to the CIO or IT Director. Sufficient time must be allowed to develop the process documents. The documents should have a description of all the data inputs, information outputs and work processes. A flow chart of the work-flow should also be included. Much thought needs to occur to ensure all interfaces and work are identified. In addition, the project plan needs to develop a process and identify a team to handle any process gaps during or immediately following implementation. The plan must include tasks to identify and train the people performing the work. The plan will vary depending upon management's decision to staff from within or look externally for the appropriate talent. Job descriptions need to be drafted and sufficient time allocated to work with the Human Resources organization to review and adopt them. Sufficient time must be built into the plan to train the FM team on the new processes and any other ITIL team that interfaces with FM. Many organizations have chosen to train all IT staff on FM processes since it impacts everyone in the IT organization. Some organizations choose to train their business managers on FM processes to promote a better understanding of IT costs and their impacts on changes in business processes and volumes. Any work regarding acquisition, consolidation and/or implementation of financial management tools will be included in the plan. If tools are to be acquired, the project manager needs to allow sufficient time in the plan for corporate acquisition policies and procedures to be followed. The project manager needs to develop a plan item to communicate the organization and its processes. Many organizations use their internal corporate communications team to accomplish this task. Due to demands on their talents, the project manager should schedule the work with corporate communications well in advance so project goals can be achieved. The project should include members of the financial team so a comprehensive implementation and ongoing operations budget can be developed. In addition, these project team members will assist in identifying current expenditures across the organization that performs Financial Management for IT functions. All the financial information is then fed into the Total Cost of Ownership (TCO) document and submitted to management with the proposed project plan. Project reports should be determined and agreed. Many organizations employ the use of a dashboard report, using traffic light colors (Green, Yellow, and Red) to signify project status. Once the project plan and the budget have been completed, the project manager and the project sponsor present the plan for approval.

#### *2.3.3.3 Step 3: Execute the Plan*

**Assign the Staff**

The FM staff should be assigned immediately. By participating from the onset, the staff is very familiar with all facets of the processes and business and technology data.

**Document and publish the Processes**

Since this is a pilot, defining and writing the processes are more work than a "normal" ITIL implementation. Interim interfaces to existing IT units have to be identified as well as those needed for end-state so work can be accomplished with a minimum of interruption while the rest of the organization rolls out. It is necessary to document the work-flow: inputs, outputs, work accomplished, steps to accomplish, who does the work, who receives the work, outside assistance needed to execute the processes. It may be advantageous to employ the services of a professional writer to do the bulk of the work with management and technical staff creating just an outline to minimize disruption to day-to-day activities. Doing so ensures the processes are documented consistently in the same format and the same language (tone and wording). Acquire and Implement the Tools Historical infrastructure performance data and reporting tools are as important as the FM staff. The accurate reporting of service performance is critical to the team's success. Without the right detailed data it is difficult for the staff to efficiently or effectively execute processes and procedures. Ideally a single tool will provide all the functions mentioned below. However economics may dictate that a number of existing products must be used and integrated. The Finance Manager must review the portfolio carefully however to ensure that data from all tools is based upon the same collection interval and that data can be easily moved between tools. Manual input of data from one tool into another can be a productivity drain and subject to errors, therefore it is desired to have automated methods of integrating the tools. Temporary means may be utilized until the Capacity Management team is implemented and more sophisticated tools become available.

**Build the Accounting and Budgeting Framework**

The budget and cost model are put in place. Generally a budget in some form is already available, it may just need more detail depending upon the new structure. Interfaces to corporate finance and financial units within the business units will be needed to obtain invoices, staffing expenses, travel, supply, vendor services and depreciation schedules. A financial calendar needs to be put in place to determine when regular analyses and review points will take place. The calendar needs to be coordinated with the business planning calendar as both work efforts will depend on each other.

**Identify, Define and Implement Chargeback Systems**

Usage data is gathered and analyzed to confirm original estimates and allocations. Any changes to add detail to the usage data gathering applications need to be put in place. Rates need to be determined and put in place. Reporting needs will be finalized and reports will be built and put in place. This work will require close coordination with the Capacity Management team as they will be the primary data provider. If charging is based upon business volumes, business data interfaces need to be put in place and tested, then integrated into the chargeback system.

**Define Metrics to Measure Success**

As with all ITIL processes, there needs to be a way to measure the success and ongoing performance of the different IT units. Metrics need to be meaningful and measurable. They should be tied to business value rather than technical measures. Metrics should be fewer in numbers yet succinct and to the point, still providing management with good representation of the effectiveness of the unit. Remember that each ITIL process will have at least one metric, which will be rolled up into an overall IT report. It is necessary to keep the metrics at a manageable level as executives and managers do not have the time or the desire to read through many pages of metrics reports. In FM, most metrics will be related to financial performance.

**Build the Training Materials and Execute the Training Plan**

As stated previously, sufficient time must be built into the plan to train not only the FM team but any other team that interfaces with Financial Management. To accomplish this, it will be necessary to develop training materials based upon the processes previously drafted. Generally the use of a presentation tool such as Microsoft PowerPoint or Adobe Acrobat is desirable since it permits self study or group presentations. Some organizations have opted to develop online training facilities, permitting staff to go through the material in a computer-based interactive environment. To ensure retention, testing should be performed. Passing the test should be made mandatory. Some organizations offer financial incentives, others tie success to future compensation and include them in staff MJOs. Once again, it cannot be stressed enough that organizations will experience fewer missteps when they spend more time testing. In most cases, the work-flows will be substantially different than the work performed today; therefore it is necessary for each staff member to understand the work for which he or she is accountable and the value of the work to the organization.

**Implement Reporting and Exception Processes and Procedures**

Financial performance cannot be assessed without some type of reporting. Two types of reporting need to be put into place. High level reporting is used to keep senior management informed of service quality. These reports are generally in the form of a "dashboard," using the colors red, yellow and green to depict service quality. It is important that each service have two measures - current status and trend. In this way management will understand the current status and where it is trending. For example, a service with a yellow current service indicator and a green trend indicator may need less attention than a service with a green current service indicator and a yellow or red trend indicator. The FM team and those staff assisting with corrective actions will need more detailed reporting to identify problematic service areas and to track results of actions taken.

### *2.3.3.4 Step 4: Initiate the Ongoing Work of FM*

Once the initial budgets and accounting spreadsheets are put in place, work to automate and produce financial reports should be started. Intelligence should be built into the reports to alert the FM team when financial targets are threatened and when substantial changes in user behavior occur. This proactive trending permits actions to be taken before financial targets are missed.

Financial review meetings should be scheduled on a regular basis to cover results. These meetings are normally held monthly or quarterly. The data presented should be concise and only address changes or trends in usage and determine corrective actions. This meeting should not be one of reading the financials line by line, citing the results. The continuous improvement process will be engaged on an annual basis to review the processes and make adjustments where necessary. This work is performed by the FM process champion.

### *2.3.3.5 Step 5: Perform Post Implementation Review*

At the end of the implementation project, the project manager should quickly put together a "lessons learned" document that identifies any changes that should be made to the process to facilitate future process migrations. Any implementation process changes should be made at this time.

Six to 12 months after completion, a post implementation audit should be performed to determine if the new processes are being adhered to and if the new organization is delivering the expected business benefit. Some of the questions that should be asked are:

- Did we accomplish what we set out to do?
- Are the metrics measuring the team's performance valid?
- Is the team communicating successfully with the organization in accordance with the FM processes?
- Are the interfaces working smoothly?
- Did we meet expectations on benefit delivered to the business?
- Does the organization as a whole have a better understanding of the makeup and costs of IT services?
- Are we capturing the right data and at the right level of detail?
- Are the processes accepted and observed by staff, both internal and external to FM?
- Are IT services more effectively used due to changes in business unit usage behaviors?

**Success Factors**

- Management needs to be very supportive of training, implementation and execution efforts. Managers at all levels need to be ITIL cheerleaders.
- All IT and Business units must be willing to work within the new processes.
- Business units must want to support Financial Management disciplines.
- The right people must be in the right positions to do the work.
- Effective tools are in place to collect the needed details of infrastructure usage and the tools have the capability to store historical data.
- Patience is needed to allow the team sufficient time to become proficient in the new processes and for old behaviors to die.
- Processes and pre-defined teams to execute them need to be in place and ready for dealing with gaps once implementation is completed. These teams will be used until all ITIL

implementations have been completed. The business work must continue in spite of the changes so when gaps occur it is essential that the gaps can be addressed before service problems occur.

- Compensation policies should be adjusted to reinforce ITIL practices and drive the appropriate behaviors. Common goals should be in place for all ITIL processes, especially financial and quality.

**Potential Inhibitors**

- Unrealistic expectations by management can erode confidence in the processes. One must remember that a large number of companies have successfully implemented ITIL framework and best practices, many considering the new organization a competitive advantage. To succeed, they ensured management expectations were set realistically.
- Some management may view this unit as purely overhead and superfluous, making it difficult to sustain the team and its value to the organization.
- Lack of patience resulting in partial or cancelled implementation. It takes staff - and those who interface with the organization - time to become familiar with new work-flows. It is essential to allow sufficient time for gaps and issues to be addressed and processes to mature.
- Lack of consistency in allocating unallocated costs across the cost centers.
- Permitting smaller business units to employ less-costly solutions that may look attractive from an individual business unit perspective but are more costly to the organization as a whole.
- Not enforcing adherence to processes – falling back to old behaviors. Two processes are more confusing and probably more detrimental than a single bad process. It is difficult as a surprising amount of work is accomplished through the influence of friends, but managers must resist the temptation and let the processes work. It may not seem like it at the time but when all implementations are completed and the staff is familiar with the new processes, work will flow through the system much faster. For example, one company saw the time needed to install a software change reduced from 45 days to 2 days due to ITIL process improvements.

## 2.3.4 Financial Management for IT Services

The goal of Financial Management for IT Services is to ensure that IT expenditures are managed to allow IT to deliver exactly the services that best support the business goals of the organization in the most cost-effective manner. This process oversees the allocation of IT financial resources to services, and manages the recovery of the costs of those services from the business customers to whom they are provided.

Financial Management for IT Services encompasses the activities that establish the expenditure expectations of the organization, the tracking of how costs are accrued and money is spent, the management of financial assets, and the association of these costs against the various service consumers within the organization. ITIL recognizes that different types of service organizations have different needs in terms of granularity and precision of financial management information. However, with the sizeable investments that most enterprises make in IT, evidence of sound governance and fiscal management practices are increasingly necessary for compliance and external regulatory purposes.

Financial Management for IT Services must address two key questions. First, "Are we doing the right things?" Do we invest in the right projects? Are the services that we provide exactly what the business needs, in terms of functionality, availability, cost and quality? What value does IT deliver to the business? Second, "Are we doing things right?" Are we delivering IT services as cost-efficiently as possible? Where can we improve? Should we do things ourselves or can someone else provide the service more efficiently? You could argue that the Financial Management for IT Services subway line supports all of the other ITIL Service Delivery processes. Availability, capacity and IT service continuity plans are generated to ensure that the organization's service levels are achieved; and, they are drafted in line with the available budget that the organization holds. Financial Management therefore acts as a "check and balance" to ensure that all service management practices are cost-effective and align with business objectives.

Budgeting, IT accounting and charging activities (or "cost allocation" if chargeback is seen as counter-cultural or infeasible) rely upon the establishment of a cost model for all IT expenditures. Subsequent reconciling activities, usage analysis and cost metrics are measured against this model. The role of technology in this context, therefore, is to ensure that the cost model can be held in some electronic form; to automatically measure usage, expenditure and activity; to aggregate and reconcile these measurements; and, finally, to allocate costs — adjusted for service quality or service consumption volumes back to cost centers or other organizational structures.

Figure 2.5 illustrates how technology can be applied to optimize each stage of the journey from the initial planning of Financial Management for IT Services to its process terminus — the efficient and cost-effective stewardship of IT assets and resources and the management of IT investments.

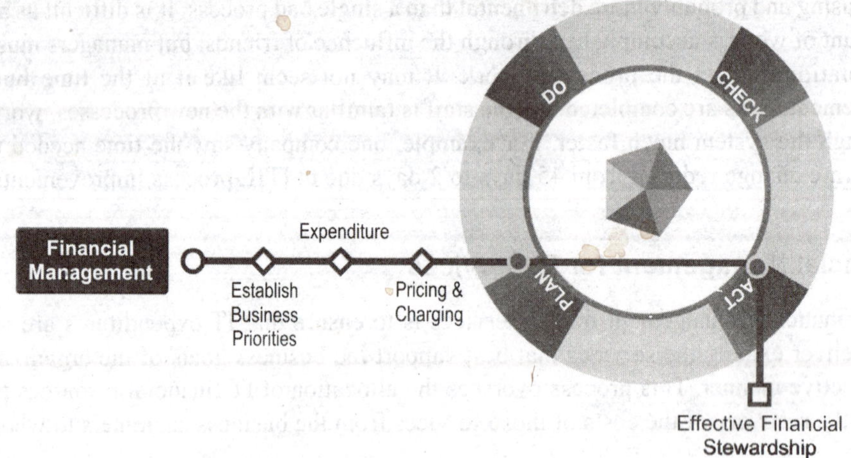


**Fig. 2.5:** Shows the Financial Management

#### *2.3.4.1 First Steps*

The Financial Management for IT Services journey begins with planning the policies, objectives, activities, disciplines and resources required to create the appropriate financial controls. At this stage, technology evaluation typically touches on existing company financial and accounting systems and project management tools. Almost any organization will have accounting practices in place and can easily report the cost of hardware, software, employment, external services, etc. But how does the organization use these resources? Can we benchmark the cost of IT services for a business process? Even if there is no intention of charging IT costs back to the business organization, there is a growing need to gain more transparency about the cost of service and resource utilization, in line with demands that IT "run more like a business." Existing accounting systems and practices need to be extended to meet IT requirements. Likewise, the organization must consider how it can leverage existing operational monitoring tools, inventory tools and service level assurance technology to provide accounting and usage information. You should further consider how you will deliver the financial information to the business and other interested parties; for example, using portal and role-oriented dashboard capabilities. The cost model may need to be representative of the goods and services offered in the IT Service Catalog, hence you may need to consider IT financial management technology in parallel with Service Level Management requirements.

#### 2.3.4.2 Establish Business Priorities

At the first step on the Financial Management for IT Services journey you establish how you should prioritize IT investments and how to allocate the IT budget. By its very nature, much of the IT infrastructure and organization will support business processes of varying or conflicting priorities. Therefore, a key technology deliverable is to enable the comparison of various IT activities and projects in multiple business-context dimensions, such as cost, efficiency, customer satisfaction, quality, growth, compliance and other corporate goals, such that IT organizations can arrive at an optimized portfolio of projects and operational activities in line with business priorities while considering the resources and budget available to IT. The IT Service Continuity line also moves through this station, since this process has a similar emphasis on establishing business priorities in terms of the vital business functions and the critical business processes that support them. All organizations need to ensure that sufficient investment is made to reduce operational risks and to manage the business continuity plans as they relate to IT activity. This activity again relies on accurate project and portfolio controls, but also has a critical reliance upon accurate inventory and related technologies — which are similarly essential in establishing an accurate cost basis for financial management.

#### 2.3.4.3 Expenditure

Having established the relative priorities of IT activities in line with business objectives, operational practices lead naturally to expenditure and cost accrual. The cost model and charging policies will dictate the granularity to which you need to track expenditure. However, in procuring IT hardware and software assets, good governance relies upon the operational view of these assets (typically focused on inventory, availability and performance) being synchronized with the service, financial and contractual views — thus ensuring that the right resources are cost-effectively deployed for the right business purposes. Integrated IT Asset Management technology plays an important role here, and is similarly important to identification and verification stages in Configuration Management. Technology integration is an important consideration as separate business systems will track other costs, and this information may need to be aggregated with resource (people) costs and hardware and software costs to deliver a complete view of expenditure. The ability to influence expenditure based on prior knowledge of the costs will also require service catalog technology that aggregates direct and indirect costs as part of the IT service description.

#### 2.3.4.4 Pricing and Charging

Many travelers on the Financial Management for IT Services journey feel that the pricing and charging station is the most congested and sometimes difficult, and some even decide to avoid it altogether. As the business naturally needs to bear the cost of IT services, issues surround the model for how the costs should be recovered, who should pay and how value for money should be measured. While it might be simpler for IT to be a "utility" cost to the business, equally shared by all, this model might skew the internal balance sheet of individual lines of business with important political consequences. Similarly, directly charging a line of business for only the activities IT conducts on its behalf and the proportion of infrastructure it uses requires a granular level of accounting which may not be cost-justified in terms of the benefits gained by the extra accuracy. Certainly, charges should be related to business transactions or activities. Reports on CPU seconds and network bandwidth utilization don't necessarily help the business users to understand and optimize their cost (although these are important metrics for the Capacity Management process). In order to provide the transparency required, you need to relate prices for services to a well-defined catalog of business-oriented IT services. A further dimension is that the price of services might be dependent on the quality of service actually delivered. The technology challenge is to associate the IT budget with the IT services offered and the IT assets used to arrive at an overall service cost; and then to associate IT activities, utilization and the quality of IT services with the consumers of these services in order to arrive at an allocation of these costs. Ideally, there should be integration with the Service Catalog technology, the service level metering and availability monitoring technology and the asset inventory with aggregated costs, along with the ability to reconcile these to the budgetary components to feed service billing technology. In-route to our next stop, we come to another intersection, which illustrates the difficulty in ensuring that the right levels of investment are managed in order to meet current and new business requirements while maintaining service levels and mitigating risks. Under-investing in any of these areas can have serious implications for all of the business; hence, technology can be leveraged to enable the IT portfolio to be optimized, which is essential to business success.

#### 2.3.4.5 Effective Financial Stewardship

Finally, we arrive at our destination — a point at which the planned budget of IT expenditure is fully accounted for by the scheduled and unscheduled deployment of IT resources and infrastructure, and where these deployment decisions are evidently cost-effective and aligned with business priorities. As a result, the business is able to see the value it receives from IT, and can trust that the IT organization is run under fiscal controls consistent with other business functions. It can see that the service levels delivered by IT are relevant to the costs of that service. Therefore, it is not enough simply to have well-managed investments. It is equally important to demonstrate that this is the case. Technology's role is to provide the automated information collection and aggregation used for service and customer-level cost allocation and service level assurance. Technology must hold and assist the creation of the IT service cost model, and it must provide reporting and visualization for both business managers and IT managers alike.

#### 2.3.4.6 Maintain Investments

The fundamental goal of Financial Management for IT Services is to ensure that IT assets and resources are obtained, deployed, utilized, changed and disposed of cost-effectively. In many organizations, there will already be technology involved in the operational aspect of these stages, but this is unlikely to extend to cover the financial management aspects. To enhance the Financial Management process, therefore, technology must provide:

- A view of the current book value of IT assets for use in cross charge or cost allocation activity
- A view of the total cost of IT assets across their entire lifecycle
- Integration with contract and license repositories in order to accommodate vendor management activity within financial management
- An ability to automate the allocation of costs for a service to a business unit or user at the point of request for that service (i.e., an inherent part of the provisioning process)
- An ability to reconcile service charges with service quality to ensure that these are in balance as far as the business is concerned
- Accommodation of flexible charging structures such as flat rate, usage based, tiered or quality-based
- The ability to take existing operational data sources to provide details of utilization and IT service quality
- A means by which to associate the elements of the cost model with the elements in the budget, with the elements in the IT service catalog that provide consistent constructs for both IT and the business.

### 2.3.4.7 Avoiding Financial Management Problems

The following suggestions may help you avoid some of the most common problems on your Financial Management for IT Services journey:

- Find an equitable charging model. Apart from fiscal diligence, one of the functions of Financial Management for IT Services is to provide evidence that IT activities and costs are aligned to business priorities. IT loses credibility and the IT/business partnership falters if the basis of charging is not equitably distributed. Hence any service charges must also show the direct and indirect breakdown of charges.
- Don't overly constrain flexibility. What decisions can the business now make on the basis of "transparent" IT cost/charge information? For example, can it control its own cost base? Can it change how and when it uses the services? If the opportunity to change behavior is limited, the cost-effectiveness of establishing complex charging and billing systems may be questionable.
- Integrate key elements. Linking the service catalog to the budget and automating service provision can dramatically simplify the Financial Management for IT Services activities, and can also feed into Service Level management automation.
- Avoid undesired side effects. Cost transparency and especially chargeback of IT cost will change the behaviors of users and customers. You need to plan (and adjust) these models carefully in order to avoid undesired results. For example, inappropriate pricing may lead to over-utilization of external resources over existing internal resources.
- Automate data gathering. A lack of conceptual planning when implementing chargeback in large, client/server environments risks creating a bottleneck due to the diversity of information being gathered and rapid rate at which it can change. Automating the collection and mediation of metrics is essential to avoid the benefits of chargeback being outweighed by the costs.

### 2.3.5 Benefits of Financial Management for IT Services

The benefits of implementing a Financial Management for IT Services process in line with ITIL best practices include:

- An accurate accounting of IT costs relative to services rendered
- Better ability to optimize the cost and value of IT services
- Better ability to keep IT priorities in alignment with business goals
- Transformation of IT from a business expense to a strategic business asset

### 2.3.6 Conclusions

The Financial Management for IT Services process strives to provide accurate and cost effective stewardship of IT assets and resources used in providing IT services. This process is concerned with planning, controlling and recovering costs for expenditures related to providing the IT services negotiated in various Service Level Agreements (SLAs). Financial Management for IT Services helps ensure that IT delivers the services that optimally support business objectives from the standpoint of functionality, availability, quality and overall cost. Its overall goal is cost-efficiency across the entire lifecycle of IT assets and services. The major activities that comprise the Financial Management for IT Services process:

- **Financial Management** — Planning the policies, objectives, activities, disciplines and resources required for the appropriate Financial Management for IT Services controls.
- **Establish Business Priorities** — Establishing how you should prioritize IT investments and how to allocate the IT budget
- **Expenditure** — Tracking expenses and cost accrual to ensure that the right resources are cost effectively deployed to address the right business priorities
- **Pricing and Charging** — Determining how IT costs should be recovered, from whom, and using what valuation Because all aspects of IT service delivery, including Availability Management, IT Service Continuity Management and Capacity Management are planned and executed with an eye on the IT budget, Financial Management for IT Services can be seen as the foundation for all the other ITIL Service Delivery processes.

## 2.4 SERVICE MANAGEMENT

### 2.4.1 Introduction

**Service Management** is integrated into **Supply Chain Management** as the joint between the actual sales and the customer. The aim of high performance Service Management is to optimize the service-intensive supply chains, which are usually more complex than the typical finished-goods supply chain. Most service-intensive supply chains require larger inventories and tighter integration with field service and third parties. They also must accommodate inconsistent and uncertain demand by establishing more advanced information and product flows. Moreover, all processes must be coordinated across numerous service locations with large numbers of parts and multiple levels in the supply chain.

Among typical manufacturers, post-sale services (maintenance, repair and parts) comprise less than 20 percent of revenue. But among the most innovative companies in Service , those same activities often generate more than 50 percent of the profits.

### 2.4.2 Uses

1. Service management is usually used in conjunction with operations support systems. Systems that use service management can include order management, inventory management, activation, maintenance, performance diagnostics and several other types of support systems to make sure that these systems are running proficiently and error free.

   There are several components of service management. Service management usually incorporates automated systems along with skilled labor. Service management also usually provides service development. For instance, it is extremely important to first simplify and then streamline services that you manage (i.e. delivery, support) into a simple work-flow. However, managing your work-flow is not enough, another component is the ability to govern automated controls from a centralized location and make sure that data security is in effect at all times.

2. Service Management is usually used with other types of management systems including Total Quality Management (TQM), Six Sigma, CMMI (Capability Maturing Model and Integration), and Business Process Management. It can be used with small scale companies or used with extremely large corporations. The discipline of service management has been around since the early 1970's and was originally part of the Operations Management discipline.

   Today, you can find many resources and service providers that help small and large businesses incorporate the principles of service management into their organization. Some of the vendors that provide service management include: IBM Service Management, Novell Zenworks, Oracle Enterprise Manager and Altrius Management Suite.

### 2.4.3 Benefits

The main drivers for a company to establish or optimize its Service Management practices are varied: High service costs can be reduced, i.e. by integrating the service and products supply chain. Inventory levels of service parts can be reduced and therefore reduce total inventory costs.

- Customer service or parts/service quality can be optimized.
- Increasing service revenue.
- Reduce obsolescence costs of service parts through improved forecasting.
- Improve customer satisfaction levels.
- Reduce expediting costs — with optimized service parts inventory, there is no need to rush orders to customers.
- Minimize technician visits — if they have the right part in hand, they can fix the problem on the first visit.

### 2.4.4 Components

Generally, Service Management comprises six different capabilities that companies should consider for optimization:

**Service Strategy and Service Offerings**

- Service Strategy Definition
- Service Offerings Definition & Positioning
- Go-To-Market Strategy
- Service Portfolio Management

**Spare Parts**

- Parts Supply Management
- Inventory Management
- Parts Demand Management
- Fulfillment Operations & Logistics
- Service Parts Management

**Returns, Repairs and Warranties**

- Warranty & Claims Management
- Reverse logistics
- Returns Processing
- Re-manufacturing

**Field Service Management or Field Force Effectiveness**

- Technician Enablement
- Mobility
- E-learning
- Activity Scheduling
- Service Billing

**Customer management**

- Order Management & Availability
- Channel & Partner Management
- Customer Insight
- Technical Documentation

**Assets, Maintenance, Task Scheduling, Event Management**

- Remote Monitoring
- Diagnostics & Testing
- Asset Management/Optimization
- Configuration Management

Service management, also called **IT service management**, is the discipline used in industries that provide services or a combination of goods and services. While widely used in the IT industry, specifically the ICT (information and Communication Technology) sector, service management can be integrated into many other industries.

### 2.4.5 IT Service Management (ITSM)

ITSM is a discipline for managing information technology (IT) systems, philosophically centered on the customer's perspective of IT's contribution to the business. ITSM stands in deliberate contrast to technology-centered approaches to IT management and business interaction. The following represents a characteristic statement from the ITSM literature:

*Providers of IT services can no longer afford to focus on technology and their internal organization, they now have to consider the quality of the services they provide and* ***focus on the relationship with customers.***

ITSM is process-focused and in this sense has ties and common interests with process improvement movement (e.g., TQM, Six Sigma, Business Process Management, CMMI) frameworks and methodologies. The discipline is not concerned with the details of how to use a particular vendor's product, or necessarily with the technical details of the systems under management. Instead, it focuses upon providing a framework to structure IT — related activities and the interactions of IT technical personnel with business customers and users.

ITSM is generally concerned with the "back office" or operational concerns of information technology management (sometimes known as operations architecture), and not with technology development. For example, the process of writing computer software for sale, or designing a microprocessor would not be the focus of the discipline, but the computer systems used by marketing and business development staff in software and hardware companies would be. Many non-technology companies, such as those in the financial, retail, and travel industries, have significant information technology systems which are not exposed to customers.

In this respect, ITSM can be seen as analogous to an enterprise resource planning (ERP) discipline for IT — although its historical roots in IT operations may limit its applicability across other major IT activities, such as IT portfolio management and software engineering.

## 2.5 CAPACITY MANAGEMENT

### 2.5.1 Capacity Management — The Meaning of Capacity

The capacity of a production unit (e.g. machine, factory) is its ability to produce or do that which the customer requires. In production and operations management, three types of capacity are often referred to:

1. **Potential Capacity:** The capacity that can be made available to influence the planning of senior management (e.g. in helping them to make decisions about overall business growth, investment etc). This is essentially a long-term decision that does not influence day-to-day production management
2. **Immediate Capacity:** The amount of production capacity that can be made available in the short-term. This is the maximum potential capacity — assuming that it is used productively.

3. **Effective Capacity:** An important concept. Not all productive capacity is actually used or usable. It is important for production managers to understand what capacity is actually achievable.

### *2.5.1.1 Measuring Capacity*

Capacity, being the ability to produce work in a given time, must be measured in **the unit of work**.

For example, consider a factory that has a capacity of 10,000 "machine hours" in each 40 hour week. This factory should be capable of producing 10,000 "standard hours of work" during a 40-hour week. The actual volume of product that the factory can produce will depend on:

— the amount of work involved in production (e.g. does a product require 1, 5, 10 standard hours

— any additional time required in production (e.g. machine set-up, maintenance)

— the productivity or effectiveness of the factory

Capacity Management is the discipline that ensures IT infrastructure is provided at the **right time in the right volume at the right price**, and ensuring that IT is used in the most efficient manner.

This involves input from many areas of the business to identify what services are (or will be) required, what IT infrastructure is required to support these services, what level of Contingency will be needed, and what the cost of this infrastructure will be.

These are inputs into the following Capacity Management processes:

- Performance monitoring
- Workload monitoring
- Application sizing
- Resource forecasting
- Demand forecasting
- Modelling

From these processes come the results of capacity management, these being the capacity plan itself, forecasts, tuning data and Service Level Management guidelines.

### 2.5.2 Constraints on Capacity

In capacity management there are usually two potential constraints — TIME and CAPACITY

**Time** may be a constraint where a customer has a particular required delivery date. In this situation, capacity managers often "plan backwards". In other words, they allocate the final stage (operation) of the production tasks to the period where delivery is required; the penultimate task one period earlier and so on. This process helps identify whether there is sufficient time to meet the production demands and whether capacity needs to be increased, albeit temporarily.

**Capacity Management** is a process used to manage information technology (IT). Its primary goal is to ensure that IT capacity meets current and future business requirements in a cost-effective manner. One common interpretation of Capacity Management is described in the ITIL framework . ITIL version 3 views capacity management as comprising three sub-processes: business capacity management, service capacity management, and component capacity management (known as resource capacity management in ITIL version 2).

## 2.5.3 ITIL Capacity Management

### 2.5.3.1 What is it?

Capacity Management is one of five components in the ITIL Service Delivery area. The work is proactive rather than reactive in nature and is responsible for ensuring that business needs and service definitions are fulfilled using a minimum of computing resources.

Capacity Management activities include:

- Monitoring, analyzing, tuning, and implementing necessary changes in resource utilization
- Managing demand for computing resources, which requires an understanding of business priorities
- Modeling to simulate infrastructure performance and understand future resource needs
- Application sizing to ensure required service levels can be met
- Storing capacity management data
- Producing a capacity plan that documents current utilization and forecasted requirements, as well as support costs for new applications or releases
- Building the annual infrastructure growth plan with input from other teams

### 2.5.3.2 Why should I implement Capacity Management?

Immediate and long term benefits include lower costs, more consistent levels of service and improved service quality. Processes allow you to:

- Get more out of existing IT resources and improve IT cost per service unit positions
- Fine tune applications and infrastructure components to improve performance, reduce consumption, and delay upgrades
- Eliminate redundant work and ensure consistent reporting
- Efficiently provision capacity
- Provide timely capacity and related cost information for more informed business decisions
- Provide more complete input to TCO of proposed new and/or major IT-related upgrades or initiatives
- Project consumption at future growth levels and uncover bottlenecks with sufficient warning to correct before business services are adversely affected Capacity management teams have close ties to ITIL Service Level Management and Financial Management areas. Through Capacity Management processes, more thorough service level and associated financial information is available to the business, permitting business leaders to make more informed decisions.

### 2.5.3.3 Why should I implement it first?

ITIL Capacity Management offers quick, early wins that have often generated enough cost savings (in the millions of dollars in our experience) to fund the remainder of your ITIL project. Recovering implementation costs early and demonstrating success also helps gain momentum for the project.

encourage senior management to stay the course, and alleviate organizational resistance. These benefits make Capacity Management a good candidate for a pilot implementation.

Capacity Management is the discipline that ensures IT infrastructure is provided at the right time in the right volume at the right price, and ensuring that IT is used in the most efficient manner. This involves input from many areas of the business to identify what services are (or will be) required, what IT infrastructure is required to support these services, what level of Contingency will be needed, and what the cost of this infrastructure will be.

**Capacity management is made up of three subprocesses:**

1. Business capacity management (BCM)
2. Service capacity management (SCM)
3. Resource capacity management (RCM)

These subprocesses all share a common set of activities that are applied from different perspectives. They include the following:

— Modeling

— Service monitoring

— Performance management

— Demand management

— Workload management

— Analysis

— Change initiation

— Optimization

— Trend analysis

These are inputs into the following Capacity Management processes:

- Performance monitoring
- Workload monitoring
- Application sizing
- Resource forecasting
- Demand forecasting· Modelling

From these processes come the results of capacity management, these being the capacity plan itself, forecasts, tuning data and Service Level Management guidelines.

As the usage of IT Services change and functionality evolves, the amount of processing power, memory etc also changes. If it is possible to understand the demands being made currently, and how they will change over time, this approach proposes that planning for IT Service growth becomes easier and less reactive. If there are spikes in, for example, processing power at a particular time of the day, it proposes analyzing what is happening at that time and make changes to maximize the existing infrastructure, for example, tune the application, or move a batch cycle to a quieter period.

These activities are intended to optimize performance and efficiency, and to plan for and justify financial investments. Capacity management is concerned with:

- Monitoring the performance and throughput or load on a server, server farm, or property
- Performance analysis of measurement data, including analysis of the impact of new releases on capacity
- Performance tuning of activities to ensure the most efficient use of existing infrastructure
- Understanding the demands on the Service and future plans for workload growth (or shrinkage)
- Influences on demand for computing resources
- Capacity planning — developing a plan for the Service

Capacity management interacts with the discipline of Performance Engineering, both during the requirements and design activities of building a system, and when using performance monitoring as an input for managing capacity of deployed systems.

#### 2.5.3.4 Why Capacity Management First?

Capacity management (CM) is one of several services that is a good candidate for a pilot implementation. Many companies already perform CM in some form or another and may just need to consolidate organizations and refine processes to migrate to the new paradigm. Existing senior technicians probably have a good idea of where performance improvement and resource reduction opportunities exist. These improvement opportunities may not have been pursued due to lack of understanding of benefits or organizational dynamics. With the new organization and its best practices, performance and/or financial benefits will be more clearly communicated and processes will drive the remediation work, resulting in relatively quick returns. For example, CM staff working with an application team could tune a database application, resulting in lower per transaction resource utilization which could delay an expensive infrastructure upgrade. The resulting budget savings will reinforce the value of implementing CM and the remaining ITIL processes. Some of the immediate benefits are: Lower costs

- Higher precision tools and more effective best practices permit existing technology assets to be driven closer to the edge, getting more out of existing resources and improving IT cost per service unit positions.
- Continuous runtime improvement processes fine tune applications and infrastructure components, thus improving performance, reducing consumption and delaying expensive capacity upgrades.
- Central performance and capacity data stores eliminate redundant work across IT units and ensures consistent reporting. Redundant tools can be decommissioned, resulting in improved staff productivity, lower software expenses and lower online data storage requirements.

**Improved Quality**

- Predictive modeling disciplines more efficiently provision capacity and provide more timely capacity and related cost information to the business for more informed decisions.
- More comprehensive input to Total Cost of Ownership analyses improve accuracy so more informed decisions can be made regarding proposed new and/or major IT-related upgrade initiatives.
- Proactive analyses with modeling tools project consumption at future growth levels and discover bottlenecks with sufficient warning to correct before business services are adversely affected.

### 2.5.4 The Work of Capacity Management

Capacity management is responsible for ensuring that IT infrastructure resources are in place to satisfy planned business needs and that those infrastructure assets are effectively used. The desired goal for capacity management is to provide a service that is proactive rather than reactive in nature.

The **major work components** of capacity management are:

**Performance management** is a continuous improvement process that examines application and system program performance, analyzes them for possible improvements, identifies candidates for improvement, specs out the costs and requirements, commissions the corrective work, then measures and reports the results. An effective performance management team can reclaim infrastructure capacity by finding ways to improve the way applications consume resources. For example, changing the way an application reads a large database can improve response times to the end user and reclaim capacity by using fewer resources to do the same work. The performance management team works closely with quality assurance testing and performance volume stress testing teams to monitor changes to applications and catch performance problems before they are introduced into production.

**Workload management** uses data from performance monitoring tools to separate resource usage by business process rather than individual increments of usage on a particular infrastructure component. The goal is to address capacity needs on a business process basis. Since some business processes have downstream effects on other processes, this is a more efficient and more effective method of performing capacity planning. For example, selling a certain quantity of merchandise will have an immediate affect on infrastructure resources at the time of the sale, but will also have a future affect on resources as the sales will generate a certain number of customer inquiry calls after the sale. Knowing these business relationships, a capacity planner can make a much more accurate prediction of future needs.

**Building the capacity plan** is probably the most important, and most complex, piece of work the capacity management team produces. In most cases the capacity plan is produced on an annual basis and mid-course corrections are made at predetermined intervals, usually quarterly or semiannually. The plan takes into account current business volumes, projected business growth by business unit or process, budgetary considerations from the financial organization, planned projects from the applications teams and the technical support organizations, service restoration requirements from availability management teams, business contingency requirements from the disaster recovery teams, and service level agreements in place and planned.

The **capacity planning team** works with service level management and finance teams to devise the best plan that meets the business requirements at a cost the business can afford. The most important inputs to the estimation process are the business plans and metrics, and the service level agreements. Without these two important pieces, the infrastructure components cannot be accurately and efficiently designed. For most organizations this is a large effort which should not be underestimated. Sufficient time and people resources should be allocated to perform the task correctly. A well done capacity plan can have a substantial positive impact on IT expenditures by right-sizing components and employing just-in-time provisioning techniques.

The **capacity database** is a repository of all IT and business related information needed to perform the work of capacity management. The data store can also be used by other organizations, eliminating redundancy. For example, utilization data can be extracted for the financial management team in order to produce chargeback billing reports and the enterprise command center can utilize the real-time data collection facility to monitor system performance. A single data store is preferred but multiple stores can be used if data collection tools require, however doing so usually requires a significant work effort to integrate the data sources and pull the information together into a common format for reporting and modeling purposes. Examples of data captured and stored are business volumes, budgetary information and consumption data. Modeling is the process of using software that employs mathematical formulas to simulate infrastructure performance and permit business growth to be applied to the model in order to closely approximate future resource needs. Modeling can find bottlenecks in application systems before they adversely impact business processes and provide sufficient warning so corrective actions can be completed before service interruptions occur. Even with the modeling tools available to the team, this is a labor intensive effort, usually reserved for large scale projects and mission critical applications. That being said, accurate modeling can prevent productivity losses due to outages or slowdowns and can reduce or eliminate the risk of needing to purchase interim resources to maintain business as usual until corrective actions can be accomplished. Demand management relates to managing IT resources consumed by users. The capacity manager is in the unique position of seeing both the business need and the technology available to satisfy it. Where conflicts between business requirements and budgetary constraints arise, the capacity manager should know the options and trade-offs available and start dialogues between the affected parties to determine the best solution from a business point of view. The capacity manager also manages resources during extreme periods such as IT cutbacks resulting from business downturns, unexpected high business volumes, or disasters. During these extraordinary events the capacity manager is responsible for optimizing existing resources and satisfying as many business needs as possible based upon business priorities. Resource management deals with the individual resource components of workloads and business processes by:

- Accumulating them by specific platforms
- Applying recovery requirements
- Devising a capacity plan for each component at an acceptable cost

To get the best possible utilization from IT assets and the best fit when sharing platforms among applications, resource management requires substantial knowledge of individual application usage patterns. For example, a resource capacity planner may plan for a nightly batch reporting process to run on the same server and a day-time online transaction system that runs from 8 a.m. to 5 p.m. In doing so, the capacity planner takes advantage of idle capacity on the processor, satisfying the nighttime capacity need with little or no additional cost. Capacity management also provides a sizing service for new business applications and major application and infrastructure upgrade projects. The capacity team takes initial business metrics, application function and work-flow information, proposed data storage structure and volume information and produces an estimate of the resources needed to provision the new functionality or changes. Capacity then works closely with financial management to develop a 5-year TCO (Total Cost of Ownership) document to assist IT and business leaders in understanding the initial and ongoing support costs before work has started. The costs can then be compared with the business value of the new work or work-flows and an informed decision can be made whether to proceed with the project.

#### 2.5.4.1 Which Other ITIL Processes Interface with Capacity Management?

Capacity is probably the most wide ranging of all the ITIL processes, having links to virtually every area in the IT and business communities. Capacity management processes are tightly integrated with the other service delivery processes and with configuration management, business strategic planning, incident and problem management, and change management. One of the most important interfaces is to Service Level Management (SLM). Capacity management passes historical service metrics to SLM so SLAs can be appropriately sized and configured. SLM passes the detailed SLA information back to CM so that the appropriate capacity positions can be put in place to satisfy the need. Reporting processes are then set up to measure and report service results and forward to SLM for input into their processes. Another important interface is that with Cost management. This interface generally applies to chargeback efforts and the building of TCO documents. The timely and comprehensive exchange of data ensures the costs of IT services are well understood and communicated appropriately to the business. The level of detail will depend on how the business and corporate finance account for IT expenditures and charge backs.

### 2.5.5 Steps to Implement Capacity Management

All successful projects start with a project plan. Implementing capacity management is no different. A project manager with a record of success in implementing large, complex projects should be assigned. Additional staff as required by the company's project management process should be assigned at the same time. Support staff will be needed to document the progress. Since this implementation is the pilot, the support staff should be sufficient to quickly handle any anomalies during the execution of the project plan and should be the ones to make adjustments to the general implementation procedures to smooth the way for future process implementations.

#### *2.5.5.1 Gather the Data*

The first step is to identify a capacity manager. In all shops with more than 100 IT employees, this should be a full time position. The leader must be a true IT generalist. He needs to be a people person, able to communicate well and build relationships with business as well as technical staff. He needs to understand business processes and he needs a good grip on all facets of IT technology. Over time he will probably interface with every leader in the organization. He will need strong negotiation skills to initiate the work identified by him and his staff to streamline applications. He will be responsible and accountable for the entire IT infrastructure capacity budget which includes servers and associated software, networks, network connectivity equipment such as routers and modems, and telephony equipment such as PBX and VRU. The next task is to define the vision for capacity management. Although the decision has been made to implement the ITIL framework and best practices, in most cases the vision behind the decision is at a much higher level than needed to scope and develop a CM team process that meets the business needs. The team tasked to develop the vision should include senior IT management and the capacity manager. The vision will include a mission statement and desired end-state goals, processes and responsibilities. In concert with developing the vision, work can commence on creating a current state assessment. This is frequently prepared with the assistance of a consultant or facilitator however the Office of Government Commerce (OGC) does provide a self-assessment checklist that can be used to narrow the focus of the assessment work. The project team should survey the entire IT organization and discover where and to what extent capacity management work is being performed today. For example in many large companies network, server, and mainframe capacity planning are being done in different organizations under different leaders. Capacity and Performance Reports and their distribution lists should be inventoried. Existing policies and procedures should be documented. The project team should inventory the IT staff both from the perspective of those performing CM work today, but also from the perspective of finding those who have the skills necessary to perform the future CM work. A tools and software inventory should also be performed. In most organizations, different tools are used by different departments to perform monitoring, capacity planning, performance management, and chargeback work. The project team should work with the finance organization to collect the details from the various IT and business budgets that pertain to capacity management work. This is necessary to understand the differences between existing run rates and the start-up and ongoing support costs for the new organization. Once the assessment and inventories have been completed, the next step is to perform a gap analysis. The gap analysis will show the areas that need process improvements or new work to be performed and where efforts are duplicated. Staffing needs and/or skills and training requirements will be identified. The project team will identify any tools needs and any duplication. The results of the gap analysis is essential to build the project plan, define the work that needs to be accomplished, identify tools that need to be acquired, unveil staffing requirements and the costs Now that the gap analysis has revealed the changes required to migrate to the new organization, the project plan can be developed and a cost analysis completed. Staffing, tools and equipment needs will be translated into costs and included in the cost analysis.

### *2.5.5.2 Build the Plan*

Once the gap analysis has been completed, sufficient information will be available to tailor an implementation plan to attain the vision. The plan will be responsible for establishing the three major components of capacity management — people, processes and tools. The plan will also determine the costs necessary to sustain the organization, build a preliminary budget, and compare it to the current expenditures for similar function and possible spread across the organization. The components of the implementation plan are: Determine where capacity management is placed in the IT organization. The ideal placement is as a direct report to the CIO, IT Director or within the Service Management group. However a number of organizations opt to place it in the Operations area. This may not be a good choice as applications and user areas may feel capacity management will immediately take the Operations point of view rather than a neutral position. At this point in time a decision must be made as to having a formal, centralized capacity management team or have a matrixed organization. Many organizations separate network functions under entirely different management teams. Generally it is better to have a single organization. Today's applications are complex and span a number of technologies so it is necessary to examine an application with an end-to-end perspective to determine where capacity upgrades or tuning efforts are required. For example, when adding online data storage for a new database or data store, there is more to it than just buying the physical storage. A centralized capacity management team will look at the operating environment as a whole. If the storage is to be kept remotely, the capacity team will know if there is sufficient bandwidth to transmit the data for backup and recovery purposes. The capacity team will also know if sufficient backup media and equipment, such as tape drives, are available to perform the additional work within the time frames specified in the SLA. Environmental capacity (power, air conditioning, surge protection, backup generator, etc.) will also be reviewed to ensure sufficient resources exist to support the new equipment. In a split team, miscommunications can lead to omissions in researching one or more of the additional elements, resulting in unplanned service issues. Sufficient time must be allowed to develop the process documents. The documents should have a description of all the data inputs, information outputs and work processes. A flow chart of the work flow should also be included. Much thought needs to occur to ensure all interfaces and work are identified.

In addition, the project plan needs to develop a process and identify a team to handle any process gaps during or immediately following implementation. The plan must include tasks to identify and train the people performing the work. The plan will vary depending upon management's decision to staff from within or look externally for the appropriate talent. Job descriptions need to be drafted and sufficient time allocated to work with the Human Resources organization to review and adopt them. Sufficient time must be built into the plan to train not only the capacity management team but any other team that interfaces with capacity management. Many organizations have chosen to train everyone on capacity management, just as they do with service level management or financial management. Many post implementation reviews reveal that insufficient time was made for training and the implementation would have had many fewer incidents had more time been allocated. Any work regarding acquisition, consolidation and/or implementation of capacity and performance tools will be included in the plan. If tools are to be acquired, the project manager needs to allow sufficient time in the plan for corporate acquisition policies and procedures to be followed. The project manager needs to develop a plan item to communicate the processes to the organization. Many organizations use their internal corporate communications team to accomplish this task. Due to demands on their talents, the project manager should schedule the work with corporate communications well in advance so project goals can be achieved. The project should include members of the financial team so a comprehensive implementation and ongoing operations budget can be developed. In addition, these project team members will assist in identifying current expenditures across the organization that performs capacity management functions. All the financial information is then fed into the TCO document and submitted to management with the proposed project plan. Project reports should be determined and agreed upon. Many organizations employ the use of a dashboard report, using traffic lights (Green, Yellow, Red) to signify project status. Once the project plan and the budget have been completed, the Project Manager and the Project Sponsor present the plan for approval.

### *2.5.5.3 Execute the Plan*

**Build the Organization**

The first step is to write the job descriptions. The size of the organization will dictate the number and function of the positions. Job descriptions should be developed even if the work is matrixed to another organization. Job descriptions should specify the position name, salary grade, skills required to perform the work, and any previous experience required. Some of the desired skill sets for capacity management positions are: Capacity Planner — For business and service capacity management, applications and/or business analyst experience is desired as the work is usually at a higher level than a single infrastructure component. Engineers or long time technical support staff can perform the functions very effectively but must be able to rise above a detail level to be successful. Resource capacity management can be performed by staff with previous engineering, technical support or operation monitoring/command center background as they are working at individual infrastructure components that they are already familiar with. One of the goals for a capacity planner is to be trained to work across all infrastructure components rather than a single technology. Good communication skills, both verbal and written are desired for these positions. Performance — Good candidates for performance management roles are staff with experience in System Programming, Applications Performance Management, Operations Analysis, Database Support, Problem Determination and Performance Monitoring. Medium and large organizations will have a well diversified group of people to permit specialization in key areas such as database tuning and application coding techniques. Modeling – Engineers make good candidates but must be able to transition from a detailed to business focus. Mathematicians understand the modeling process but need an IT operational background to be able to ensure the models truly reflect the real life environment. Data gathering, storage and reporting – Good candidates for these positions have experience in one or more of the following areas: technical support, monitoring, chargeback, and IT reporting. A candidate with multiple infrastructure platform experience is a plus. Process champion – This person audits the process on an annual basis and is responsible for making appropriate process changes as dictated by changes in the work-flow. This is usually not a full time position and can be filled by any capacity management team member with good writing skills.

**Document and Publish the Processes**

Since this is a pilot example, it is more work as interim interfaces and goals have to be identified so work can be accomplished with a minimum of interruption while the rest of the organization rolls out. Writing the processes is a lot of work. It is necessary to document the work-flow: inputs, outputs, work accomplished, steps to accomplish, who does the work, who receives the work, outside assistance needed to execute the processes. It may be advantageous to employ the services of a professional writer to do the bulk of the work with management and technical staff creating just an outline to minimize disruption to day-to-day activities. Doing so ensures the processes are documented consistently, in the same format and in the same language (tone and wording). Although an organization can structure the work in many different ways, the most common components of capacity management where processes need to be documented are:

- **Performance management** — continuous performance improvement of applications, performance trend analysis and analysis of chronic application performance problems.
- **Capacity planning/capacity plan** — building of the capacity plan, resource management, demand management, capacity management.
- **Modeling** – forecast future needs through use of simulation tools and proactive bottleneck discovery.
- **Performance data collection, storage and reporting** – without the data, little of the work of capacity management can be accomplished and communicated.
- **New Application and major upgrade sizing.**

**Acquire and Implement the Tools** — Capacity and performance tools are as important as people to capacity management. The gathering and processing of infrastructure utilization and performance data is critical to the team's success. Without the right detailed data it is difficult for the staff to efficiently or effectively execute processes and procedures. Ideally a single tool will provide all of the functions mentioned below. However economics may dictate that a number of existing products must be used and integrated. The capacity manager must review the portfolio carefully to ensure that data from all tools is based upon the same collection interval and that data can be easily moved between tools. Manual input of data from one tool into another can be a productivity drain in most shops. Manual input is tedious, subject to change, and very time consuming for servers that have numerous peripheral devices attached such as hundreds on online data storage volumes. Therefore it is necessary to have automated methods of integrating the tools if capacity management productivity is to be maintained at expected levels. Tools required to successfully and efficiently execute capacity management processes have the following functions and capabilities:

**Monitor and infrastructure utilization data collection tools** — These tools are required for real-time monitoring of infrastructure components and to harvest the associated utilization data, storing it for future analysis. The collection tools should have the ability to segregate data based upon user-defined categories, associating usage by user, application and/or business process. The tools should have automation built in so staff support is necessary for the day-to-day functions of the tool. The tools should be able to collect detailed application performance data such as CICS, DB2, Oracle, Java, SAP, Email, Network packets and other major applications. The user interface to the tools should be intuitive and easy to use with minimal training requirements. In Wintel and Midrange systems, the tools should not be kernel intrusive so operating system integrity can be maintained and maintenance processes simplified. From a database management perspective, the tools should have data management processes built in or employ common database systems such as DB2, Sybase, and Oracle where existing data center tools can be used.

**Reporting** — The reporting functions within the tools should be easy to use. They should provide greater flexibility, permitting detailed reporting for a single device or higher level reporting for a business process. Reporting should have automation built in so regularly scheduled reports can be produced with minimum staff intervention. In today's environment, reporting tools that provide web-based displays of reports are a plus as they eliminate the need for costly printing and distribution.

**Analysis functions** —The tools need to be able to assist performance management and capacity planning staff in analyzing infrastructure utilization data. They need to be able to perform trend analysis to determine when resources will be needed or to spot performance anomalies before they impact service. They should be able to process large amounts of data and present them in abbreviated form based upon the users needs. The tools should have the ability for a wide view, from an individual application on a server to an end-to-end application or business process. Artificial intelligence is available with some tool sets, especially in the mainframe and network areas. This can reduce analysis time when researching a performance problem and can permit less knowledgeable staff to identify problems quickly. However one needs to be careful with automation in complex environments. For example, artificial intelligence could mistakenly diagnose a problem because different problems or interacting problems could exhibit similar characteristics.

**Modeling tools** — This tool or set of tools should permit simulation of utilization changes to the IT infrastructure components. Again, the tools should have a wide span of operation, permitting simulation of a single device to an end-to-end view of a particular business application or business process. The tool should be easy to use. It should have some automation built in such as automatic calibration of baseline models (those models developed to simulate the current infrastructure components at current business volumes). The model should have the ability to import data from the data collection tools with minimum effort. The tool should also have the ability to easily generate reports of the simulation results. Analytic and Discrete Event Simulation (DES) are two types of simulation tools available on the market today. Analytic modeling uses mathematical formulas based upon Queuing Theory to simulate computing environments. DES is much more detailed and simulates the actual running of the individual processes on processors and the transmission of individual packets on network lines and devices. Each method has its own strengths and weaknesses and its own place in the capacity Manager's toolbox. If we look at the most effective tools on the market today, there are probably more analytic tools than DES.

**Define Metrics to Measure Success**

As with all ITIL processes, there needs to be a way to measure the success and ongoing performance of the different IT units. Metrics need to be meaningful and measurable. They should be tied to business value rather than technical measures. Metrics should be fewer in number yet succinct and to the point, still providing management with good representation of the effectiveness of the unit. Remember that each ITIL process will have at least one metric, which will be rolled up into an overall IT report. It is necessary to keep the metrics at a manageable level as executives and managers do not have the time or the desire to read through many pages of metrics reports. Examples of metrics are:

- **Performance management** — Due to the nature of the work, results are not known until corrective actions have been completed. Generally a productivity or SLA conformance metric is used.
- **Capacity Planning** — generally metrics showing adherence to the plan, cost related or SLA conformance are used.
- **Modeling** — accuracy is the major metric used and productivity is not a good measure due to the varying complexity of work.
- **Data Collection and Reporting** — metrics that show completeness and timeliness of data collection and reporting are the most commonly used.
- **Application sizing** — probably the most difficult to measure. The work is usually accomplished with a minimum of technical or business data so accuracy measurements generally are not well-suited. Productivity measures such as completing a sizing within a standard period of time is the most common metric employed. Build the Training Materials and Execute the Training Plan  s stated previously, sufficient time must be built into the plan to train not only the capacity management team but any other team that interfaces with capacity management. To accomplish this, it will be necessary to develop training materials based upon the processes previously drafted. Generally the use of a presentation tool such as Microsoft PowerPoint or Adobe Acrobat is desirable since it permits self study or group presentations. From previous experience, self study seems to work well in a busy IT environment, however managers must ensure that each member of their staff has sufficient time to read and comprehend the information. Some organizations have opted to develop online training facilities, permitting staff to go through the material in a computer based interactive environment. To ensure retention, testing should be performed. Passing the test should be made mandatory. Some organizations offer financial incentives while others tie success to future compensation and include them in staff Major Job Objectives. Once again, it cannot be stressed enough that organizations increase their chances for success when more time is spent testing. In most cases, the work-flows will be substantially different than the work performed today; therefore it is necessary for each staff member to understand the work for which he or she is accountable and the value of the work to the organization.

### 2.5.5.4 Open for Business

The initial focus should be directed toward performance management. With the capacity database just filling with data, time is needed before sufficient historical data is available before more complex work can be performed in the capacity planning areas. Begin by choosing a highly visible but less complex piece of work. Since this is the ITIL pilot for the entire organization, it is better to have a small victory than a large defeat. When choosing work, ask yourself, "If the customer doesn't see the problem, is it really a problem and should we address it now?" For example, if a web application is operating in a cluster and servers need to be rebooted during the day due to memory leaks or other similar causes, the customer probably doesn't know it happened as they just refreshed the browser and the page came back, albeit from a different server. This is a problem that only impacts operations with no customer impact; thus not a good candidate to demonstrate the benefits of capacity management. To start, attack problems that are low risk, have wide visibility and where correction efforts provide significant benefit to the company. During this time, you will have everyone's attention. It is easier to get things done during this period as everyone is flush with ITIL training and eager for success. Initial roadblocks associated with process implementation are easier to break now than at a later date. If needed business data is not available or resistance is encountered, now is the time to escalate. At least 30 days of historical performance data should be gathered before developing any kind of trend or model. Start simple (platform specific) then work up to end-to-end application transactions and then business processes. This will take time. Some organizations have taken several years to reach end-state yet ITIL benefits were enjoyed from the start. Keep a good customer focus. Your business partners in most cases will welcome you when you say you want to understand their processes. They are as proud of what they do as you are of your work.

#### 2.5.5.5 Post Implementation Review

At the end of the implementation project, the project manager should quickly put together a "lessons learned" document that identifies any changes that should be made to the process to facilitate future process migrations. Any implementation process changes should be made at this time. 6-12 months after completion, a post implementation audit should be performed to determine if the new processes are being adhered to and if the new organization is delivering the expected business benefit. Some of the questions that should be asked are:

- Did we accomplish what we set out to do?
- Are the metrics measuring the teams' performance valid?
- Is the team communicating successfully with the organization in accordance with the capacity management processes?
- Are the interfaces working smoothly?
- Did we meet expectations on benefit delivered to the business?
- Has capacity/performance improved overall?
- Have the cost goals been attained?
- Are we capturing the right data?
- Are the processes accepted and observed by staff, both internal and external to capacity management?

**Success Factors**

- Management needs to be very supportive of training, implementation and execution efforts. Managers at all levels need to be ITIL cheerleaders.

- Business units must be willing to work within the new processes.
- The right people must be in the right positions to do the work.
- Behavior of staff used to working around processes may need modifying. Working outside the processes slows work, disrupts day-to-day and generally has negative impact on service delivery. If people cannot adjust to the new work-flows and continue to disrupt work-flows, their ongoing value to the organization needs to be seriously assessed and the appropriate Human Resources actions taken.
- Centralized organization is essential to the effectiveness of capacity management. When the organization is spread out across IT, it is subject to missed handoffs, politics and conflicting goals.
- Patience is needed to allow teams sufficient time to become proficient in the new processes and for old behaviors to die.
- Processes and pre-defined teams to execute them need to be in place and ready for dealing with gaps once implementation is completed. These teams will be used until all ITIL implementations have been completed. The business work must continue in spite of the changes so when gaps occur it is essential that the gaps can be addressed before service problems occur.
- Compensation policies should be adjusted to reinforce ITIL practices and drive the appropriate behaviors. Common goals should be in place for all ITIL processes, especially financial and quality.

**Potential Pitfalls**

- Unrealistic expectations by management can erode confidence in the processes. One must remember that a large number of companies have successfully implemented ITIL framework and best practices, many considering the new organization a competitive advantage. To succeed, they ensured management expectations were set realistically.
- Substantial misses on predictions can cause loss of confidence in the capacity management organization. Attention to detail and additional work reviews in the initial implementation will reduce the risk of missing on predictions. If a prediction is missed, it is important to quickly determine the reasons and make appropriate changes to the processes to avoid shortcomings in the future.
- Lack of patience resulting in partial or cancelled implementation. It takes staff, and those who interface with the organization, time to become familiar with new work-flows. It is essential to allow sufficient time for gaps and issues to be addressed and processes to mature.
- Not enforcing adherence to processes and falling back to old behaviors. Two processes are more confusing and potentially more detrimental than a single bad process. It is difficult as a surprising amount of work is accomplished through the influence of informal networks. but managers must resist the temptation and let the processes work. It may not seem like it at the time but when all implementations are completed and the staff is familiar with the new processes, work will flow through the system much faster. For example, one company saw the time needed to install a software change reduce from 45 days to 2 days due to ITIL process improvements.

## 2.6 AVAILABILITY MANAGEMENT

### 2.6.1 Introduction

The objective of Availability Management is to provide a cost-effective and defined level of service availability that enables the business to reach its objectives. Availability Management can be met through process, technology and people, resource planning and implementation. In general, Availability Management is the process of ensuring IT Services are available when required, has the capacity to recover quickly and not liable to malfunction. Availability Management is about understanding and meeting the needs of the business. Meeting these needs is accomplished by managing the availability, serviceability, maintainability and reliability of IT services.

- **Availability.** Services provided according to agreed upon service times with the customer, response times, etc.
- **Serviceability.** The expected availability of a component where a service is provided by a third party supplier.
- **Maintainability.** The ease with which an IT component can be maintained (which can be both remedial and preventative).
- **Reliability.** The time for which an IT component can be expected to perform under specific conditions without failure.

Fig. 2.6: Shows the Availability Management

Good Availability Management is also about proactively designing for the availability of the IT infrastructure, as documented in Service Level Agreements, rather then reactively trying to make services available. Availability Management also serves to make services available at optimum costs in order to support the business objectives. This business and IT alignment creates the environment needed to maximize the availability of IT related components thereby increasing customer satisfaction, and empowering the business to design for availability rather than fire fight to make services available, reactively. Availability management is also the cornerstone of Information Security in ITIL, being one of the three major building blocks confidentiality, integrity, availability) of any security strategy.

#### 2.6.1.1 *What is it?*

Availability Management is one of five components in the ITIL Service Delivery area. It is responsible for ensuring application systems are up and available for use according to the conditions of the Service Level Agreements (SLAs).

The Availability Management team reviews business process availability requirements and ensures the most cost effective contingency plans are put in place and tested on a regular basis to ensure business needs are met. For example, Internet applications supporting online ordering systems may have 30-minute or less recovery requirements, so they may be provisioned with infrastructure components providing several levels of redundancy. Less critical, non-customer-facing applications used by a few users in small offices with a 5-day recovery period may be provisioned on less expensive infrastructure with limited redundancy capabilities.

Availability Management is also the lead in Component Failure Impact Analysis and Service Outage Analysis initiatives, determining cause, analyzing trends and taking any appropriate actions to ensure service availability meets SLAs.

Availability Management activities include:

- Ensuring service availability meets SLAs
- Determining the cause of availability failures
- Reviewing business requirements for availability of business systems
- Cataloging business requirements
- Ensuring proper contingency plans are in place and tested
- Establishing high-availability, redundant systems to support mission-critical applications

#### 2.6.1.2 *Why should I implement Availability Management?*

Benefits to implementing Availability Management processes include:

- Services are available for use during expected timeframes as specified in SLAs.
- Services are provisioned on specific infrastructure depending upon their availability needs. This avoids unnecessary costs due to provisioning services with longer recovery times on more expensive high-availability platforms.
- Potential service availability issues are identified and corrected before they negatively impact services.

Availability Management processes are tightly integrated with Service Level Management, Capacity Management, IT Service Continuity Management, and Incident Management.

### 2.6.2 Benefits of Availability Management

The **benefits of Availability Management** include:

- Reduced cost of downtime
- Systems are managed according to business availability targets
- There is a greater level of control over IT systems

- New systems are produced according to the availability requirements rather than designing availability around the new systems
- An increased level of support for the core business operations
- A reduction in the level of reactive support for IT systems

There are a number of critical activities of Availability Management that this paper will focus on. These activities include planning for IT/Business Plans, new services, design and recovery requirements; measuring availability, reliability and maintainability metrics; and automated monitoring and improving IT services against measurements. The key activities of Availability Management are represented in Figure below, and include:

- Monitor
- Record an impact
- Analyze
- Maintain Resilience and security

The Availability Management subway line crosses all of the major Service Delivery lines because of its focus on proper design, implementation, measurement and management of the IT Infrastructure availability to ensure the stated business requirements for availability are consistently met. Availability Management should create and maintain a proactive availability plan aimed at improving the overall availability of IT services and infrastructure components, and ensuring that any capability gaps are quickly identified and rectified. By travelling along this line, and by continuously optimizing activities, IT organizations can reduce the frequency and duration of incidents that impact IT Availability and thereby helping to achieve the process objective of ensuring IT services are available when required.

### 2.6.2.1 Monitor

The journey of Availability Management begins with monitoring the current state of IT service availability. This stage involves determining what infrastructure components should be monitored, setting up a monitoring plan and identifying appropriate monitoring tools. Key tasks at this stage include collecting and monitoring key metrics of infrastructure availability, including:

- **Availability.** Accumulated downtime over given periods of time.
- **Reliability.** The frequency of downtime.
- **Maintainability.** How well the organization maintains IT services in an operational state
- **Serviceability.** Identical to maintainability, but involves monitoring external service providers. During the monitoring stage of Availability Management it is critical to measure as much information as possible, so as to be able to verify service levels agreements, identify problem areas, and present proposals for availability improvements. All good IT Service Management requires ongoing monitoring and reporting on the process environment and the Availability Management journey is no different.

Appropriate monitoring will help identify incidents and provide the information to anticipate, or predict IT failures, thereby empowering IT staff to act in a preventative rather than reactive manner. Automation of monitoring activities will improve the IT organizations ability to control the environment by providing accurate and detailed reports. The organizational benefits include minimizing the impact on perceived quality, improved user satisfaction and enhanced business reputation.

In order to support the monitoring of service availability, monitoring applications can collect the data and automatically correlate that data against pre defined thresholds that reflect the true business, user and IT perspectives. This data can then be used in trend analysis and helping identify unacceptable levels of services and promoting a dialog to rapidly correct them.

#### *2.6.2.2 Record Impact*

Even with the best hardware, systems and software failures will occur within the operational infrastructure, resulting in deviations from normal service. Once we understand and can measure availability from our monitoring activities, the next objective is to align any outage to an IT service and document the impact of the outage. The outage, or unavailability impact, will allow us to identify the infrastructure components causing availability problems and help us to understand where we may be incurring excessive costs, unplanned expenditure and, additional costs charged by suppliers, etc. It is important to note that a sometimes overlooked area of availability management is the management of suppliers, since few organizations manage and maintain their entire infrastructure. For example, a call centre or Service Desk is often externally managed. These supplier relationships should include associated service level agreements because these are vital to managing the availability of the complete service and understanding the impact of unavailability.

#### *2.6.2.3 Analyze*

The IT Organization traditionally has extensive usage and availability information although often not organized in a format that can be utilized for good availability analysis. At this stage on the Availability Management line, it is important to identify, analyze and manage the current data to assess and identify areas of improvement. In performing a structured analysis the objective is to create an availability matrix with the relevant information about provided services and components. To accomplish this task a broad spectrum of methods and techniques are available:

- **Component Failure Impact Analysis (CFIA)** can assist identify key components and their roles in each service.
- **Fault Tree Analysis (FTA)** can be used to identify the chain of events leading to failure.
- **CCTA Risk Analysis and Management Method (CRAMM)** provide the means of identify justifiable countermeasures to protect IT services against performance and security breaches.
- **Service Outage Analysis (SOA)** is a technique used to identify the causes of faults, investigate the IT organization effectiveness, and provide recommendations for improvements.
- **The Technical Observation Post (TOP)** method is based on a dedicated team of IT specialists that will investigate a single aspect of availability when where routine applications provide insufficient information.

These methods can provide inputs to availability calculations, based on pre-defined metrics, which can be used as input to the service availability agreements that will be included on Service Level Agreement (SLA) for a related IT service agreed with its customers.

#### 2.6.2.4 Maintain Resilience and Security

Tools and best practices exist today that rapidly detect service degradation and ensure systems resilience before users are impacted by IT service outages. The mission of Availability management is to leverage the information from monitoring and analysis in order to establish a secure environment to support sustainable services. It is important to realise that security and reliability are closely linked. For example, insufficient security planning and design can affect the availability of the service. During the service availability planning stage and development of availability plan, security issues must be considered. The impact on the service provisioning like authorized access to secure areas and critical authorizations, should be addressed.

### 2.6.3 Optimizing the Availability Management

Successful Availability Management depends on the business clearly defining their availability objectives and service requirements. Optimization of the Availability Management process is possible with the integration of Service Level Management (SLM). Optimizing the Availability Management journey should include defining Service Level Agreements (SLA) with availability components, since SLM will serve to formalize the relationship between IT and customers of IT thereby demonstrating the benefits of IT services availability. An example quality metric based on the core objective of Availability Management is to measure the % of service availability to ensure that it is within a SLA negotiated requirement. When implemented with relevant and meaningful metrics Availability Management can influence the way IT services are designed, implemented and managed. By understanding the business processes and how IT supports those processes you are able increase customer satisfaction by eliminating constraints that can affect service performance which will intern make a positive impact on the culture of your organizations Avoiding Availability Management Issues and Problems Availability Management often suffers from misunderstandings that may inhibit its establishment and deployment in an organization. The most common barriers include:

- Perception: There is a difference in the level of availability of systems and the availability of services; for example, IT can report to the business that the percentage availability of the Lotus Notes system is 97.5% and the availability of NT Servers is 99% and think that they are doing a great job. However, if the availability of the 'Printing Service' is at 65%, then the perception by the business is that IT is not providing the required level of availability so perhaps they should outsource.
- Relevant Availability metrics should be presented to the business and not simply raw IT availability data.
- Lack of understanding how Availability Management will make a significant improvement, especially when disciplines such as Incident Management, Problem Management and Change Management are being implemented without looking at the bigger picture.
- Current levels of Availability are considered "acceptable" so managers see little value of embarking on the Availability Management journey.
- IT staff sees availability as a responsibility of all senior managers and offers resistance on point who will be empowered and soon responsible for manage IT service availability.

## 2.7 ITIL SERVICE DELIVERY PROCESSES

**Table 2.1:** Shows the Different ITIL Service Delivery Processes

| S.No. | Process | Brief Process Description |
|---|---|---|
| 1. | Service Level Management | Service level management provides a mechanism to align the IT services with the business requirements. Service level management provides a structured way for customers and providers of IT services to meaningfully discuss and assess how well a service is being delivered. The primary objective of service level management is to provide a mechanism for setting clear expectations with the customer and user groups with respect to the service being delivered. Activities included in the process are creating a catalog of services, identifying requirements, negotiating SLAs, and managing service continuity, availability, capacity, and workforce. |
| 2. | Financial Management | Financial Management process introduces the concept of Budgeting, Accounting and Charging for IT services delivered to the customers. Budgeting and Accounting involves understanding the cost of providing various services. Financial management ensures that any IT service proposed is justified from a cost and budget standpoint. This is often referred to as a cost-benefit analysis. Activities performed within the function include such standard accounting practices as budgeting, cost allocations, and others. The concept of charge back allows internal IT departments to function as a business unit, controls non essential demands from customers and allows customers to demand value for money. |
| 3. | Availability Management | The goal of availability management is to ensure that the IT services are available to users when they need them. Availability is calculated and reported as percentage of the agreed service hours for which the service was available |
| 4. | Capacity Management | Capacity management activities include planning, sizing, and controlling service solution capacity to satisfy user demand within the performance levels set forth in the SLA. This requires the collection of information about usage scenarios, patterns, and peak load characteristics of the service solution, as well as stated performance requirements. These data collection activities are included in the Capacity Management process. |
| 5. | IT Service Continuity Management | IT service continuity management, also known as contingency management, focuses on minimizing the disruptions to business caused by the failure of mission-critical systems. This process deals with planning to cope with and recover from an IT disaster. It also provides guidance on safeguarding the existing systems by the development and introduction of proactive and reactive countermeasures. IT service continuity management also considers what activities need to be performed in the event of a service outage not attributed to a full-blown disaster. |

## 2.8 SUMMARY

Implementing the Service Level Management framework and best practices takes work and determination but the benefits make it worth the efforts. Once processes mature, your customers will be delighted as expectations have been set, they understand what service they will receive and the roles and responsibilities of the parties involved. Management will applaud the effective use of IT resources achieved by efficiencies produced through the right-sizing and business justification of the levels of service provided.

Implementing the Financial Management framework and best practices takes work and determination but the benefits make it worth the efforts. Once processes mature, your customers will be delighted as expectations have been set, they understand what service they will receive and the roles and responsibilities of the parties involved. Management will applaud the effective use of IT resources achieved by efficiencies produced through the right-sizing and business justification of the levels of service provided.

Implementing the capacity management framework and best practices takes work and determination but the benefits make it worth the efforts. Once processes mature, your customers will be delighted with the improved quality of IT services as a result of the improved performance and capacity management processes. Management will applaud the lower costs achieved by efficiencies produced through the execution of ITIL capacity management best practices.

CHAPTER 3

# Service Support and Storage Management

## 3.1 SERVICE SUPPORT PROCESS

The Service Support ITIL discipline is focused on the User and is primarily concerned with ensuring that they have access to the appropriate services to support the business functions.

To a business, customers and users are the entry point to the process model. They get involved in service support by:

Asking for changes.

Needing communication, updates.

Having difficulties, queries.

Real process delivery.

The major processes in this area are:

### 3.1.1 Service Desk or Help Desk

The Service Desk is the single point of focus for all IT services clients to request services and report problems. The service desk processes include tracking and escalation procedures. In addition, the Service Desk is responsible for disseminating information to the organization regarding planned outages and/ or implementation of changes impacting production services.

### 3.1.2 Incident Management

The primary focus of Incident Management (IM) is the restoration of services following an incident. IM is primarily a reactive process; its processes provide guidance on diagnostic and escalation procedures required to quickly restore services. IM processes are closely integrated with Help Desk, Problem Management and Change Management processes.

### 3.1.3 Problem Management

The primary focus of Problem Management (PM) is to identify the causes of service issues and commission corrective work to prevent recurrences. PM processes are reactive in responding to incidents and proactive in identifying and preventing future incidents. Its processes are closely integrated with Incident Management, Change Management and Availability Management (AM). Although AM performs the lead role in component failure and system outage analyses, PM performs an important role in obtaining data and analyzing it in support of the studies.

### 3.1.4 Configuration Management

Configuration Management (CfM) processes guide the collection, archiving and report of individual infrastructure component specifications. The Configuration Database is the single repository of configuration information for the enterprise. In addition to configuration information, the database contains information regarding the relationships and dependencies among infrastructure components. CfM processes closely integrate with Change Management processes, because risk assessments must take into consideration any relationships and dependencies that may be affected by requested changes to production operations. CfM databases are also used by Capacity, Availability and IT Service Continuity Management processes to accurately perform their work.

### 3.1.5 Change Management

Change Management (ChM), as the name implies, manages change being introduced into the IT infrastructure. ChM teams assess risks of individual changes, use configuration information to identify dependencies and other impacted applications and systems, and after analyzing the information, authorize or deny change requests. The goal of ChM is to identify application code, functional and performance defects and intercept them before customers are impacted by them. Change Management teams are judged successful when changes are introduced into production operations without impact to business units or their customers.

### 3.1.6 Release Management

Release Management is closely integrated with Change Management. Release Management addresses large-scale changes to the environment such as installing a new database management system or managing widespread changes to a business application. As a result, Release Management is concerned with managing a large number of changes that will be introduced simultaneously into the production operating environment.

The Service Support (Figure 3.1) represents a journey of improving day-to-day IT service support processes that lay the operational foundation needed upon which to build business value.

## 3.2 CONFIGURATION MANAGEMENT

Configuration Management (CfM) is one of the components in the ITIL Service Support area. The primary focus of CfM is to identify, maintain and verify information on IT assets and configurations in the enterprise.

CfM stores up-to-date information about Configuration Items (CIs), which are simply IT infrastructure components as you define them such as hardware, software, documentation, or even personnel. CIs are stored in a Configuration Management Database, or CMDB. The CMDB contains a variety of information on CIs such as version and location, as well as relationships between CIs.

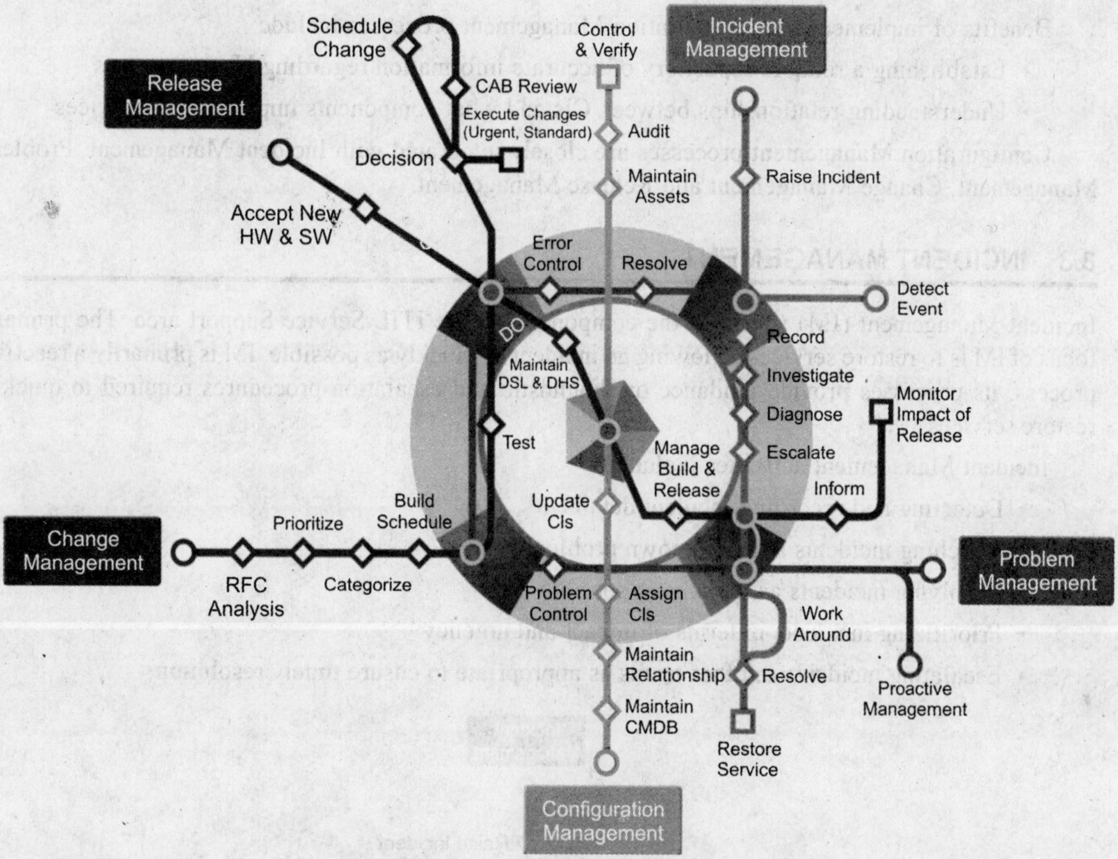

**Fig. 3.1:** Shows the Service Support Process

Configuration Management activities include:

- Defining the scope - the depth and breadth - of the CMDB
- Identifying CIs and entering them into the CMDB
- Collecting, recording and maintaining accurate information

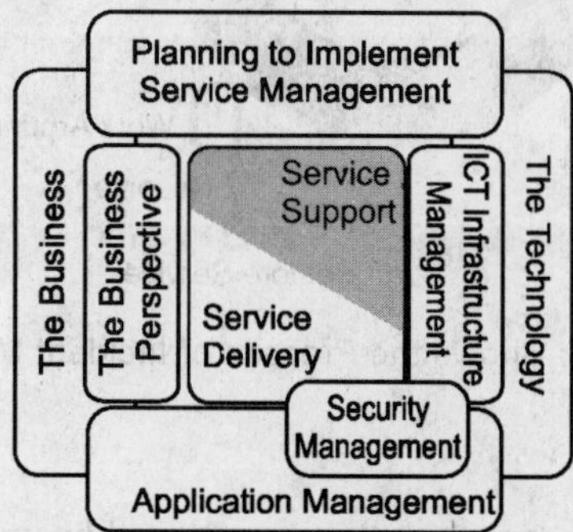


**Fig. 3.2:** The process of Configuration Management

Benefits of implementing Configuration Management processes include:

- Establishing a reliable repository of accurate information regarding IT components
- Understanding relationships between CIs and what components impact which services

Configuration Management processes are closely integrated with Incident Management, Problem Management, Change Management and Release Management.

## 3.3 INCIDENT MANAGEMENT

Incident Management (IM) is one of the components in the ITIL Service Support area. The primary focus of IM is to restore services following an incident as quickly as possible. IM is primarily a reactive process; its processes provide guidance on diagnostic and escalation procedures required to quickly restore services.

Incident Management activities include:

- Detecting and recording incident details
- Matching incidents against known problems
- Resolving incidents as quickly as possible
- Prioritizing incidents in terms of impact and urgency
- Escalating incidents to other teams as appropriate to ensure timely resolution

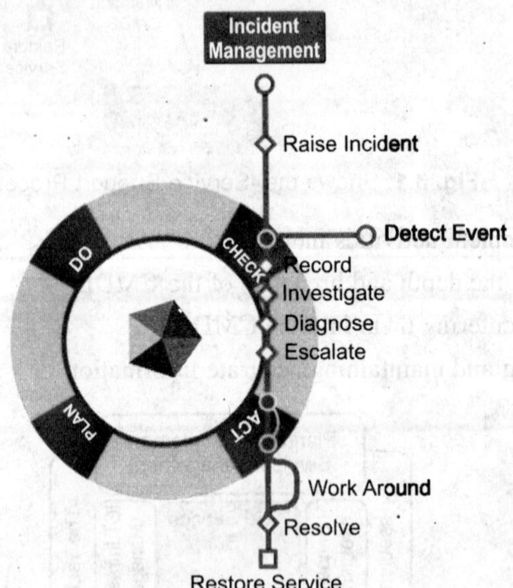


**Fig. 3.3:** Shows the Process of Incident Management

### 3.3.1 Benefits

- Timely resolution of incidents resulting in reduced business impact
- Improved user satisfaction

- More efficient utilization of Service Desk and other staff
- Enhanced ability to measure and monitor IT performance relative to SLAs
- Better data to support executive decisions regarding service quality
- Improved ability to track incidents and service requests efficiently
- Proactive identification of process enhancements

The objective of Incident Management is to rapidly restore services in support of service level agreements. Unlike Problem Management, whose focus is on finding the root cause of problems, Incident Management is essentially about getting things back up and running quickly, even if this means performing work arounds and quick fixes.

Technology can play a critical role in optimizing the Incident Management process, by automating the actual process activities themselves (such as incident recording and classification), and by accessing the outputs from other related processes. Integration with other processes (especially Problem Management, Change Management, Configuration Management and Service Level Management) is vitally important to ensure that incidents are kept to a minimum and that the highest levels of availability and service are maintained.

### 3.3.2 Raise Incident

Incident Management starts with an Incident, which ITIL defines as an occurrence that is not part of the standard operation of a service and which causes, or may cause, an interruption or reduction in service quality. Incidents can include hardware and software errors; as well as user service requests, which are typically not associated with IT infrastructure failures. Examples of service requests include functional questions or requests for information, or a request to have a password reset.

### 3.3.3 Detect Event

An event is similar to an incident but is detected within the IT infrastructure rather than being reported by a user. The first activity along the Incident Management process journey is the mechanism to detect events as they occur within the IT infrastructure and result in deviations from normal service. Users of IT services are often the first to detect service deviations. However, with appropriate automation, IT can rapidly detect incidents before they adversely affect IT services as users experience them (that is, from the viewpoint of business processes). The goal is to detect events and solve the underlying problem(s) quickly, before they affect IT service levels or impact the business.

### 3.3.4 Record

In most cases incidents will be recorded by a Service Desk function, which should record all incidents to ensure that compliance with service level agreements can be reported correctly. The nature of an incident will determine who or what reports it. Naturally, users should have a facility to incidents quickly and easily, supplying all information to the front line analyst. A truly effective reporting function, however, also should enable the system itself to automatically record incidents as they occur.

Many Service Desk solutions provide self-help and knowledge-based capabilities, but even if users resolve the issue themselves, they should record the incident. This is important, since the IT function can pro-actively leverage an accurate base of recorded incidents to facilitate improvements in other ITSM processes. Also, giving users the ability to log incidents that are not time-critical through a web-enabled interface, combined with a knowledge management tool to provide self-service answers to questions, greatly reduces the number of calls made to the Service Desk.

- Categorizing the incident should also be tart of the Incident Management recording function. Effective categorization of incidents has two aspects:
- Classification to determine incident type (e.g., IT Service = degraded)
- Matching against the IT Service or Configuration Items (CIs) affected (e.g. Order Entry Service), to determine if a similar incident has occurred previously.

During this phase, Service Desk analysts review previous incident activity to understand the reason for the incident. Technology can help by providing front line support with information pertaining to the CIs supporting the user who recorded the incident. The analyst should also have the means to correctly classify the incident using appropriate, standardized coding criteria. Many organizations mistakenly combine the IT Service/CI into the incident type. As a result, their incident classification methodology becomes far too complicated and a high percentage of incidents are incorrectly classified.

After classification, it is important to properly prioritize the incident. Service Desk solutions can help by automatically determining the priority based on the type of the incident (e.g. IT Service = Outage), and the business services that are affected. You can also use current SLAs to help determine priority. After classification, the analyst should use incident matching to see whether a similar incident has occurred previously; and whether there is a solution, work around or known error. If there is, then the Service Desk function can bypass the investigation and diagnosis stages, and initiate resolution and recovery procedures.

If the incident has high priority and cannot be resolved immediately, the incident manager should create a linked problem record and initiate Problem Management process activities. It is interesting to note that Problem Management has a different focus from Incident Management, which can potentially result in conflicts. That is, Incident Management is charged with restoring the IT service, while Problem Management is charged with determining a root cause and updating the status of the incident to a known error. In the majority of cases where there is a conflict, the Incident Management should take priority, since it is often more critical to restore normal service levels, even with work arounds, than to ferret out root causes.

### 3.3.5 The Check Junction

Before continuing along our Incident Management process journey, it is worth considering how the effective detection, recording and classification of incidents (achieved thus far) can facilitate an optimum journey along other ITIL process lines. Figure 3.4 shows that, after the detection and recording activities, the Incident Management process arrives at a critical point—the Check junction.

The Check junction illustrates how Incident Management outputs derived from the timely detection and accurate reporting of incidents provide the means to be more proactive and optimize the Problem Management process. For example, the accurate recording of all incidents will assist Problem Management with the rapid identification of underlying errors. Where justified, Problem Management will strive to permanently correct these errors, and reduce the amount of repeat incidents. Alternatively, the Check junction enables Incident Management to take inputs from Problem Management to further streamline the overall process. For example, by delivering information about known errors (from an integrated known error database) the "journey time" to the ultimate destination—service restoration—will be reduced dramatically. Naturally, technology can play a key role, integrating both Incident and Problem Management within a single solution.

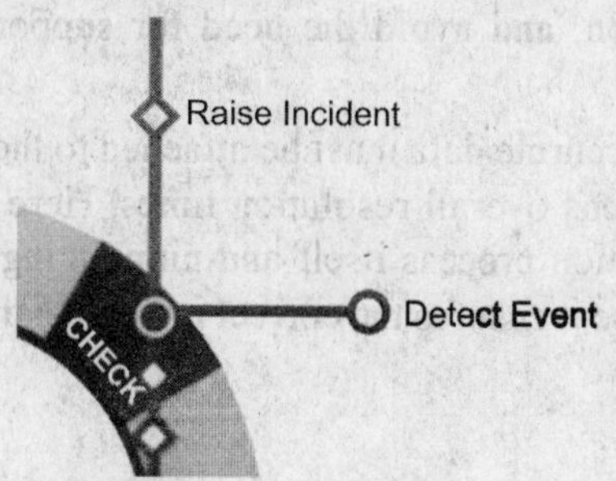


Fig. 3.4: Shows Incident Management process arrives at a critical point

### 3.3.6 Investigate and Diagnose

During the investigation and diagnosis phase, support analysts will collect updated incident details and analyze all related information (especially configuration details from a Configuration Management Database (CMDB) linked to the Service Desk). During this phase, the support staff must have access to comprehensive historical incident, problem and knowledge data, centralized and maintained within the Service Desk. Also critical is the capability to augment incident management records with diagnostic data supplied by or via integrated management technologies. Management technologies can play a key role here in correctly identifying and routing incidents to the appropriate SMEs. By its very nature, investigation and diagnosis of incidents is an iterative process, and may involve multiple Level 1, 2 and 3 groups as well as external vendors. This demands discipline and a rigorous approach to maintaining records, actions, work arounds and corresponding results. Integrated Service Desk technology can help in this process by providing:

- Flexible routing of Incident Management data according to geographic region, time, etc.
- Automatic linkage and extraction of CMDB data for the examination of failed items
- A strong knowledge base and tools to expedite the diagnostic function
- Management dashboards and reports to provide an overall status of Incident Management
- Controls to ensure process conformance and provide comprehensive audit logs

### 3.3.7 Escalate

Having conducted investigation and diagnosis, the Incident Management journey arrives at the Escalation station. Critical here is the ability to rapidly escalate incidents according to agreed service levels, and to allocate more support services if necessary.

Escalation can follow two paths; horizontal (functional) or vertical. Horizontal escalation is needed when the incident needs to be escalated to different SME groups better able to perform the Incident

Management function. If not closely monitored, horizontal escalation can lead to incidents bouncing around the system without anyone taking ownership; which, in turn, increases the likelihood of breeching service level agreements. This is why it is so important to have a proactive approach and use process automation to correctly route incidents to the appropriate SME groups. Vertical escalation is where the incident needs to gain higher levels of priority. As part of the activity, it is essential that rules are clearly in place to ensure timely escalation, and avoid the need for support analysts to work out when to escalate—a recipe for disaster.

For every resolution attempt, accurate data must be attached to the incident detail to save repeating recovery procedures, which lengthens overall resolution times. Here technology can play yet another key role, by automating the escalation process itself and pinpointing the exact source of errors. This latter capability is important because it ensures the correct incident hand-off to appropriate SME groups early in the support cycle.

### 3.3.8 The Act Junction

At this stage of the journey, the Incident Management process line has arrived at the Act junction (see Figure 3.5). Here, iterative investigation and diagnosis will have determined the nature of the incident, and what actions need to be initiated to resolve the problem. Customer service must be restored as quickly as possible (through work arounds if necessary), and incidents should be escalated to Problem Management to detect the underlying cause of the problem, provide resolutions and prevent incidents from reoccurring.

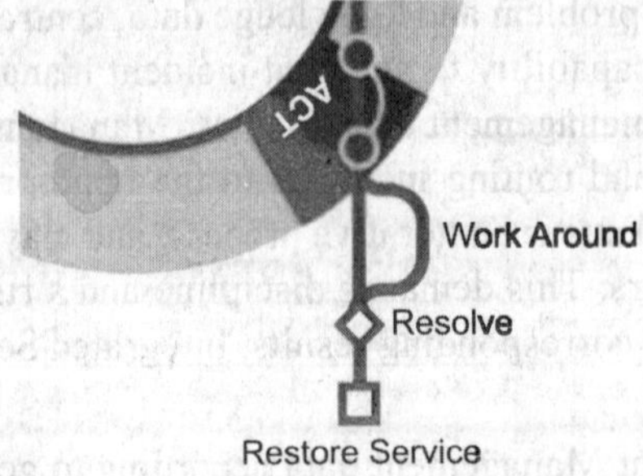


**Fig. 3.5:** Shows Act Junction

### 3.3.9 Resolve

The final stage along the Incident Management journey is Resolution and Recovery. Here the main activities include resolving the incident with solutions or work arounds obtained from previous activities. For some solutions, a Request for Change (RFC) will need to be submitted, so it is vital that automation supports the timely and accurate transference of incident details to a Change Management process. Once the SME groups resolve the solution, the incident is routed back to the Service Desk function, which confirms with the initiator of the incident that the error has been rectified and that the incident can be closed. During this phase, integrated processes must support a number of service improvement functions, such as providing restricted access to the incident closing function, and ensuring that incidents are matched to known errors or problem records.

## 3.4 PROBLEM MANAGEMENT

### 3.4.1 Introduction

Problem Management (PM) is one of the components in the ITIL Service Support area. The primary focus of PM is to identify causes of service issues and commission corrective work to prevent recurrences. PM processes are both reactive and proactive - reactive in solving problems in response to incidents, and proactive in identifying and solving potential incidents before they occur.

Problem Management activities include:

- Recording, managing and escalating service problems as appropriate
- Analyzing historical data to identify and eliminate potential incidents before they occur
- Identifying underlying causes of incidents and preventing recurrences
- Developing work arounds or other solutions to incidents
- Submitting change requests to Change Management as required to eliminate known problems

The objective of the Problem Management process is to find the root cause of problems and initiate actions to improve or correct the situation. The major activities within Problem Management include:

- **Problem Control** for identifying problems and investigating their causes
- **Error Control** for monitoring known errors through to successful resolution
- **Proactive Problem Management** for identifying and eliminating problems before incidents occur
- **Providing Support Information** or **delivering problem information** to other process areas and to IT management

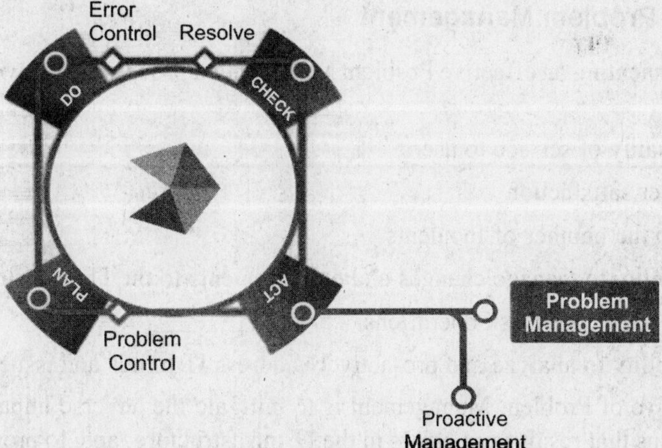


**Fig. 3.6:** Process of Problem management

Notably, Problem Management differs from Incident Management, which is focused on restoring service as quickly as possible. But many organizations struggle to control these distinct processes because they mistakenly try to combine them. One challenge is that the investigation of a problem's root cause may require periods of unplanned downtime, which Incident Management tries to avoid. By separating the two processes, responsibilities become clearer and the IT organization becomes more efficient.

Although the goals of Incident and Problem Management differ, the processes have a strong relationship. Problem Management supports the Incident Management process by providing work arounds and quick fixes. Incident Management supports Problem Management by providing comprehensive incident records to facilitate problem identification.

Problem Management includes both reactive and proactive activities. Reactive Problem Management aims to identify the root causes of Incidents and present proposals for resolution by submitting Request for Changes (RFCs). Proactive Problem Management aims to prevent Incidents by working to identify weaknesses in the infrastructure and correct them before they cause service disruption. Many IT organizations spend too much time in reactionary, day-today problem resolution. Business value increases when IT becomes more proactive, providing problem-free IT services through preventative measures and controls.

Problem Management requires several roles to ensure effective functioning. The Problem Process owner is responsible for determining the structure of the Problem Management team, as well as the tasks within the Problem Management process. The Problem Manager is responsible for managing the process while providing the mechanism for proper execution.

The Problem Manager also works with the Incident Manager to determine the criteria by which a single Incident warrants the opening of a Problem. Also, and based on agreed-upon criteria, certain authorized staff within the Incident Management team can determine if a Problem actually exists; and, if so, can involve the Problem team to perform root-cause analysis while the Incident team concentrates on restoring the service.

### 3.4.2 Benefits of Problem Management

The benefits of implementing an effective Problem Management process in line with ITIL best practices include:

- Improved quality of service to users
- Improved user satisfaction
- Reduction in the number of Incidents
- Improved ability to manage changes and enhancements to the IT infrastructure
- More efficient Service Desk operations
- Enhanced ability to analyze and pro-actively address IT trends and issues

The main objective of Problem Management is to mitigate the adverse impact on the business of Incidents and Problems that result from errors in the IT infrastructure; and, to prevent Incidents related to these errors from occurring. To achieve this objective, Problem Management attempts to discover the root cause of Incidents and Problems, and then to initiate actions to improve or correct the situation.

The Problem Management process includes both reactive and proactive activities. The reactive actions address problems that arise in response to one or more Incidents. Proactive actions are those that help identify and solve Problems and Known Errors before Incidents occur or SLAs are impacted.

Technology can play a critical role in optimizing the Problem Management process, by automating the activities themselves (such as classifying problems), and by integrating the flow of data between Problem Management and related Service Delivery processes like Incident Management, Change Management, Configuration Management and Service Level Management. This integration is key to leveraging ITIL best practices to drive greater business alignment and cost reductions across the IT environment.

### 3.4.3 Problem Management Integration Points

Before examining the Problem Management process in detail, it is important to review critical process integration points. The Problem Management process line crosses each of the Plan, Do, Check and Act junction points of the continuous process improvement cycle. During problem diagnosis, the process integrates with Incident Management (at the Act junction) to provide information about Known Errors, work arounds, and quick fixes so that IT can restore services faster and with minimal disruption. When Known Errors have been identified, Problem Management must integrate with Change Management (at the Plan and Do junctions) to ensure that RFCs are raised and implemented to resolve these Problems. Once the Change has been implemented, Problem Management again integrates with Incident Management (at the Check junction) to gather and analyze Incident data to pro-actively identify Problems.

#### *3.4.3.1 Problem Control*

Problem Management starts with Problem Control, which is responsible for identifying Problems, investigating the root cause, and the Configuration Items (CIs) that are at fault. Problem Control also provides the Service Desk function and Incident Management with information and advice on work arounds. The goal of Problem Control is to advance Problems to become Known Errors by diagnosing the unknown underlying root cause of the Problem.

The first phase of Problem Control is to identify and record the Problem. Problems can occur when events captured by Incident Management have an unknown root cause. In general, any Incident with an unknown cause should be associated with a Problem, but this practice is only worthwhile if there is a serious Incident, or if the Incident occurs repeatedly.

During this phase, the Problem Management team gathers information from Incident Management and from other processes for analysis. Strong process linkages must be in place to ensure that problem instances can be identified quickly.

Based upon the information gathered during the analysis phase, the Problem Management team will begin to determine the Problem's root cause. To be successful, any Problem Management system must have the capability to link all associated Incidents and CIs from the Configuration Management Database (CMDB) to the problem. Here, it may be necessary to create a parent Problem with subsequent associated Problems, so as to break up the multitude of potential problem areas for proper analysis and tracking.

Ensuring that single or multiple Incidents can be linked to the Problem, and that Problems are linked to other associated Problems, is critical for an effective Problem Management process. At the same time, the process must integrate with Change Management by initiating RFCs to address any Known Errors identified.

#### 3.4.3.2 Problem Classification

After Incident data has been collected for analysis, and a Problem has been determined, it must be properly classified according to the category, impact, urgency, priority and status. Problem category identifies the problem area (for example, hardware or software), and all the CIs that affect the Problem. Classification is accompanied by impact analysis on IT services (via the CMDB) to determine the seriousness of the Problem, and the extent to which deferral of a solution is acceptable (urgency). Impact, urgency and business risk help determine the priority of the problem, as with Incident Management.

#### 3.4.3.3 Problem Investigation and Diagnosis

After the problem has been classified, the Problem Management journey begins an iterative process of problem investigation and diagnosis. The Problem Management process line may be traveled several times before the root cause can be determined. During this phase, rapid response teams may meet to jointly investigate and diagnose, the root cause of severe problems. Technology plays a critical role in this activity, helping pinpoint root cause across the technology domains that support IT services, such as Web services, applications, databases, servers and networks. During the investigation and diagnosis phase, it is especially critical to have access to data on the status and the attributes of associated CIs (for example, access to information such as operating system level, and security patches). Combined with the number and type of incidents and problems associated with the CI, this information can enable the Problem Management team to determine root causes and initiate error control activities more quickly.

If no immediate work around or Known Error is available, then the Problem Management team continues to gather additional information for further diagnosis. Effective diagnosis of the underlying cause of the problem requires access to CI attributes (as discussed above) as well as any documentation or troubleshooting information from the Incident Management team. The Incident and the Problem Management system should be integrated to make this process seamless.

Throughout the Problem Management process, other groups outside of the Problem Management team, such as application support, may be brought in to assist with Problem diagnosis. In such cases, however, care must be taken to ensure that such teams work collaboratively to resolve Problems, avoiding the more traditional and inefficient practices of attempting to resolve problems "silo by silo." Here again, advanced analytic and diagnostic tools can help pinpoint the problem to a specific area and avoid unnecessary and time consuming Problem investigation.

#### 3.4.3.4 Problem Escalation

If no immediate solutions are available it may be necessary to escalate the Problem. Escalation schemes are essential to successful Problem Management. When Problem Managers meet with Incident Managers, escalated problems must be evaluated not only to expedite their resolution, but also to indicate potential future impacts to the business.

Escalation schemes should also allow for the fact that classification of a given Problem may change during its lifecycle (for example, when a seemingly minor Problem becomes more critical after additional Incidents are reported).

### 3.4.3.5 Error Control

Once the cause of a Problem and associated CI has been identified, it is assigned "Known Error" status and the Error Control activity begins. Error Control monitors Known Errors until they are resolved. This is achieved by raising RFCs to the Change Management process and by evaluating the effectiveness of changes in a Post Implementation Review (PIR).

During this phase, developing a Known Error database in accordance with Knowledge Management principles is critical to ensuring efficient and effective Incident Management and Service Desk activities. The Service Desk function coordinates Incident and Problem Management activities and must leverage information contained within a Knowledge Database, which catalogs Known Errors and work arounds. Therefore, a knowledge tool is necessary that allows for flexible creation of Known Error records in a manner that ensures data accuracy and consistency.

Other mechanisms can also save time and money during Error Control. For example, once a Known Error or work around has been used to resolve an Incident, the Incident should be automatically linked back to the Problem associated with the Known Error or work around. This ensures that Problem Management teams can immediately see the effectiveness of work arounds and quick fixes. If an RFC has been issued and completed, a PIR should be initiated to ensure that everything went as planned and that the problem was truly resolved. Prior to actually initiating an RFC, the duration of the resolution process must be determined, together with the anticipated costs, and the cost/benefit to the business. If the business benefit is minimal, but the cost is high, then the resolution may be documented but not actually initiated.

### 3.4.3.6 Proactive Problem Management

Another important aspect of Problem Management is Proactive Problem Management. While Proactive Problem Management takes a similar route to the "reactive" journey discussed above, it aims to prevent Incidents by identifying weaknesses and creating proposals to eliminate them. To build proactive capability, the Problem Management team can examine the Incident repository and, via analysis of both current and past Incidents, determine if a Problem in the environment exists and group these Incidents into one Problem.

Technology can support the Problem Management process by determining whether there are relationships between Incidents and then automatically creating a Problem. Obviously, such tools need strong analytical capability to determine trends and then create Problems and links to the evidence (Incidents).

Proactive Problem Management also uses trend analysis to identify potential Problems, and analyze situations where a CI under investigation could cause a failure elsewhere in the infrastructure. It should also support better protection of IT services when failures have occurred in other areas. IT can better realize these benefits when data from a Knowledge Management tool facilitates faster associations, matching and resolution.

Integrated Knowledge Management tools enable the automatic population of attributes into an Incident when a Known Error is associated with that Incident. This improves the accuracy of metrics by ensuring consistency. One example is the proper classification of the category for the Incident, which may have been originally misdiagnosed. Another example is automatically linking the Incident back to the original Problem to keep gathering evidence and allowing greater visibility into the impact.

### 3.4.4 Selecting the Appropriate Problem Management Solution

Tools that help enhance the Problem Management process should provide:

- Support for development of trend information for more proactive Problem Management
- The ability to view CMDB attributes and relationships to assist in the Problem resolution process
- Mechanisms (e.g., reports and service dashboards) to report Key Performance Indicators on the Problem Management process, including:
  - Total number of Problems
  - Average Problem resolution time (and by priority)
  - Number of Incidents resolved by Problems
- Data that can help measure IT performance and efficiency, such as:
  - Percentage of Problems resulting in a RFC
  - Percentage of RFCs based on Problems that had to be backed out
  - Known Error effectiveness (number of Incidents tied to Known Errors)
  - Number of Problems as a direct result of failed or unapproved changes
  - Number of work arounds created and Known Errors created
  - Number of Problems resolved by analyst group, individual analyst, etc.

### 3.4.5 Keys to Success in Problem Management

The following are some of the most important areas to focus on within the Problem Management process:

#### *3.4.5.1 Effective Communication*

Everyone involved in the Problem Management process must understand the importance of their role in the overall effort. Ensuring that each team member understands the proper handling of information regarding associated Incidents, Problems, Changes and CI information is critical to understanding the impact of a Problem. Also, effective communication allows each role to know the status and progress of a Problem. It is also important that team members communicate information regarding Problems back to the affected users and management.

#### *3.4.5.2 Effective Known Error Creation*

The Problem Management team must understand what data is necessary for effective Known Error creation, categorization and work flow. Having a standard for required data types within the Known Error database is critical to effective management of information based on Known Errors.

#### *3.4.5.3 Access To Trend Data*

Ensure that the information needed for trending analysis is tracked and available. A fully integrated toolset allows organizations to readily see information contained within the Incident Management solution, information on the CIs as well as access to the Known Error and knowledge databases. Also important is a management dashboard illustrating what is happening in the organization in near real-time.

## 3.5 CHANGE MANAGEMENT

### 3.5.1 Introduction

Change is an intrinsic aspect of every business — especially healthy businesses that innovate and readily adapt to shifts in the market. For a business to remain healthy, its IT organization must be capable of effectively and efficiently handling change. It must be able to execute change with minimal cost and minimal risk of business disruption. IT must also be able to keep its infrastructure and services well-aligned with changing business goals and priorities.

In today's fast-moving markets, the ability to easily and appropriately handle change is even more important. That is why IT organizations need to implement and automate best practices for the entire end-to-end Change Management lifecycle, from "Plan" through "Do" (see Figure). Only IT organizations that embrace this disciplined approach to change management will be able to deliver the operational agility essential for service excellence.

If Incident and Problem Management represent the "heart" of Service Support, then Change Management is the process that controls the "heart rate." Optimized Change Management results in fewer incidents and problems, and helps ensure that strategic improvement requests are quickly processed and implemented.

### 3.5.2 Benefits

- Faster, more predictable change implementation
- Reduce risk to the business of implementing new technologies
- Improve IT agility even in the face of changing business needs and competitive pressures
- Increase visibility into the change process
- Improve service levels, including reduced downtime across the IT infrastructure
- Enhance user satisfaction

### 3.5.3 Process of Change Management

Let's review the Change Management process journey illustrated in Figure 3.7 assessing each critical process activity (or station), and examining how technology can be applied to optimize every stage of the journey. Note that, while technology can greatly enable the automation of the Change Management process, it cannot do much to improve the value to the business of a process that is functioning poorly.

#### *3.5.3.1 Request for Change*

The journey of Change Management starts with a Request for Change (RFC). What is the difference between a service request and a change? Basically, a service request may involve making a change to the environment, but generally that change is operational and doesn't impact business services. A number of related service requests could generate a change if they require impact analysis or touch the production environment.

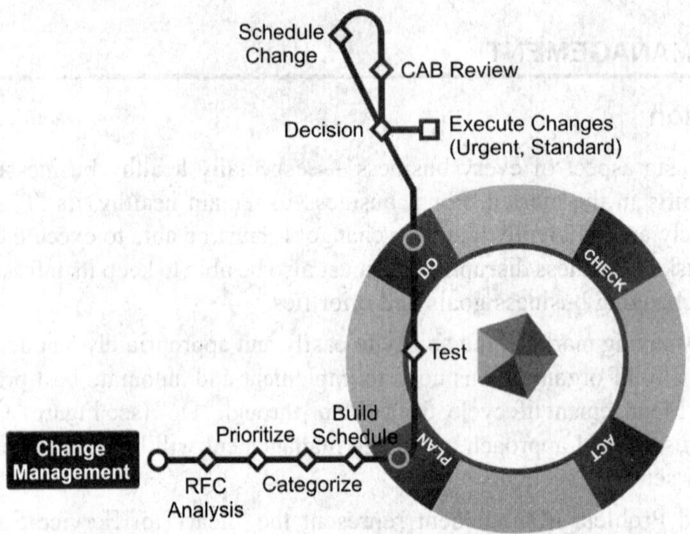


**Fig. 3.7:** Shows the process of Change Management

A Request for Change (RFC) could be triggered by such activities as a customer request via the Service Desk, the introduction or removal of a Configuration Item (CI), or the output of a development project. It could also be triggered by Problem Management activities. To prevent a situation where there are too many entry points into the change process, you should document who can create RFCs, what those RFCs are intended to do, and what information is required in them. Technology can help by ensuring that requestors have a simple way of submitting RFCs. The tool should drive them through the important steps and ensure that the correct level of detail is captured. It is also important to understand the business importance of the change.

Remember, the goal of Change Management is to facilitate all change requests by using clear procedures, automation and simple checks and balances. ITIL suggests that any member of the organization should be able to submit an RFC. If not managed properly, this could lead to ungated demand and possible misuse of the Change Management system. A more appropriate approach would be to use service requests for routine standardized demands that need not be controlled by Change Management, and to use IT or business relationship managers to submit RFCs.

#### *3.5.3.2 RFC Analysis*

The RFC Analysis phase is intended to perform an initial evaluation of the information provided for completeness and feasibility. An automated system can significantly shorten this phase by allowing the tool to apply business rules to determine what information is required. A key requirement for such a system is the ability to ensure that adequate change lead times are in place, and are in line with policy.

#### 3.5.3.3 Change Prioritization

After performing the initial RFC analysis, the next step is to prioritize the change. This occurs by analyzing the impact of the problem and the urgency of the fix (if the change was generated from a problem) or the importance to the organization of whatever the change is implementing. If this can't be agreed upon, the Change Advisory Board (CAB) may need to intervene. When the change priority is determined, it is used to determine resource requirements and change scheduling windows. In a resource-constrained environment, business units can use it to internally prioritize demand. Risk assessment should also be determined at this stage. Measuring risk can be defined as the actual risk associated with implementing the change versus the risk of possible failures if changes are not implemented. Both types of risks should be evaluated and cost-analyzed. Another aspect of determining risk relates to the impact of the change on other components of the environment. Today, in a highly shared environment, an individual cannot track all of the touch points between technology and business services. For example, if a change requires a clustered web server to be rebooted, what business services are affected and what is the impact on Service Level Agreements (SLAs)? Integration of Change Management with Configuration Management can help by allowing you to work through "what if" scenarios to determine the impact of a technology change on business services.

#### 3.5.3.4 Categorize

The Categorize station is actually a major hub for a number of activities. Categorization involves evaluating the size of the change from a resource requirements perspective, the risk associated with the change, as well as the priority, and then deciding what process steps you will follow. Categorization is an extremely important activity, since it is assigned according to business impact, and therefore determines the level of change authorizations and financial and resource requirements. During this stage, IT must collaborate with the business to ensure the correct categorization of changes and to avoid problems further down the line.

The bulk of Change Management work is done at this station, with many checks and balances to ensure that change approval becomes relatively straightforward. Here, organizations can realize the major benefits of Change Management; for example, by utilizing technologies to help determine change categories (based on criteria agreed upon with the business), to quickly absorb large volumes of changes, and to determine the costs of changes before they are incurred. For a minor change, a small number of work flow tasks should be completed that, for the most part, will involve approvals and implementation scheduling. A minor change is appropriate only where a small amount of effort and risk is involved. Similar categorization can be used for significant changes. This is another area where technology can streamline and automate the process itself, using business rules to insert the correct process flow into the change and then report conformance against the work flow while also providing an audit trail.

#### 3.5.3.5 Build and Test Change

This stage includes building the schedule for provisioning hardware and software and performing the work needed to put the change together. The change needs to be tested in a pre-production environment to make sure that it has every chance of success.

#### 3.5.3.6 Change Advisory Board Review

Once this work of Categorization has been performed, a decision is made on whether to proceed.

This will happen at a Change Advisory Board meeting. The CAB should consist of all the interested parties for active changes, both from IT and the business. The CAB should meet regularly and utilize formal meeting procedures, including meeting minutes and communication. The CAB should review all proposed and implemented changes (for which this constitutes the Post Implementation Review).

For new changes, there should be agreement on the need, resource allocation and available funds. A considerable amount of work may be required after CAB approval, which is why it is important to automate as much as possible of what can be complex processes. Minor changes should be authorized prior to the CAB meetings, which should focus on change requests that have higher risk and associated costs. Again, this is why the business must be involved from the design phase of process development. Everyone needs to understand what is critical to the business to determine changes that can be pre-approved and those that need to be analyzed further. The CAB should also review implemented changes to determine the quality of the process and whether the changes were implemented correctly. Determining that the technical aspect of the change was successfully implemented is insufficient. What is required is to determine whether the change achieved its purpose.

More mature organizations will wait for a specified period before "closing" a change. IT should demonstrate its engagement with the customer at the CAB stage by ensuring that business users affected by changes are fully involved in the decision making process. The CAB has responsibility for approving or rejecting changes. They also should perform the due diligence and, in instances where there is not enough information, make a decision to send the change back to the requester. Approval must be gained at three levels: technical, business and financial. Since these CAB meetings can require significant time and resources, technology can be supportive; for example, by giving CAB members electronic access to RFCs for electronic approval. Once the CAB approves the change, the "Do" phases of scheduling, building, testing and implementation begin. The CAB has to be financially responsible and strike a balance between managing risk and controlling costs.

Once all approvals are given, it is appropriate to schedule the change. More activities need to happen before a change window can be selected. In cases of major releases, an organization may be restricted to certain maintenance windows and should put a place holder in the Forward Schedule of Changes (FSC) calendar. These key activities are best controlled by using best practice project management. This is one of the key steps in increasing the value of Change Management and taking advantage of the proactive potential. The key stakeholders should work out scheduling to ensure that all the implementation steps required to institute the change are achievable. Automated technology helps keep everyone informed of what needs to be done and when it is needed. Providing visibility into when changes are to be implemented is critical. In this scheduling phase, the FSC should be updated. This should take the form of a generally available calendar view indicating when you've scheduled all change windows. Within each window it should clearly state any (business) services or technologies that will be impacted, along with the start and end time of the implementation. The FSC is important for a number of reasons. First, it allows changes to be implemented together where there is an opportunity to do so (for example where there is common infrastructure being affected). Secondly, it provides the ability to quickly spot change conflicts or situations where the time of the planned change could have a detrimental affect on the business. For example, if the business is running a sales campaign it would be inconvenient if certain Web services were unavailable during that time. Thirdly, the FSC makes the Service Desk aware of planned change and service outages so they can place an advance notice on the bulletin board and are prepared to answer the influx of calls. Otherwise, the Service Desk might waste time trying to diagnose the increase in incidents caused by the service outage or implemented change.

#### 3.5.3.7 Implementation

The implementation station is the next step. Only the changes that are approved and scheduled in the change window can be implemented. This is not an opportunity for people to introduce unauthorized changes. The entire premise of the Change Management process is to protect the production environment; unauthorized changes put this objective at risk. An output at this stage will be an implementation report that will be reviewed at the next CAB meeting to ensure that the business goals were met and the risks and costs to the business were minimized. Including business stakeholders in the implementation process allows for continuous improvement because you are constantly engaged to ensure the change process is aligned with business goals. If they are not, you may not meet the business objectives and thus be forced to refine your process to make the necessary changes.

#### 3.5.3.8 Emergency Changes

All the discussion above has been in the context of a well-planned process where forewarning is embedded into the change process. In a dynamic operational environment there will often be times when high-impact incidents and problems need to have fixes applied that will involve a change to the production environment. This is not an opportunity to bypass the change process as there should also be a process in place to handle urgent or emergency changes. Change approval is still a prerequisite in these cases, but the standard process will generally be condensed and some of the CAB approvals will be delegated. Organizations that have not fully developed their Change Management processes will see a high volume of emergency changes, most likely because of timing. This is normally due to lead times not being enforced, with changes continuously and mistakenly viewed as emergencies. A good metric to gauge whether a change is an emergency is to determine if there is a high impact incident or problem open that this change will fix. If this is not the case, then you must question whether it's an emergency change. The last step is to review the Change Management process as an entire unit. Change Management is an iterative process that requires constant review and adjustment for continuous improvement. This is why the process owner should constantly be reviewing changes to look for ways to make the process better and to consult with the business often to ensure their needs are being met.

## 3.6 RELEASE MANAGEMENT

### 3.6.1 Introduction

Release Management oversees the controlled distribution of software and hardware components into the production environment. It provides a structured approach to the management of releases from initial policy and release planning, through design, building and release configuration, to testing, release distribution and installation. Release Management activities that are aligned with ITIL best practices increase the quality of the production environment, by ensuring that formal procedures are followed when implementing new versions. Release Management works closely with Change Management to build implement changes from authorized Request for Changes (RFCs). But unlike Change Management, which focuses on change verification and control, Release Management is concerned with the actual implementation of changes.

### 3.6.2 Benefits

Improved quality of services due to better integration of hardware, software and documentation

- A better ability to correlate business processes with underlying services
- Fewer calls to the Service Desk
- A higher percentage of first-contact fixes, due to an up-to-date CMDB and embedded Change Management supporting Release Management
- Increased control on over- and under-licensing, ultimately resulting in significant cost savings
- Better planning of releases leading to reduced impact of new release rollouts on business users
- Improved quality and professionalism at the Service Desk

Figure 3.8 illustrates the Release Management process journey. The sections that follow describe each of the critical process activities.

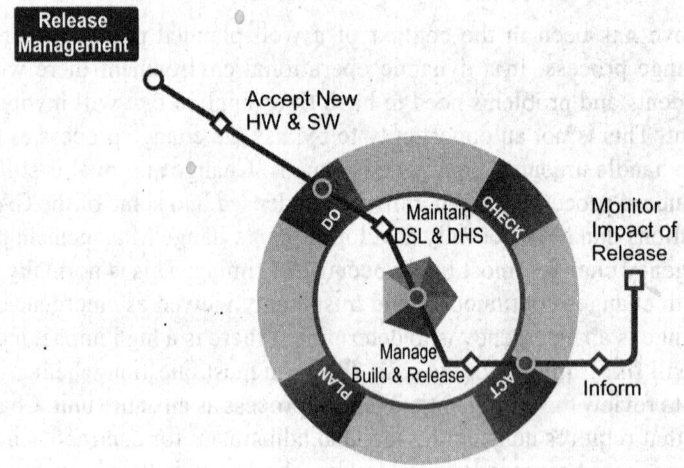


**Fig. 3.8:** Shows Release Management

#### *3.6.2.1 Accept New Software & Hardware*

Release Management must be engaged early in the development lifecycle, before new hardware and software components can be accepted into the live environment. Ideally, any development that results in changes to the production environment should be controlled by Change Management, with all RFCs reviewed and approved by both Development and Operations and managed through a single change process. This approach improves communication and increases the percentage of successful releases.

To optimize the effectiveness of the process, it is also important to create policies defining how and when releases are configured, and to make recommendations addressing any concerns and issues, such as the level of IT infrastructure controlled by Release Management, release blackout periods, back-out plans and testing, naming conventions and documentation.

Since Release Management affects every process area in a live environment, preparation and planning requires a structured project management approach. Every release is a project with a lifecycle that starts with a Request for Change (RFC) and ends with a Post Implementation

Since the process manages many releases simultaneously, ITIL recommends the use of a formal project management methodology to increase the chance of success for every release, and for Release Management as a whole. Since many development groups adopt project management disciplines, the Release Management process should adopt similar principles to improve the coordination of activities between operations and software development.

### 3.6.2.2 Maintain DSL & DHS

The next stage of the Release Management process involves the design, construction and configuration of a potential release using standard procedures in a controlled and reproducible manner. The output of this activity should be a release, complete with installation instructions, a test plan and a blackout plan stored in the DSL and DHS.

### 3.6.2.3 Manage Build & Release

A release may be based on components developed in-house, or purchased and configured. Installation and configuration instructions should always form part of the release, and should be treated as configuration items (CIs) under the control of Change Management and Configuration Management. From a software perspective, this process activity is often called Build Management, which can be extremely time-consuming and error-prone if performed manually. Fortunately, technology is available to automate procedures and ensure that software executables are created the same way every time. During this stage, hardware components may need to be assembled, and similar procedures need to be applied to ensure reproducible configurations. Here again, technology can be used to automate the installation of operating system and application software.

A back-out plan should be produced toward the end of this stage to define the activities that need to be performed if something goes wrong with the release. While Change Management may have responsibility for drawing up back-out plans for each change, Release Management must ensure that all back-outs can be practically applied. There are two common approaches to back-outs, and a combination of both may be used: First, a failed release is reversed. This step is critical for a full release, and preferable for a partial or delta release. Second, if a release cannot be rolled back, disaster recovery plans are initiated to recover service.

### 3.6.2.4 Acceptance Testing

The next Release Management activity involves acceptance testing in a controlled test environment. Lack of adequate testing is the most common cause of release failures by far. To avoid this situation before implementation, any release should undergo both functional user testing, as well as operational testing by IT staff. Once development testing is completed, the release is logged in the DSL, and the development team should update the known-error database to reflect any errors identified during development testing. The release is then checked out of the DSL for testing in the controlled environment by the operations team.

Operational testing is an area that is often neglected, and the IT organization needs to ensure rigorous testing of technical operations, performance within the IT infrastructure and other operational aspects. These tests should also include tests on installation procedures and backout plans. A formal list of acceptance of each step is submitted to Change Management for authorization, with the final stage being authorization of the release for implementation.

At this point, Release Management works closely with Change Management to determine a schedule for the implementation and Post Implementation Review, and publishes to the Change Management Forward Schedule of Changes. When final authorization is provided, Release Management will then implement the change into the live production environment on the date and time specified.

### 3.6.2.5 Inform

Before you distribute and install releases, you should advise customers and appropriate support staff on the release details and how this release affects them. This is normally accomplished through a series of joint training sessions and release acceptance activities. Communicate any changes that need to be made during distribution and installation to all parties to set appropriate expectations. This activity normally includes running a series of rollout planning meetings with all of the stakeholders to ensure that the plans are properly reviewed, with responsibilities agreed upon and understood. You may also need to communicate changes to hardware or software support contracts to the relevant staff. This is the responsibility of the Service Desk, but Release Management may be better positioned to undertake detailed communications. Release distribution and installation manages the purchase, storage, transport, delivery and handoff of software and hardware. The processes for procurement, storage, dispatch, receipt and disposal of goods should ensure that equipment is delivered safely to its destination in its expected state. The Configuration Management process requires checks on the receipt of goods against supporting delivery documentation.

Wherever possible, you should use automated tools for software distribution should to expedite installation, increase quality and free up resources. These tools also will facilitate verification of successful releases and provide automated mechanisms to back out failed or partially completed releases.

### 3.6.2.6 Installing Releases

Installing the software releases is the final step in the process. Here, it is common to distribute a new version of a software application to a target installation so that it remains dormant until activated. This should be accomplished by following the tested installation procedures, and may involve running automated installation routines or other one-offs. To ensure a smooth rollout, an automated check of the target platform is required to ensure it meets hardware and software prerequisites. Here again, automated technologies can assist with the process.

The CMDB should be updated following installation or disposal of hardware or software, to ensure that it reflects the final position after a release. It may also be necessary to retrieve old versions of software that have been superseded, to prevent software license rules from being violated.

After a successful installation, the Configuration Management records should be updated with the location and the owner of the hardware and software. This will help support staff to locate equipment and resolve any subsequent incidents and problems. Finally, Change Management is notified and takes responsibility for conducting Post Implementation Reviews and closing the associated RFC.

### 3.6.3 Conclusions

Release Management strives to implement approved changes into the live or production environment with minimal negative impact on the business. Release Management works best when integrated with Change Management and Configuration Management to drive continuous improvement in IT service quality. Release Management works with Change Management to ensure that only approved changes are implemented, and with Configuration Management to ensure that records are updated and accurate.

**To further ensure that Release Management functions optimally, it is helpful to observe these additional best practices guidelines:**

- Any activity (Design, Building, Testing, Training and Communication, Implementation) must ensure that all release criteria have been met and are in line with the business objectives and service agreements.
- Sign-off should take place at the end of each phase. Random audits may be necessary to ensure that the release criteria sign-offs are being met rigorously.
- Requirements of the Service Desk should not be taken lightly. The Service desk must be involved in the sign-off process.
- The supporting deliverables of the release that directly affect the Service Desk must be complete. This includes thorough documentation and complete and accurate escalation lists.
- The Service Desk should receive formal training on any new release or major upgrade. This training may be developed in-house or provided by a third party in advance of the release

## 3.7 STORAGE MANAGEMENT

### 3.7.1 Introduction

The administration of any or all of backup, archival, disaster recovery and hierarchical storage management (HSM) procedures within an organization.

**Memory management** is the act of managing computer memory. In its simpler forms, this involves providing ways to allocate portions of memory to programs at their request, and freeing it for reuse when no longer needed. The management of main memory is critical to the computer system.

Memory management systems on multi-tasking operating systems usually deal with the following issues.

#### *3.7.1.1 Relocation*

In systems with virtual memory, programs in memory must be able to reside in different parts of the memory at different times. This is because when the program is swapped back into memory after being swapped out for a while it can not always be placed in the same location. The virtual memory management unit must also deal with concurrency. Memory management in the operating system should therefore be able to relocate programs in memory and handle memory references in the code of the program so that they always point to the right location in memory.

#### 3.7.1.2 Protection

Processes should not be able to reference the memory for another process without permission. This is called memory protection, and prevents malicious or malfunctioning code in one program from interfering with the operation of other running programs.

#### 3.7.1.3 Sharing

Even though the memory for different processes is normally protected from each other, different processes sometimes need to be able to share information and therefore access the same part of memory. Shared memory is one of the fastest techniques for Inter-process communication.

#### 3.7.1.4 Logical Organization

Programs are often organized in modules. Some of these modules could be shared between different programs, some are read only and some contain data that can be modified. The memory management is responsible for handling this logical organization that is different from the physical linear address space. One way to arrange this organization is segmentation.

#### 3.7.1.5 Physical Organization

Memory is usually divided into fast primary storage and slow secondary storage. Memory management in the operating system handles moving information between these two levels of memory.

#### 3.7.1.6 Hierarchical Storage Management

Hierarchical Storage Management (HSM) is a data storage technique which automatically moves data between high-cost and low-cost storage media. HSM systems exist because high-speed storage devices, such as hard disk drive arrays, are more expensive (per byte stored) than slower devices, such as optical discs and magnetic tape drives. While it would be ideal to have all data available on high-speed devices all the time, this is prohibitively expensive for many organizations. Instead, HSM systems store the bulk of the enterprise's data on slower devices, and then copy data to faster disk drives when needed. In effect, HSM turns the fast disk drives into caches for the slower mass storage devices. The HSM system monitors the way data is used and makes best guesses as to which data can safely be moved to slower devices and which data should stay on the fast devices.

#### 3.7.1.7 Tiered storage

Tiered storage is a data storage environment consisting of two or more kinds of storage delineated by differences in at least one of these four attributes: Price, Performance, Capacity and Function.

Any significant difference in one or more of the four defining attributes can be sufficient to justify a separate storage tier.

Examples:

- Disk and Tape: Two separate storage tiers identified by differences in all four defining attributes.
- Old technology disk and new technology disk: Two separate storage tiers identified by differences in one or more of the attributes.

- High performing disk storage and less expensive, slower disk of the same capacity and function: Two separate tiers.
- Identical Enterprise class disk configured to utilize different functions such as RAID level or replication: A separate storage tier for each set of unique functions.

## 3.8 BACKUP & STORAGE

In information technology, **backup** refers to making copies of data so that these additional copies may be used to restore the original after a data loss event. These additional copies are typically called "backups." Backups are useful primarily for two purposes. The first is to restore a state following a disaster (called disaster recovery). The second is to restore small numbers of files after they have been accidentally deleted or corrupted. Data loss is also very common. 66% of internet users have suffered from serious data loss.

Since a backup system contains at least one copy of all data worth saving, the data storage requirements are considerable. Organizing this storage space and managing the backup process is a complicated undertaking. A data repository model can be used to provide structure to the storage. In the modern era of computing there are many different types of data storage devices that are useful for making backups. There are also many different ways in which these devices can be arranged to provide geographic redundancy, data security, and portability.

Before data is sent to its storage location, it is selected, extracted, and manipulated. Many different techniques have been developed to optimize the backup procedure. These include optimizations for dealing with open files and live data sources as well as compression, encryption, and de-duplication, among others. Many organizations and individuals try to have confidence that the process is working as expected and work to define measurements and validation techniques. It is also important to recognize the limitations and human factors involved in any backup scheme.

### 3.8.1 Storage, the Base of a Backup System

#### *3.8.1.1 Data Repository Models*

Any backup strategy starts with a concept of a data repository. The backup data needs to be stored somehow and probably should be organized to a degree. It can be as simple as a sheet of paper with a list of all backup tapes and the dates they were written or a more sophisticated setup with a computerized index, catalog, or relational database. Different repository models have different advantages. This is closely related to choosing a backup rotation scheme.

#### *3.8.1.2 Unstructured*

An unstructured repository may simply be a stack of floppy disks or CD-R/DVD-R media with minimal information about what was backed up and when. This is the easiest to implement, but probably the least likely to achieve a high level of recoverability.

#### *3.8.1.3 Full + Incremental*

A Full + Incremental repository aims to make storing several copies of the source data more feasible. At first, a *full* backup (of all files) is taken. After that, any number of *incremental* backups can be taken.

There are many different types of incremental backups, but they all attempt to only backup a small amount of data relative to the full backup. Restoring a whole system to a certain point in time would require locating the full backup taken previous to that time and the incremental backups that cover the period of time between the full backup and the particular point in time to which the system is supposed to be restored. The scope of an incremental backup is typically defined as a range of time relative to other full or incremental backups. Different implementations of backup systems frequently use specialized or conflicting definitions of these terms.

#### *3.8.1.4 Continuous Data Protection*

This model takes it a step further and instead of scheduling periodic backups, the system immediately logs every change on the host system. This is generally done by saving byte or block-level differences rather than file-level differences. It differs from simple disk mirroring in that it enables a roll-back of the log and thus restoration of old image of data.

### 3.8.2 Computer Data Storage

**Computer data storage**, often called **storage** or **memory**, refers to computer components, devices, and recording media that retain digital data used for computing for some interval of time. Computer data storage provides one of the core functions of the modern computer, that of information retention. It is one of the fundamental components of all modern computers, and coupled with a central processing unit (CPU, a processor), implements the basic computer model used since the 1940s.

In contemporary usage, memory usually refers to a form of semiconductor storage known as random — access memory (RAM) and sometimes other forms of fast but temporary storage. Similarly, storage today more commonly refers to mass storage — optical discs, forms of magnetic storage like hard disk drives, and other types slower than RAM, but of a more permanent nature. Historically, *memory* and *storage* were respectively called *primary storage* and *secondary storage*.

1 GB of SDRAM mounted in a personal computer. An example of *primary* storage.

Fig. 3.9: Shows SDRAM

40 GB hard disk drive (HDD); when connected to a computer it serves as *secondary* storage (Fig. 3.10).

160 GB SDLT tape cartridge, an example of *off-line* storage. When used within a robotic tape library, it is classified as *tertiary* storage instead (Fig. 3.11).

Fig. 3.10: Hard disk drive

Fig. 3.11: SDLT tape

### 3.8.3 Purpose of Storage

Many different forms of storage, based on various natural phenomena, have been invented. So far, no practical universal storage medium exists, and all forms of storage have some drawbacks. Therefore a computer system usually contains several kinds of storage, each with an individual purpose.

A digital computer represents data using the binary numeral system. Text, numbers, pictures, audio, and nearly any other form of information can be converted into a string of bits, or binary digits, each of which has a value of 1 or 0. The most common unit of storage is the byte, equal to 8 bits. A piece of information can be handled by any computer whose storage space is large enough to accommodate the binary representation of the piece of information, or simply data. For example, using eight million bits, or about one megabyte, a typical computer could store a short novel.

Traditionally the most important part of every computer is the central processing unit (CPU, or simply a processor), because it actually operates on data, performs any calculations, and controls all the other components.

Without a significant amount of memory, a computer would merely be able to perform fixed operations and immediately output the result. It would have to be reconfigured to change its behavior. This is acceptable for devices such as desk calculators or simple digital signal processors. Von Neumann machines differ in that they have a memory in which they store their operating instructions and data. Such computers are more versatile in that they do not need to have their hardware reconfigured for each new program, but can simply be reprogrammed with new in-memory instructions; they also tend to be simpler to design, in that a relatively simple processor may keep state between successive computations to build up complex procedural results. Most modern computers are von Neumann machines.

In practice, almost all computers use a variety of memory types, organized in a storage hierarchy around the CPU, as a tradeoff between performance and cost. Generally, the lower a storage is in the hierarchy, the lesser its bandwidth and the greater its access latency is from the CPU. This traditional division of storage to primary, secondary, tertiary and off-line storage is also guided by cost per bit.

### 3.8.4 Hierarchy of Storage

Various forms of storage, divided according to their distance from the central processing unit. The fundamental components of a general-purpose computer are arithmetic and logic unit, control circuitry, storage space, and input/output devices. Technology and capacity as in common **home computers** around 2005.

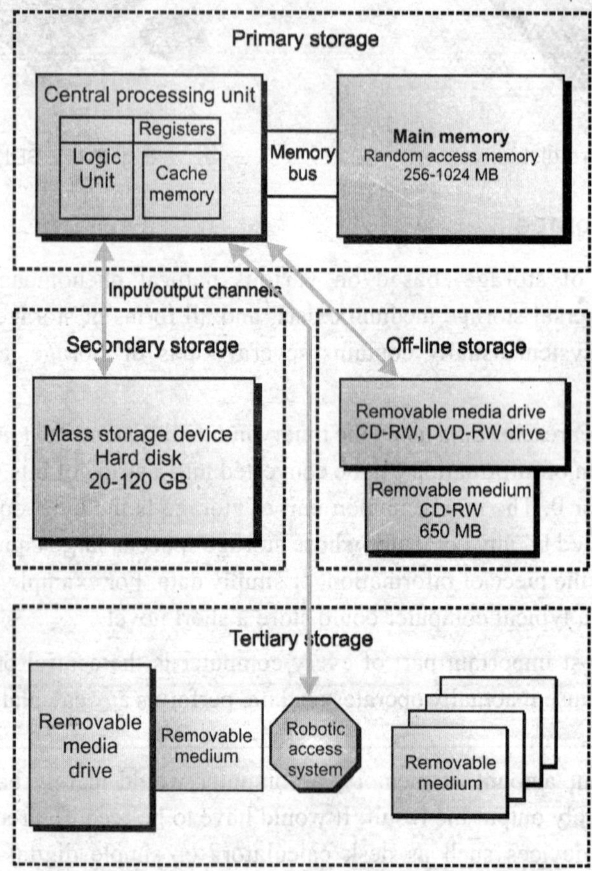


**Fig. 3.12:** Shows Hierarchy of storage

#### 3.8.4.1 Primary Storage

**Primary storage**, presently known as **memory**, is the only one directly accessible to the CPU. The CPU continuously reads instructions stored there and executes them as required. Any data actively operated on is also stored there in uniform manner.

Historically, early computers used delay lines, Williams tubes, or rotating magnetic drums as primary storage. By 1954, those unreliable methods were mostly replaced by magnetic core memory, which was still rather cumbersome. Undoubtedly, a revolution was started with the invention of a transistor, that soon enabled then-unbelievable miniaturization of electronic memory via **solid-state** silicon chip technology.

This led to a modern random-access memory (RAM). It is small-sized, light, but quite expensive at the same time. (The particular types of RAM used for primary storage are also **volatile**, i.e. they lose the information when not powered).

As shown in the diagram, traditionally there are two more sub-layers of the primary storage, besides main large-capacity RAM:

- Processor registers are located inside the processor. Each register typically holds a word of data (often 32 or 64 bits). CPU instructions instruct the arithmetic and logic unit to perform various calculations or other operations on this data (or with the help of it). Registers are technically among the fastest of all forms of computer data storage.
- Processor cache is an intermediate stage between ultra-fast registers and much slower main memory. It's introduced solely to increase performance of the computer. Most actively used information in the main memory is just duplicated in the cache memory, which is faster, but of much lesser capacity. On the other hand it is much slower, but much larger than processor registers. Multi-level hierarchical cache setup is also commonly used — *primary cache* being smallest, fastest and located inside the processor; *secondary cache* being somewhat larger and slower.

Main memory is directly or indirectly connected to the CPU via a *memory bus*. It is actually comprised of two buses (not on the diagram): an address bus and a data bus. The CPU firstly sends a number through an address bus, a number called memory address, that indicates the desired location of data. Then it reads or writes the data itself using the data bus. Additionally, a memory management unit (MMU) is a small device between CPU and RAM recalculating the actual memory address, for example to provide an abstraction of virtual memory or other tasks.

As the RAM types used for primary storage are volatile (cleared at start up), a computer containing only such storage would not have a source to read instructions from, in order to start the computer. Hence, non-volatile primary storage containing a small startup program (BIOS) is used to bootstrap the computer, that is, to read a larger program from non-volatile *secondary* storage to RAM and start to execute it. A non-volatile technology used for this purpose is called ROM, for read-only memory (the terminology may be somewhat confusing as most ROM types are also capable of *random access*).

Many types of "ROM" are not literally *read only,* as updates are possible; however it is slow and memory must be erased in large portions before it can be re-written. Some embedded systems run programs directly from ROM (or similar), because such programs are rarely changed. Standard computers do not store non-rudimentary programs in ROM, rather use large capacities of secondary storage, which is non-volatile as well, and not as costly.

Recently, *primary storage* and *secondary storage* in some uses refer to what was historically called, respectively, *secondary storage* and *tertiary storage*.

### 3.8.4.2 Secondary Storage

A hard disk drive with protective cover removed (Fig. 3.13).

**Secondary storage** in popular usage, differs from primary storage in that it is not directly accessible by the CPU. The computer usually uses its input/output channels to access secondary storage and transfers the desired data using intermediate area in primary storage. Secondary storage does not lose the data when the device is powered down — it is non-volatile. Per unit, it is typically also an order of magnitude less expensive than primary storage. Consequently, modern computer systems typically have an order of magnitude more secondary storage than primary storage and data is kept for a longer time there.

**Fig. 3.13:** Shows a hard disk drive with protective cover removed

In modern computers, hard disk drives are usually used as secondary storage. The time taken to access a given byte of information stored on a hard disk is typically a few thousandths of a second, or milliseconds. By contrast, the time taken to access a given byte of information stored in random access memory is measured in billionths of a second, or nanoseconds. This illustrates the very significant access-time difference which distinguishes solid-state memory from rotating magnetic storage devices: hard disks are typically about a million times slower than memory. Rotating optical storage devices, such as CD and DVD drives, have even longer access times.

Some other examples of secondary storage technologies are: flash memory (e.g. USB flash drives or keys), floppy disks, magnetic tape, paper tape, punched cards, stand alone RAM disks, and Iomega Zip drives.

The secondary storage is often formatted according to a file system format, which provides the abstraction necessary to organize data into files and directories, providing also additional information (called metadata) describing the owner of a certain file, the access time, the access permissions, and other information.

Most computer operating systems use the concept of virtual memory, allowing utilization of more primary storage capacity than is physically available in the system. As the primary memory fills up, the system moves the least-used chunks (pages) to secondary storage devices (to a swap file or page file), retrieving them later when they are needed. As more of these retrievals from slower secondary storage are necessary, the more the overall system performance is degraded.

### 3.8.4.3 Tertiary Storage

Large tape library. Tape cartridges placed on shelves in the front, robotic arm moving in the back. Visible height of the library is about 180 cm (Fig. 3.14)

**Tertiary storage** or **tertiary memory**, provides a third level of storage. Typically it involves a robotic mechanism which will mount (insert) and dismount removable mass storage media into a storage device according to the system's demands; this data is often copied to secondary storage before use. It is primarily used for archival of rarely accessed information since it is much slower than secondary storage (e.g. 5–60 seconds vs. 1-10 milliseconds). This is primarily useful for extraordinarily large data stores, accessed without human operators. Typical examples include tape libraries and optical jukeboxes.

**Fig. 3.14:** Shows Large Tape Library

When a computer needs to read information from the tertiary storage, it will first consult a catalog database to determine which tape or disc contains the information. Next, the computer will instruct a robotic arm to fetch the medium and place it in a drive. When the computer has finished reading the information, the robotic arm will return the medium to its place in the library.

## 3.8.5 Characteristics of Storage

Storage technologies at all levels of the storage hierarchy can be differentiated by evaluating certain core characteristics as well as measuring characteristics specific to a particular implementation. These core characteristics are volatility, mutability, accessibility, and addressibility. For any particular implementation of any storage technology, the characteristics worth measuring are capacity and performance.

### *3.8.5.1 Volatility*

1. **Non-volatile Memory:** Will retain the stored information even if it is not constantly supplied with electric power. It is suitable for long-term storage of information. Nowadays used for most of secondary, tertiary, and off-line storage. In 1950s and 1960s, it was also used for primary storage, in the form of magnetic core memory.
2. **Volatile Memory:** Requires constant power to maintain the stored information. The fastest memory technologies of today are volatile ones (not a universal rule). Since primary storage is required to be very fast, it predominantly uses volatile memory.

### *3.8.5.2 Differentiation*

1. **Dynamic Random Access Memory:** A form of volatile memory which also requires the stored information to be periodically re-read and re-written, or refreshed, otherwise it would vanish.
2. **Static memory**: A form of volatile memory similar to DRAM with the exception that it never needs to be refreshed.

#### *3.8.5.3 Mutability*

1. **Read/write Storage or Mutable Storage:** Allows information to be overwritten at any time. A computer without some amount of read/write storage for primary storage purposes would be useless for many tasks. Modern computers typically use read/write storage also for secondary storage.
2. **Read Only Storage:** Retains the information stored at the time of manufacture, and **write once storage** (Write Once Read Many) allows the information to be written only once at some point after manufacture. These are called **immutable storage**. Immutable storage is used for tertiary and off-line storage. Examples include CD-ROM and CD-R.
3. **Slow Write, Fast Read Storage:** Read/write storage which allows information to be overwritten multiple times, but with the write operation being much slower than the read operation. Examples include CD-RW and flash memory.

#### *3.8.5.4 Accessibility*

1. **Random Access:** Any location in storage can be accessed at any moment in approximately the same amount of time. Such characteristic is well suited for primary and secondary storage.
2. **Sequential Access:** The accessing of pieces of information will be in a serial order, one after the other; therefore the time to access a particular piece of information depends upon which piece of information was last accessed. Such characteristic is typical of off-line storage.

#### *3.8.5.5 Addressability*

1. **Location-addressable:** Each individually accessible unit of information in storage is selected with its numerical memory address. In modern computers, location-addressable storage usually limits to primary storage, accessed internally by computer programs, since location-addressability is very efficient, but burdensome for humans.
2. **File addressable:** Information is divided into files of variable length, and a particular file is selected with human-readable directory and file names. The underlying device is still location-addressable, but the operating system of a computer provides the file system **abstraction** to make the operation more understandable. In modern computers, secondary, tertiary and off-line storage use file systems.
3. **Content-addressable:** Each individually accessible unit of information is selected with a hash value, or a short identifier with a number pertaining to the memory address the information is stored on. Content-addressable storage can be implemented using software (computer program) or hardware (computer device), with hardware being faster but more expensive option.

#### *3.8.5.6 Capacity*

1. **Raw Capacity:** The total amount of stored information that a storage device or medium can hold. It is expressed as a quantity of bits or bytes (e.g. 10.4 megabytes).
2. **Memory Storage Density:** The compactness of stored information. It is the storage capacity of a medium divided with a unit of length, area or volume (e.g. 1.2 megabytes per square inch).

#### 3.8.5.7 Performance

1. **Latency:** The time it takes to access a particular location in storage. The relevant unit of measurement is typically nanosecond for primary storage, millisecond for secondary storage, and second for tertiary storage. It may make sense to separate read latency and write latency, and in case of sequential access storage, minimum, maximum and average latency.
2. **Throughput:** The rate at which information can be read from or written to the storage. In computer data storage, throughput is usually expressed in terms of megabytes per second or MB/s, though bit rate may also be used. As with latency, read rate and write rate may need to be differentiated. Also accessing media sequentially, as opposed to randomly, typically yields maximum throughput.

### 3.8.6 Backup Types

Backup types are: **full backup**, **differential backup**, **incremental backup** and **mirror backup**. Below you can find an overview of the **backup types**.

#### 3.8.6.1 Full Backup

**Full backup** is the starting point for all other types of backup and contains all the data in the folders and files that are selected to be backed up. Because **full backup** stores all files and folders, frequent full backups result in faster and simpler restore operations. Remember that when you choose other **backup types**, restore jobs may take longer.

#### 3.8.6.2 Differential Backup

**Differential backup** contains all files that have changed since the last **FULL backup**. The advantage of a **differential backup** is that it shortens restore time compared to a **full backup** or an **incremental backup**. However, if you perform the **differential backup** too many times, the size of the **differential backup** might grow to be larger than the baseline **full backup**.

#### 3.8.6.3 Incremental Backup

**Incremental backup** stores all files that have changed since the last **FULL, DIFFERENTIAL OR INCREMENTAL backup**. The advantage of an **incremental backup** is that it takes the least time to complete. However, during a restore operation, each **incremental backup** must be processed, which could result in a lengthy restore job.

#### 3.8.6.4 Mirror Backup

**Mirror backup** is identical to a **full backup**, with the exception that the files are not compressed in zip files and they can not be protected with a password. A **mirror backup** is most frequently used to create an exact copy of the backup data. It has the benefit that the backup files can also be readily accessed using tools like Windows Explorer.

In information technology, **backup** refers to making copies of data so that these additional copies may be used to restore the original after a data loss event. These additional copies are typically called "backups." Backups are useful primarily for two purposes. The first is to restore a state following a disaster (called disaster recovery). The second is to restore small numbers of files after they have been accidentally deleted or corrupted. Data loss is also very common. 66% of internet users have suffered from serious data loss. Since a backup system contains at least one copy of all data worth saving, the data storage requirements are considerable. Organizing this storage space and managing the backup process is a complicated undertaking. A data repository model can be used to provide structure to the storage. In the modern era of computing there are many different types of data storage devices that are useful for making backups. There are also many different ways in which these devices can be arranged to provide geographic redundancy, data security, and portability. Before data is sent to its storage location, it is selected, extracted, and manipulated. Many different techniques have been developed to optimize the backup procedure. These include optimizations for dealing with open files and live data sources as well as compression, encryption, and de-duplication, among others. Many organizations and individuals try to have confidence that the process is working as expected and work to define measurements and validation techniques. It is also important to recognize the limitations and human factors involved in any backup scheme.

## 3.9 ARCHIVE

An **archive** is a collection of historical records, and the location in which the collection is kept.. Archives contain records (primary source documents) which have accumulated over the course of an individual or organization's lifetime.

The archives of an individual may include letters, papers, photographs, computer files, scrapbooks, financial records or diaries created or collected by the individual – regardless of media or format. The archives of an organization (such as a corporation or government) tend to contain other types of records, such as administrative files, business records, memos, official correspondence and meeting minutes.

In general, archives consist of records which have been selected for permanent or long-term preservation, due to their enduring research value. Archival records are normally unpublished and almost always unique, unlike books or magazines for which many identical copies exist. This means that archives (the places) are quite distinct from libraries with regard to their functions and organization, although archival collections can often be found within library buildings.

Archives are sometimes described as information generated as the "by-product" of normal human activities, while libraries hold specifically authored information "products". A person who works in archives is called an archivist. The study and practice of organizing, preserving, and providing access to information and materials in archives is called archival science.

Archivists tend to prefer the term 'archives' (with an S) as the correct terminology to serve as both the singular and plural, since 'archive,' as a noun or a verb, has meanings related to computer science.

### 3.9.1 Information Retrieval

**Information retrieval (IR)** is the science of searching for documents, for information within documents and for metadata about documents, as well as that of searching relational databases and the World Wide Web. There is overlap in the usage of the terms data retrieval, document retrieval, information retrieval, and text retrieval, but each also has its own body of literature, theory, praxis and technologies.

IR is interdisciplinary, based on computer science, mathematics, library science, information science, information architecture, cognitive psychology, linguistics, statistics and physics.

## 3.10 DISASTER RECOVERY

**Disaster recovery** is the process, policies and procedures related to preparing for recovery or continuation of technology infrastructure critical to an organization after a natural or human-induced disaster.

Disaster recovery planning is a subset of a larger process known as business continuity planning and should include planning for resumption of applications, data, hardware, communications (such as networking) and other IT infrastructure. A business continuity plan (BCP) includes planning for non-IT related aspects such as key personnel, facilities, crisis communication and reputation protection, and should refer to the disaster recovery plan (DRP) for IT related infrastructure recovery / continuity.

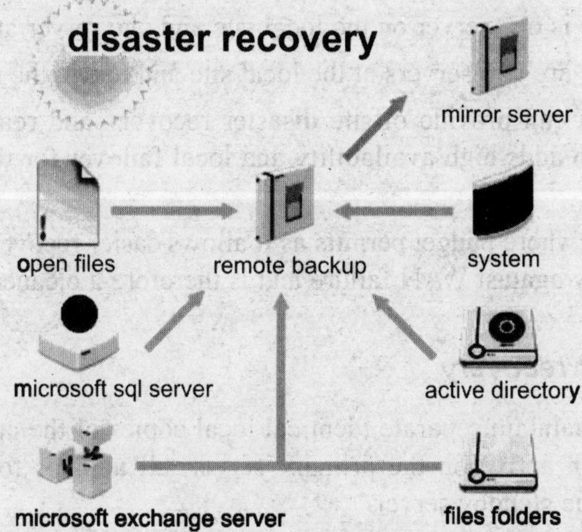


**Fig. 3.15:** The Disaster recovery

### 3.10.1 Introduction

With the increasing importance of information technology for the continuation of business critical functions, combined with a transition to an around-the-clock economy, the importance of protecting an organization's data and IT infrastructure in the event of a disruptive situation has become an increasing and more visible business priority in recent years.

It is estimated that most large companies spend between 2% and 4% of their IT budget on disaster recovery planning, with the aim of avoiding larger losses in the event that the business cannot continue to function due to loss of IT infrastructure and data. Of companies that had a major loss of business data, 43% never reopen, 51% close within two years, and only 6% will survive long-term

### 3.10.2 Classification of Disasters

Disaster can be classified in two broad categories. Viz, 1) Natural disasters- Preventing a natural disaster is very difficult, but it is possible to take precautions to avoid losses. These disasters include flood, fire, earthquake, hurricane, etc 2) Man made disasters- These disasters are major reasons for failure. Human error and intervention may be intentional or unintentional which can cause massive failures such as loss of communication and utility. These disasters include accidents, walkouts, sabotage, burglary, virus, intrusion, etc.

### 3.10.3 Disaster Recovery Solutions

The disaster recovery solution enables the use of remote standby servers to take over an application in case of server or application failure. Data is replicated in real-time to the remote site by using data replication software or storage devices.

Life Keeper sits on all servers in the cluster monitoring the health of the systems and active applications. When a failure is detected, recovery procedures are started automatically. There are currently two options available for disaster recovery:

- **2 node:** where there is one server on the local site and one server at the recovery site.
- **3 node:** where there are two servers at the local site and one at the recovery site.

A basic 2-node solution can provide offsite disaster recovery and real time backups, the more sophisticated 3-node solution adds high availability and local failover for those not-quite-disasterous occasions.

The 3 node is preferable where budget permits as it allows easier recovery for non-disaster related failures, and high availability against WAN failure and is therefore a cleaner overall solution.

#### *3.10.3.1 2-node disaster recovery*

Data replication is used to maintain separate identical local copies of the application data on the two servers. With the application active on the primary server, all updates to the application data are automatically replicated to the standby server.

When a failure occurs, the application is automatically started on the standby server, it continues its operations using a mirrored copy of the data. If the primary server is returned to service, the direction of the data replication can be reversed, and after an initial resynchronization process to bring the primary server up-to-date with any data changes which may have occurred while it was unavailable, returned to front line service.

## 3.11 DISK SPACE MANAGEMENT

Every Windows user knows that no matter how big your hard drive is, data will eventually take all of it. Modern software and multimedia content have become really greedy in terms of gigabytes. To make matters worse, many applications create temporary and / or system files that might be huge and difficult to locate. In many cases they clean up the mess. But as time moves on, more and more unerased trash starts to slow down your computer. And you have to do that again: reinstall Windows, format your disks to have a few months of freedom on your PC.

Beside such extreme methods of disk space management, you surely have come across some traditional tools to organize and manage files and folders. Standard programs are fine as long as you use standard folders and do standard things. The problem with people, though, is that we are not that standard about our hard drive needs. We might get impulsive when we create a folder with a tongue-twisting name. The impulse might go, but the folder we create stays. And that is when standard programs work badly.

First, you have to find large files and folders and traditional programs make this job surprisingly difficult. It takes ages to view folder size. You may have to manually search around to find files that occupy the most space on your drive. Sometimes these files are so well hidden, that they are virtually impossible to be located. One more problem is navigation. These days a typical computer will have thousands of different directories, which makes it not so easy to locate data. Using standard applications, you may have to scroll down a lot of screens before you get somewhere. Is there a better way? There is a small but efficient application called Directory Size that can help you manage your files much more efficiently.

The program features an intuitive interface to help you get through all these files and folders. Another benefit is that it turns data into pictures and graphs allowing you to conduct visual disk space analysis. Our mind can structure and process visuals much faster than pure numbers and bits of text.

Another important issue is speed. Directory Size operates in the background. It creates a map of where things are. That is why when you need to get somewhere around all those gigabytes, Directory Size offers you a navigation map that makes finding things pretty easy.

The program helps you save money. When you can efficiently organize your data, you do not need to get into the hype for more gigabytes. It is much more comfortable to live in a neat apartment than in a huge but messy house where you stumble every time you want to find the remote control or even the way to the bathroom.

And you know what; size does matter when we speak of files and folders on your hard disk drives. Directory Size helps you locate and keep an eye on the biggest space eaters on your computer. You can even arrange folders according to their size. Thus you can always see what programs and files occupy your precious disk space and take appropriate action when necessary.

## 3.12 DATABASE PROTECTION

### 3.12.1 What it is a Database?

A database is a collection of independent components, such as pieces of information, data, or works, arranged in a systematic or methodical way and which are individually accessible by electronic or other means. The content of a database can include literary, musical, artistic, or other works or material such as text, sound, images, numbers, facts, and raw data. Multimedia resources also fall under this definition but computer programs do not. Database protection applies to electronic and non-electronic databases.

### 3.12.2 Grounds for Database Protection

There are two main bases for database protection: copyright protection (under the condition of creativity) and new *sui generis* protection (under the condition of substantial investment). Copyright protection has an international character (databases are protected in almost all countries in the world), whereas *sui generis* protection is obtained for persons from the EU only in EU countries. Persons from outside the

EU may obtain protection only under the condition of reciprocity if, in their country, such protection is introduced. For example, the USA does not provide *sui generis* protection as such. Under EU law, cumulative protection of databases is possible under copyright and the *sui generic*right.

Neither copyright protection nor *sui generis* protection creates a new or additional protection for each individual element of a database. Database protection provides protection for a database only as a compilation.

### 3.12.3 Copyright Protection of a Database

Copyright protection applies to databases that are creative in selection or/and arrangement. Copyright exists for those databases that constitute their authors' own intellectual creation in the selection and/or arrangement.

Copyright protection is owned by the author and expires 70 years after the author's death.

## 3.13 BARE MACHINE RECOVERY

### 3.13.1 Introduction

Bare metal recovery is the process of re-building a machine when the machine fails due to catastrophic failure of the boot disk. Typically, the failed disk is replaced and then special recovery software is run that allows the image of the original disk to be copied from a backup image to the new hard drive and the system is restored. The recovery software must boot and be able to access the new hard drive as well as access the backup image. This means that the recovery software must have appropriate drivers for a large variety of hardware. In some cases the system being recovered may be obsolete and it may be difficult to build a bootable image. In other cases the process of repairing the hardware may require the replacement of components for which the drivers in the backup image may not be correct.

Since the beginning of the computing age, it has been universally understood that backup is a critical element in protecting against data loss. With the mountains of data being entered in today's online environment, the ability to recover lost data is not a luxury, but a fundamental part of doing business.

Bare Metal Recovery (BMR) is most often considered a supplemental layer of protection that can help insulate an organization against unnecessary downtime. While file-by-file backup and restore software is excellent at protecting against data loss, there is an inherent disadvantage in being able to quickly return an unbootable machine to a fully operational state. The shortcomings are the many steps required to perform a file-by-file recovery, and the lack of guarantee that every operating system (OS) change has been reinstated even after a restore. Thus, BMR should actually be a vital part of any company's disaster recovery plan, not just an afterthought.

### 3.13.2 The History Of Bare Metal Recovery

In the early days, the cost of storage was so high that individual transactions were printed on punch cards, paper tape, or ledger cards. Customer transaction totals were stored on a magnetic stripe on the back of a ledger card, tape cassette, or, for those who could afford big iron, disk. Because of the high expense for tiny amounts of storage, and since hardware frequently failed, systems were designed to allow companies to limp along using paper as a fall back during what were often long repair periods.

As technical advances in storage brought the cost per byte down, more data could be kept online. This meant that backup vendors had to keep pace by creating better technology. In some cases advancements were a requirement, and not just produced out of a desire to invent the next big thing. A good example of a necessary development was bare metal disaster recovery.

BMR was a mandatory function for Digital Equipment Corporation VAX users, back when DEC was a major player in the minicomputer market. This was because a VAX only supported one OS. Computers from other manufacturers often supported multiple OS drives so, if one failed (for any reason), you could simply boot from another drive. BMR was a technology born of a requirement by VAX end users to quickly and easily restore a "dead" machine that had lost its ability to boot. This is also often referred to as "cold" booting a machine.

When Microsoft developed Windows NT, they too designed a machine that only supported one OS drive. Windows end users had the same problem as VAX users – it was no easy task to re-install an OS and get a machine restored to the same point it was before an unbootable type of failure. It wasn't long before VAX users, who had converted to Windows NT, started asking for a BMR equivalent. The third party software community that specializes in backup was slow to understand the significance of BMR. For many users, an OS failure had never been a large issue for the equipment they supported before moving over to NT. However, as more sophisticated end users moved to the new OS, demand for a method to quickly and easily restore a failed machine gained momentum. In order to create this solution, vendors were required to think beyond the traditional file-by-file backup and restore methods that were so prevalent up until just a few years ago. Therefore, the BMR products available in today's market have been greatly influenced by the success of Windows in the business environment.

Over the past five years there has been an explosion of new hardware and software options for end users that offer better protection. Due to the amount of choices available, it is not surprising many end users are unsure as to which data protection approaches are critical and should be funded, versus what might be optional for their unique environment. Computer downtime is a leading contributor to overall business failure so it is prudent to minimize this risk. However, a major problem is balancing a viable solution cost against acceptable levels of downtime since it is extremely costly to buy and implement a non-stop computing system.

### 3.13.3 The Windows Nt Era

When Microsoft released Windows NT, nearly the entire user population regularly backed up to tape using the built-in backup product. As third party backup solutions began to emerge, UltraBac Software introduced the first Windows server backup product that not only backed up to tape, but was actually designed to write to disk as a storage option. As the price of disk storage continued to fall in the late 1990's, every competitive backup product in the Windows market released some type of disk-to-disk functionality. Consumer demand had inspired this move to a different and more stable form of backup media, as tape had often proved to be less than completely reliable. These requests for alternate storage only accelerated as the price of disks continued to fall.

As end users became more reliant on the faster disk-to-disk backups, they realized there was a huge hole in their file-by-file restores. The ability to back up to disk more rapidly than tape created the expectation of faster restores. However, with traditional restore methods this was not possible.

When it took five hours to back up to tape, recovering a failed machine in five hours as well was considered normal if not outstanding. When backup times were cut in half, the technology to restore a totally failed machine in a timely manner had to be created.

Once Windows NT was released, customers frequently experienced what was labeled "The Blue Screen of Death." A blue screen event normally did not cause any data loss; the machine just became unbootable and therefore was unusable until recovered. To recover, an administrator had to install a temporary operating system, install the backup software, use the backup software to restore the operating system partition, and then reboot. Backup and restore was almost always performed to and from tape with a common problem — a restored backup often did not have key information that had been layered on the machine since installation. Aside from how long a restore took, the fact that a failed machine typically was not completely restored to the full status at which it failed, initiated the demand for a better way to recover. This led to the development of BMR for Windows. Unfortunately, many end users initially resisted investing in this software technology because of perceived lack of functionality and high cost assumptions.

### 3.13.4 Time Is Money

While the definition (and monetary value) of a timely recovery of a failed machine can vary from organization to organization, one unarguable fact is that downtime costs money. Actual system downtime loss is an expense that is usually not well perceived in most organizations – it can even vary by the time of day. Downtime for Company A might cost $5,000 an hour while the cost for Company B could be $100,000 an hour. Even the rate between individual servers within a company can be vastly different depending on the critical nature of the applications being run. Here is a very simple formula to estimate downtime:

(Employee costs per hour) ×
(Fraction of employees affected by outage + Average income per hour) ×
(Fraction of income affected by outage)
= ***Estimated average cost of one hour of downtime***

Downtime costs fall into two broad categories: tangible and intangible. Calculating tangible costs such as employee wages, operating costs, and office expenses are straight forward and can be estimated with great accuracy using a simple formula like the one provided above. The difficultly lies in factoring all of the potential intangible costs such as lowered employee morale, missed opportunities, forgone sales, and loss of customer goodwill. These are hard to assign accurate costs. The bottom line is all companies recognize computer downtime means lost money. Regrettably, most don't realize how much it truly costs.

### 3.13.5 Decreasing Restore Times — Increasing Availability

Organizations can significantly decrease server downtime by implementing a quality bare metal recovery solution. Standard file-by-file recovery methods simply cannot bring a server back online quickly or easily. BMR software offers an economical way to eliminate unnecessary downtime, making machine failures less expensive. In some cases, the first use of a BMR solution can provide the user their full return on investment.

There are many expensive hardware and software products on the market that are designed to offer non-stop computing. They do a fine job, but do not eliminate or even help with unbootable events. For example, no matter the quality of a RAID device, or how reliable a cluster server or replication product, none of these can help overcome installing a bad driver that causes a blue screen. In a situation such as this, replication software simply becomes 'double trouble' because the bad driver is replicated to the fail-over machine, making it unbootable as well.

### 3.13.6 Defining Bare Metal Recovery

Organizations can significantly decrease server downtime by implementing a quality bare metal recovery solution. Standard file-by-file recovery methods simply cannot bring a server back online quickly or easily. BMR software offers an economical way to eliminate unnecessary downtime, making machine failures less expensive. In some cases, the first use of a BMR solution can provide the user their full return on investment.

Bare metal recovery is essentially the process of taking a low-level snapshot of a machine's operating system partition and storing it where it can be quickly and easily accessed when required. A BMR solution has two parts. The first is a program that is set up to periodically snapshot an OS partition using image backup technology. This is installed as a service and comes with a scheduler. The scheduler is then programmed to take backups of the live machine without any requirement to shut down services, close applications, or go offline. Image backups re normally stored to a UNC path, SAN, or NAS device for online storage and quick access when needed.

The second part of a BMR solution is the process used to boot a dead machine. This enables users to connect to the online location where the image backups have been stored and initiate a restore. Once the OS partition has been restored (which can take between 5 to 30 minutes), the only remaining steps necessary to complete the disaster recovery are to remove the boot media and reboot the machine. This latter phase takes approximately two minutes before the machine is back to the exact state at which the image backup was performed.

Static image backups are typically performed every 24 hours, with options for incremental and differential backups between full backups. The newest functionality for BMR is continuous image protection, or CIP. CIP can also be referred to as CDP, or continuous data protection, but the term CDP does not differentiate between block or file protection. Many CDP products on the market today only provide continuous data protection for applications such as SQL or Exchange, whereas CIP offers comprehensive protection for all applications on a disk. The advantage both CDP and CIP do offer is the ability to restore a machine to a closer point-in-time to the actual root cause of an unbootable failure, as opposed to a standard image backup that might be 23 hours old.

Using regular file-by-file backup software, restoring a failed server takes most organizations anywhere between two hours to two days to accomplish. By implementing a BMR solution, restoring the same OS partition that took hours using a regular file-based restore might be accomplished in under 10 minutes. Not only is BMR fast, but it is simple when compared to a file-based restore. A sophisticated BMR product can also be fully scripted — even a security guard on the night shift could recover a strategic 24 × 7 server.

### 3.13.7 What To Look For In A Bare Metal Recovery Solution

When image-based disaster recovery first appeared in the Windows environment, the majority of users were astonished at how fast and simple recovering failed servers became. Unfortunately, certain restrictions applied. In order to restore the saved backup image files, they were required to be restored to the same or nearly identical hardware. As BMR software has evolved, key features were introduced to make this solution truly flexible.

The technology has become an integral disaster recovery application for more and more enterprise level businesses, and now the SMB market is realizing that it is as vital to them as it is for larger companies. When considering which software application is right for a company, here are some key features to look for in a bare metal recovery solution:

1. Dissimilar hardware restore
2. Virtual consolidations and disaster recovery
3. Restore to larger partitions and disks
4. Restore to smaller partitions and disks
5. The ability to safely restore Active Directory and Domain Controllers
6. Full, incremental, and differential options
7. Continuous image protection (CIP) 8. Fully scripted backups and restores
9. Remote management
10. Backup and restore using FTP/SFTP
11. Backup and restore using IBM Tivoli Storage Manager
12. Backup and restore using any local or remote tape drive
13. Backup and restore using any local or remote library
14. Backup and restore using any local disk, UNC path, SAN, NAS, USB, or FireWire device
15. Backup and restore using CD, DVD, USB Key, or PXE/RIS
16. Backup and restore through tightly locked down firewalls
17. Disk-to-disk-to-tape options for redundant and off-site storage

### 3.13.8 How Bare Metal Recovery Saves Money

Every minute of machine downtime costs an organization time and money. Therefore, everyone should be able to agree that limiting downtime is highly desirable, particularly if it is reasonably affordable. To demonstrate the return on investment (ROI), here is a BMR scenario:

If the national average for Windows server downtime is $15,000 an hour (and this is a fairly modest sum), then this would mean that every minute of downtime equals $250. If it then takes a standard bare metal disaster recovery solution approximately 20 minutes, as opposed to 40 minutes using file-by-file backup and restore, the 20 minute savings using the BMR solution equates to a $5,000 dollar savings in downtime cost with its first use.

Expanding on this, if the price of a premium BMR solution is $1,000 per server, an organization could subtract the price of the BMR software from the money they saved on restore times.

Bottom line, the company would still be left with a $4,000 cost savings. Not many products offer a ROI like this, particularly after just a first time use. In a real production environment, the time savings is more like a 6-to-1 ratio, leading to even greater savings as opposed to the 2-to-1 ratio used in this example.

### 3.13.9 The Bare Metal Recovery Steps

To give organizations a better understanding of how the two backup methods differ, we have provided a procedure comparison between using file-based backups and restores versus image-based backups and restores.

File-by-file restore example:

1. Install EISA Partition (53 minutes)
2. Install Windows OS (45 minutes)
3. Install Backup Software (5 minutes)
4. Create Data Partitions (10 minutes)
5. Restore System 4GB drive (35 minutes)
6. Restore System State/Registry (1 hour)
7. Reboot Server (2 minutes)

**Total Restore Steps = 7 Restore Time = 3 ½ hours**

Bare Metal Recovery example using UltraBac Software's UBDR Gold:

1. Boot server using UBDR Gold Restore Media (5 min)
2. Connect to a UNC path and initiate a 10 GB OS partition restore with a conservative 2 GB/minute transfer rate (8 minutes)
3. Reboot Server (2 min)

**Total Restore Steps = 3 Restore Time = 15 minutes**

As the example demonstrates, a BMR solution can easily restore a failed machine's 10GB OS partition in 15 minutes using a conservative 2 GB/minute restore speed on a Gigabit network connection. Fast systems can experience over 5 GB/minute restore speed. Organizations using the BMR process now "complain" that the machine boot time takes longer than the physical restore. When comparing file-by-file methods with BMR, there simply is no comparison.

## 3.14 DATA RETENTION

Defines the policies of persistent data and records management for meeting legal and business data archival requirements. A data retention policy weighs legal and privacy concerns against economics and need to know concerns to determine both the retention time, archival rules, data formats, and the permissible means of storage, access, and encryption.

### 3.14.1 Access to Retained Data

The bodies which are able to access retained data in the United Kingdom are listed in the Regulation of Investigatory Powers Act 2000 (RIPA). These are :

- Police forces (as defined in section 81(1) of RIPA)
- National Criminal Intelligence Service
- National Crime Squad

- HM Customs and Excise
- Inland Revenue
- Security Service
- Secret Intelligence Service
- Government Communications Headquarters

### 3.14.2 Reasons for Accessing Retained Data

The justifications for accessing retained data in the United Kingdom are set out in the Regulation of Investigatory Powers Act 2000 (RIPA). They are:

- in the interests of national security;
- for the purpose of preventing or detecting crime or of preventing disorder;
- in the interests of the economic well-being of the United Kingdom;
- in the interests of public safety;
- for the purpose of protecting public health;
- for the purpose of assessing or collecting any tax, duty, levy or other imposition, contribution or charge payable to a government department;
- for the purpose, in an emergency, of preventing death or injury or any damage to a person's physical or mental health, or of mitigating any injury or damage to a person's physical or mental health;
- for any purpose (not falling into the above) which is specified for the purposes of this subsection by an order made by the Secretary of State.

### 3.14.3 Protection Against Data Retention

The current directive proposal (see above) would force ISPs to record the internet communications of its users. The basic assumption is that this information can be used to identify with whom someone, whether innocent citizen or terrorist, communicated throughout a specific timespan. Believing that such as mandate would be useful is ignoring that some very committed community of crypto professionals has been preparing for such legislation for decades. Below are some strategies available today to anyone to protect themselves, avoid such traces, and render such expensive and legally dubious logging operations useless.

### 3.14.4 VPNs

Several organizations have set up VPNs so their employees can safely access the private data of the company. In this case the only data retained is the connection to the VPN server, that will contain all the data served to the EU citizen encrypted.

The connections, if the company is in the EU, will be recorded as a company access, mixed with all the other employees access. To single out any user, the company would have to be tapped and that the citizen would have to use it after it's been tapped. In practice that would mean that data retention would be of the same use that the present tapping legislation, so it presents only a cost with no benefit.

### 3.14.5 Anonymizing Proxy Services: Web

There are anonymizing proxies that provide slightly more private web access. Proxies must use HTTPS encryption in order to provide any level of protection at all. Unfortunately, proxies require the user to place a large amount of trust in the proxy operator (since they see everything the user does over HTTP), and may be subject to traffic analysis.

### 3.14.6 Webmail

Most hosting companies (Pair Networks, Inc. in the US, for instance), provide a secure interface to their webmail system. This means that any EU citizen that pays for their services can read and send email without any information about it being recorded, other than a secure (e-commerce like) connection to the hosting company.

### 3.14.7 P2P Communications

Some P2P services, being it file transfer or voice over IP, use other computers to allow communication between computers behind firewalls. This means that trying to follow a call between two citizens might, mistakenly, identify a third citizen unaware of the communication.

### 3.14.8 Privacy Enhancing Tools

For security conscious citizens, using tools like Tor, mixmaster and the cryptography options integrated into any major mail client these days is always an option. Though, in practice, not everyone has the knowledge to employ the techniques described above.

Tor is a project of the US non-profit Tor Project to develop and improve an onion routing network to shield its users from traffic analysis. Mixmaster is a remailer service that allows anonymous email sending.

JAP is a project very similar to Tor. It is designed to route web requests through several proxies to hide the end users Internet address. Tor support has been included into JAP.

CHAPTER 4

# Security Management

## 4.1 SECURITY MANAGEMENT

### 4.1.1 Introduction

**Security Management** is a broad field of management related to asset management, physical security and human resource safety functions. It entails the identification of an organization's information assets and the development, documentation and implementation of policies, standards, procedures and guidelines.

In network management it is the set of functions that protects telecommunications networks and systems from unauthorized access by persons, acts, or influences and that includes many sub-functions, such as creating, deleting, and controlling security services and mechanisms; distributing security-relevant information; reporting security-relevant events; controlling the distribution of cryptographic keying material; and authorizing subscriber access, rights, and privileges.

Management tools such as information classification, risk assessment and risk analysis are used to identify threats, classify assets and to rate system vulnerabilities so that effective control can be implemented.

### 4.1.2 The Security Management Process

The security management process consists of activities that are carried out by the security management itself or activities that are controlled by the security management.

Because organizations and their information systems constantly change, the activities within the security management process must be revised continuously, in order to stay up-to-date and effective. Security management is a continuous process and it can be compared to the Quality Circle of Deming (Plan, Do, Check, Act).

The inputs are the requirements which are formed by the clients. The requirements are translated into security services, security quality that needs to be provided in the security section of the service level agreements. This means that both the client and the plan sub-process have inputs in the SLA and the SLA is an input for both the client and the process. The provider then develops the security plans for his/hers organization. These security plans contain the security policies and the operational level agreements. The security plans (Plan) are then implemented (Do) and the implementation is then evaluated (Check). After the evaluation then both the plans and the implementation of the plan are maintained (Act).

The activities, results/products and the process are documented. External reports are written and sent to the clients. The clients are then able to adapt their requirements based on the information received through the reports. Furthermore, the service provider can adjust their plan or the implementation based on their findings in order to satisfy all the requirements stated in the SLA (including new requirements).

#### *4.1.2.1 Control*

The first activity in the security management process is the "Control" sub-process. The Control sub-process organizes and manages the security management process itself. The Control sub-process defines the processes, the allocation of responsibility the policy statements and the management framework.

The security management framework defines the sub-processes for: the development of security plans, the implementation of the security plans, the evaluation and how the results of the evaluations are translated into action plans. Furthermore, the management framework defines how should be reported to clients.

The activities that take place in the Control process are summed up in the following table, which contains the name of the (sub) activity and a short definition of the activity.

**Table 4.1**

| Activities | Sub-Activities | Descriptions |
|---|---|---|
| Control | Implement policies | This process outlines the specific requirements and rules that have to be met in order to implement security management. The process ends with policy statement. |
| | Setup the security organization | This process sets up the organizations for information security. For example in this process the structure the responsibilities are set up. This process ends with security management framework. |
| | Reporting | In this process the whole targeting process is documented in a specific way. This process ends with reports. |

The meta-modeling technique was used in order to model the activities of the control sub-process. The following figure is the meta-process model of the control sub-process. It is based on a UML activity diagram and it gives an overview of the activities of the Control sub-process. The grey rectangle represents the control sub-process and the smaller beam shapes inside of the grey rectangle represent the activities that take place inside the control sub-process. The beams with a black shadow indicate that the activity is a closed (complex) activity. This means that the activity consists of a collection of (sub) activities but these activities are not expanded because they are not relevant in this particular context. The white beam without shadow indicates that the reporting activity is a standard activity. This means that reporting does not contain (sub) activities.

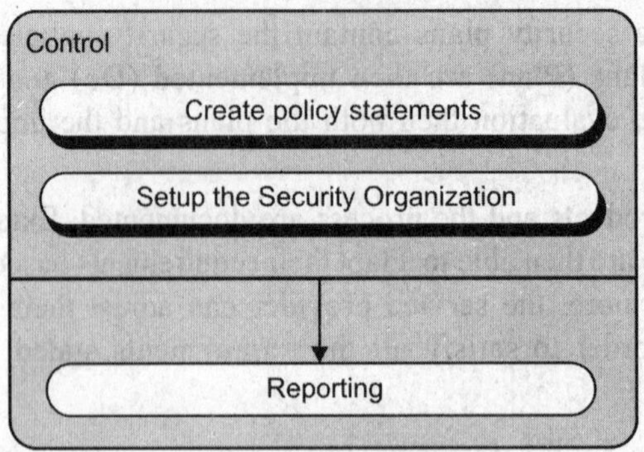


**Fig. 4.1:** Meta-process Model Control Sub-process

Furthermore, it is noticeable that the first two activities are not linked with an arrow and that there is black stripe with an arrow leading to the reporting activity. This means that the two first activities are not sequential. They are unordered activities and after these two activities have taken place the reporting activity will sequentially follow. For a more extensive explanation of the meta-modeling technique consult the Meta-modeling

The following table (table 4.2) is a concept definition table.

**Table 4.2:** Concept and Definition Control Sub-process Security Management

| Concept | Description |
|---|---|
| CONTROL DOCUMENTS | Control is a description of how SECURITY MANAGEMENT will be organized and how it will be managed. |
| POLICY STATEMENTS | POLICY STATEMENTS are documents that outlines specific requirements or rules that must be met. In the information security realm, policies are usually point-specific, covering a single area. For example, an "Acceptable Use" policy would cover the rules and regulations for appropriate use of the computing facilities. |
| SECURITY MANAGEMENT FRAMEWORK | SECURITY MANAGEMENT FRAMEWORK is an established management framework to initiate and control the implementation of information security within your organization and to manage ongoing information security provision. |

The meta-data model of the control sub-process is based on a UML class diagram. In figure 4.2 is the meta-data model of the control sub-process.

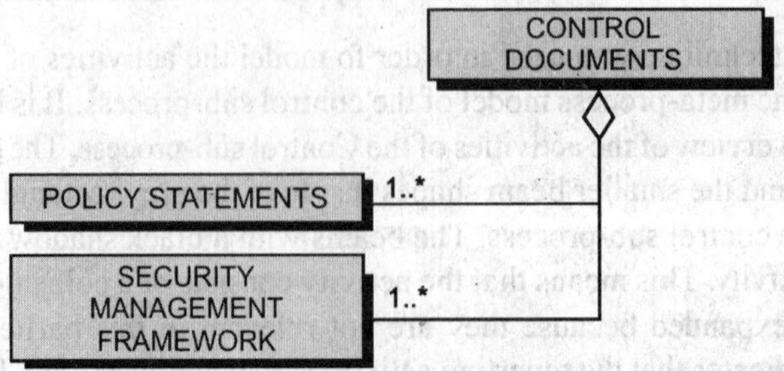


**Fig. 4.2:** Meta-process Model Control Sub-process

The CONTROL rectangle with a white shadow is an open complex concept. This means that the CONTROL rectangle consists of a collection of (sub) concepts and these concepts are expanded in this particular context.

The following picture (figure 4.3) is the process-data model of the control sub-process. This picture shows the integration of the two models. The dotted arrows indicate which concepts are created or adjusted in the corresponding activities.

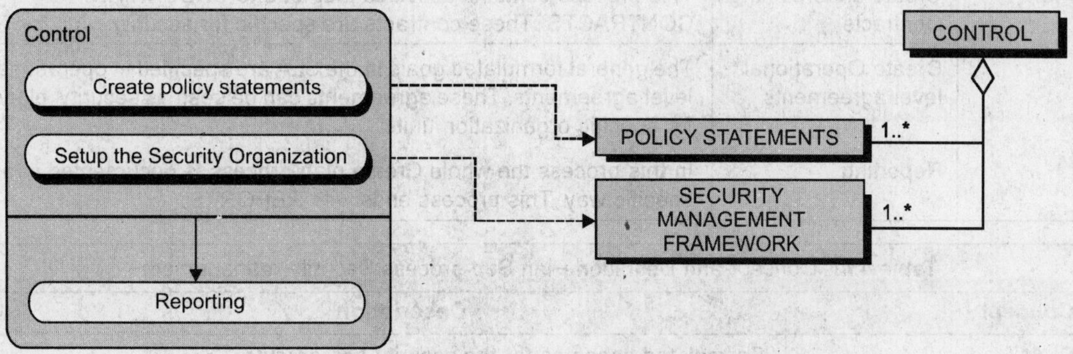


**Fig. 4.3:** Process-data Model Control Sub-process

#### *4.1.2.2 Plan*

The Plan sub-process contains activities that in cooperation with the Service Level Management lead to the (information) Security section in the SLA. Furthermore, the Plan sub-process contains activities that are related to the underpinning contracts which are specific for (information) security.

In the Plan sub-process the goals formulated in the SLA are specified in the form of Operational Level Agreements (OLA). These OLA's can be defined as security plans for a specific internal organization entity of the service provider.

Besides the input of the SLA, the Plan sub-process also works with the policy statements of the service provider itself. As said earlier these policy statements are defined in the control sub-process.

The Operational Level Agreements for information security are setup and implemented based on the ITIL process. This means that there has to be cooperation with other ITIL processes. For example if the security management wishes to change the IT infrastructure in order to achieve maximum security, these changes will only be done through the Change Management process. The Security Management will deliver the input (Request for change) for this change. The change Manager is responsible for the Change Management Process itself. Table 4.3 shows the activity plan the (sub) activities and their definition.

As well as for the Control sub-process the Plan sub-process has been modeled using the meta-modeling technique. The meta-process model of the Plan sub-process is given in the figure 4.4.

As you can see the Plan sub-process consists of a combination of unordered and ordered (sub) activities. Furthermore, it is noticeable that the sub-process contains three complex activities which are all closed activities and one standard activity. Table 4.4 consists of concepts that are created or adjusted during the plan sub-process. The table also gives a definition of these concepts.

**Table 4.3:** (Sub) activities and descriptions Plan sub-process ITIL Security Management

| Activities | Sub-Activities | Descriptions |
|---|---|---|
| Plan | Create Security section for SLA | This process contains activities that lead to the security agreements paragraph in the service level agreements. At the end of this process the *Security* section of the service level agreement is created. |
| | Create underpinning Contracts | This process contains activities that lead to UNDERPINNING CONTRACTS. These contracts are specific for security. |
| | Create Operational level agreements | The general formulated goals in the SLA are specified in operational level agreements. These agreements can be seen as security plans for specific organization units. |
| | Reporting | In this process the whole Create plan process is documented in a specific way. This process ends with REPORTS. |

**Table 4.4:** Concept and Definition Plan Sub-process Security management

| Concept | Description |
|---|---|
| PLAN | Formulated schemes for the security agreements. |
| SECURITY SECTION OF THE SECURITY LEVEL AGREEMENTS | The security agreements paragraph in the written agreements between a Service Provider and the customer(s) that documents agreed Service Levels for a service. |
| UNDERPINNING CONTRACTS | A contract with an external supplier covering delivery of services that support the IT organisation in their delivery of services. |
| OPERATIONAL LEVEL AGREEMENTS | An internal agreement covering the delivery of services which support the IT organization in their delivery of services. |

Just as the Control sub-process the Plan sub-process is modeled using the meta-modeling technique. The figure 4.4 is the meta-data model of the Plan sub-process.

The Plan rectangle is an open (complex) concept which has an aggregation type of relationship with two closed (complex) concepts and one standard concept. The two closed concepts are not expanded in this particular context.

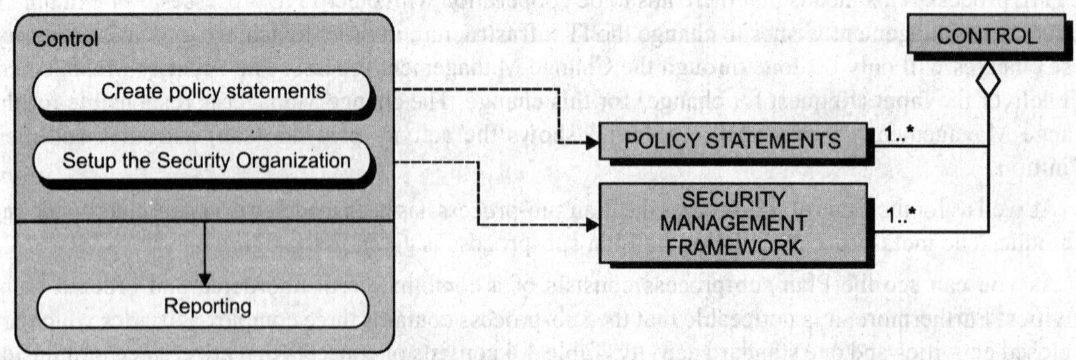


**Fig. 4.4:** Process-data model Plan sub-process

The figure 4.4 is the process-data diagram of the Plan sub-process. This picture shows the integration of the two models. The dotted arrows indicate which concepts are created or adjusted in the corresponding activities of the Plan sub-process.

### *4.1.2.3 Implementation*

The Implementation sub-process makes sure that all measures, as specified in the plans, are properly implemented. During the Implementation sub-process no (new) measures are defined nor changed. The definition or change of measures will take place in the Plan sub-process in cooperation with the Change Management Process.

The activities that take place in the implementation sub-process are summed up in the following table (table 4.5). The table contains the name of the (sub) activity and a short definition of the activity.

**Table 4.5:** (Sub) activities and descriptions Implementation sub-process ITIL Security Management

| Activities | Sub-Activities | Descriptions |
|---|---|---|
| | Classifying and managing of IT applications | Process of formally grouping configuration items by type, e.g., software, hardware, documentation, environment, application. Process of formally identifying changes by type e.g., project scope change request, validation change request, infrastructure change request this process leads to asset classification and control documents. |
| | Implement personnel security | Here measures are adopted in order to give personnel safety and confidence and measures to prevent a crime/fraud. The process ends with personnel security. |
| Implement | Implement security management | In this process specific security requirements and/or security rules that must be met are outlined and documented. The process ends with security policies. |
| | Implement access control | In this process specific access security requirements and/or access security rules that must be met are outlined and documented. The process ends with access control. |
| | Reporting | In this process the whole implement as planned process is documented in a specific way. This process ends with reports. |

The figure 4.5 is the meta-process model of the Implementation phase. The four labels with a black shadow mean that these activities are closed concepts and they are not expanded in this context. It is also noticeable that there are no arrows connecting these four activities this means that these activities are unordered and the reporting will be carried out after the completion of all the four activities.

During the implementation phase there are a number of concepts that are created and /or adjusted. See table 4.6 for an overview of the most common concepts and their description.

The concepts created and/or adjusted are modeled using the meta-modeling technique. The figure 4.5 is the meta-data model of the implementation sub-process.

The implementation documents are an open concept and is expanded upon in this context. It consists of four closed concepts which are not expanded because they are irrelevant in this particular context.

**Table 4.6:** Concept and Definition Implementation Sub-process Security Management

| Concept | Description |
|---|---|
| Implementation | Accomplished security management according to the security management plan. |
| Asset classification and control documents | A comprehensive inventory of assets with responsibility assigned to ensure that effective security protection is maintained. |
| Personnel security | Well defined job descriptions for all staff outlining security roles and responsibilities. |
| Security policies | Security policies are documents that outlines specific security requirements or security rules that must be met. |
| Access control | Network management to ensure that only those with the appropriate responsibility have access to information in the networks and the protection of the supporting infrastructure. |

In order to make the relations between the two models clearer the integration of the two models are illustrated in figure 4.5. The dotted arrows running from the activities to the concepts illustrate which concepts are created/ adjusted in the corresponding activities.

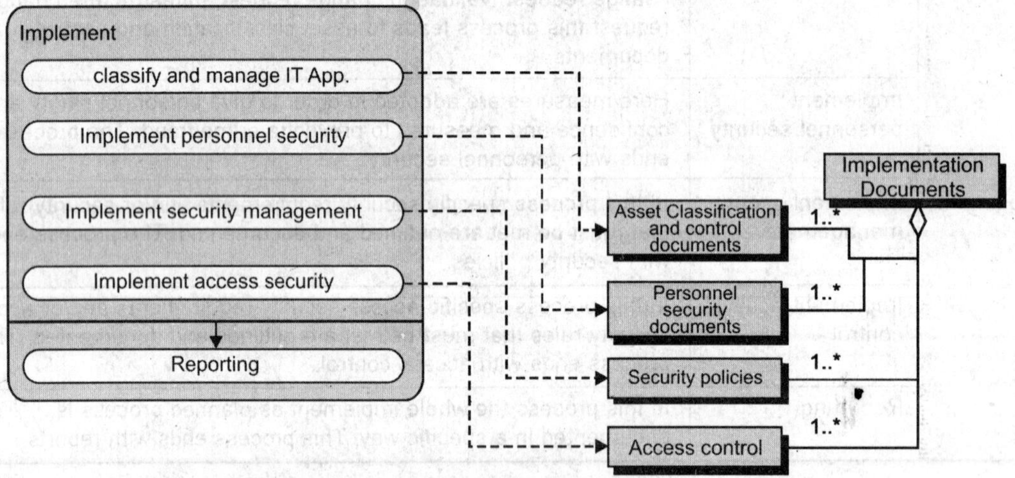


**Fig. 4.5:** Process-data model Implementation sub-process

### *4.1.2.4 Evaluation*

The evaluation of the implementation and the plans is very important. The evaluation is necessary to measure the success of the implementation and the Security plans. The evaluation is also very important for the clients (and possibly third parties). The results of the Evaluation sub-process are used to maintain the agreed measures and the implementation itself. The request for change is then defined and it is then send to the Change Management process.

Mainly there are three sorts of evaluation; the Self assessment; internal audit, and external audit.

The self assessment is mainly carried out in the organization of the processes. The internal audits are carried out by internal IT-auditors and the external audits are carried out by external independent IT-auditors. Besides, the evaluations already mentioned an evaluation based on the communicated security incidents will also take place. The most important activities for this evaluation are the security monitoring of IT-systems; verify if the security legislation and the implementation of the security plans are complied; trace and react to undesirable use of the IT-supplies.

The activities that take place in the evaluation sub-process are summed up in the following table (Table 4.7). The table contains the name of the (sub) activity and a short definition of the activity.

**Table 4.7:** (Sub) Activities and Descriptions Evaluation Sub-process ITIL Security Management

| Activities | Sub-Activities | Descriptions |
|---|---|---|
| Evaluate | Self assessment | In this process an examination of the implemented security agreements is done by the organization of the process it self. The result of this process is SELF ASSESSMENT DOCUMENTS. |
| | Internal Audit | In this process an examination of the implemented security agreements is done by an internal EDP auditor. The result of this process is INTERNAL AUDIT. |
| | External audit | In this process an examination of the implemented security agreements is done by an external EDP auditor. The result of this process is EXTERNAL AUDIT. |
| | Evaluation based on security incidents | In this process an examination of the implemented security agreements is done based on security events which is not part of the standard operation of a service and which causes, or may cause, an interruption to, or a reduction in, the quality of that service. The result of this process is SECURITY INCIDENTS. |
| | Reporting | In this process the whole Evaluate implementation process is documented in a specific way. This process ends with REPORTS. |

The process-data diagram illustrated in the figure 4.6 consists of a meta-process model and a meta-data model. The Evaluation sub-process was modeled using the meta-modeling technique. The dotted arrows running from the meta-process diagram (left) to the meta-data diagram (right) indicate which concepts are created/ adjusted in the corresponding activities. All of the activities in the evaluation phase are standard activities. For a short description of the Evaluation phase concepts see Table 4.8 where the concepts are listed and defined.

**Table 4.8:** Concept and definition evaluation sub-process Security management

| Concept | Description |
|---|---|
| EVALUATION | Evaluated/checked implementation. |
| RESULTS | The outcome of the evaluated implementation. |
| SELF ASSESSMENT DOCUMENTS | Result of the examination of the security management by the organization of the process itself. |
| INTERNAL AUDIT | Result of the examination of the security management by the internal EDP auditor. |

| | |
|---|---|
| EXTERNAL AUDIT | Result of the examination of the security management by the external EDP auditor. |
| SECURITY INCIDENTS DOCUMENTS | Results of evaluating security events which is not part of the standard operation of a service and which causes, or may cause, an interruption to, or a reduction in, the quality of that service. |

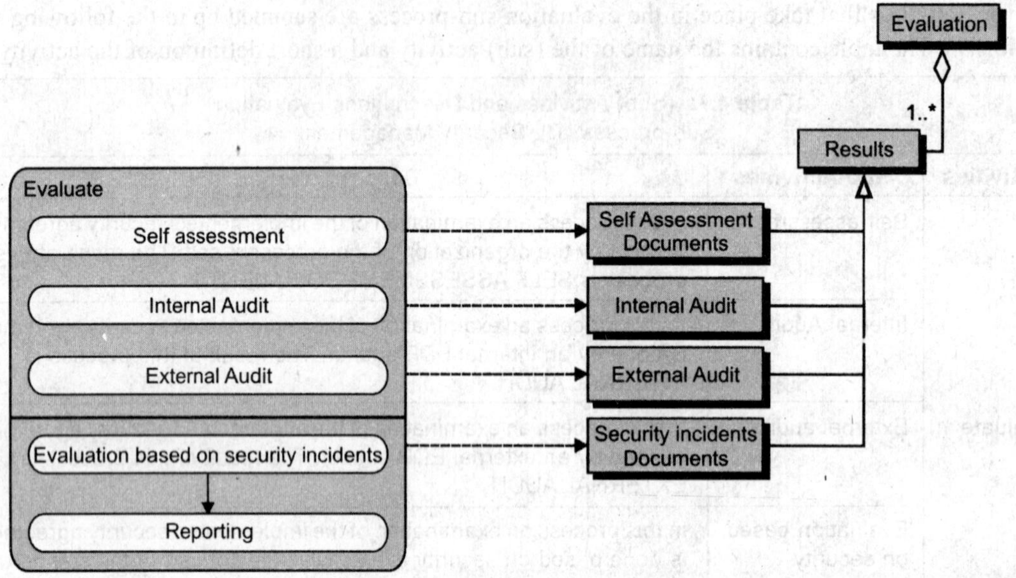


**Fig. 4.6:** Process-data Model Evaluation Sub-process

### 4.1.2.5 Maintenance

It is necessary for the security to be maintained. Because of changes in the IT-infrastructure and changes in the organization itself security risks are bound to change over time. The maintenance of the security concerns both the maintenance of the security section of the service level agreements and the more detailed security plans.

The maintenance is based on the results of the Evaluation sub-process and insight in the changing risks. These activities will only produce proposals. The proposals serve as inputs for the plan sub-process and will go through the whole cycle or the proposals can be taken in the maintenance of the service level agreements. In both cases the proposals could lead to activities in the action plan. The actual changes will be carried by the Change Management process. The activities that take place in the maintain sub-process are summed up in the following table (Table 4.9). The table contains the name of the (sub) activity and a short definition of the activity.

Figure 4.7 is the process-data diagram of the implementation sub-process. This picture shows the integration of the meta-process model (left) and the meta-data model (right). The dotted arrows indicate which concepts are created or adjusted in the activities of the implementation phase.

| **Table 4.9:** (Sub) activities and descriptions Maintenance sub-process ITIL Security Management | | |
|---|---|---|
| **Activities** | **Sub-Activities** | **Descriptions** |
| Maintain | Maintenance of Service level agreements | This is a process to keep the service level agreements in proper condition. The process ends with MAINTAINED SERVICE LEVEL AGREEMENTS. |
| | Maintenance of operational level agreements | This is a process to keep the operational level agreements in proper condition. The process ends with MAINTAINED OPERATIONAL LEVEL AGREEMENTS. |
| | Request for change to SLA and/or OLA | Request for a change to the SLA and/or OLA is formulated. This process ends with a REQUEST FOR CHANGE. |
| | Reporting | In this process the whole maintain implemented security policies process is documented in a specific way. This process ends with REPORTS. |

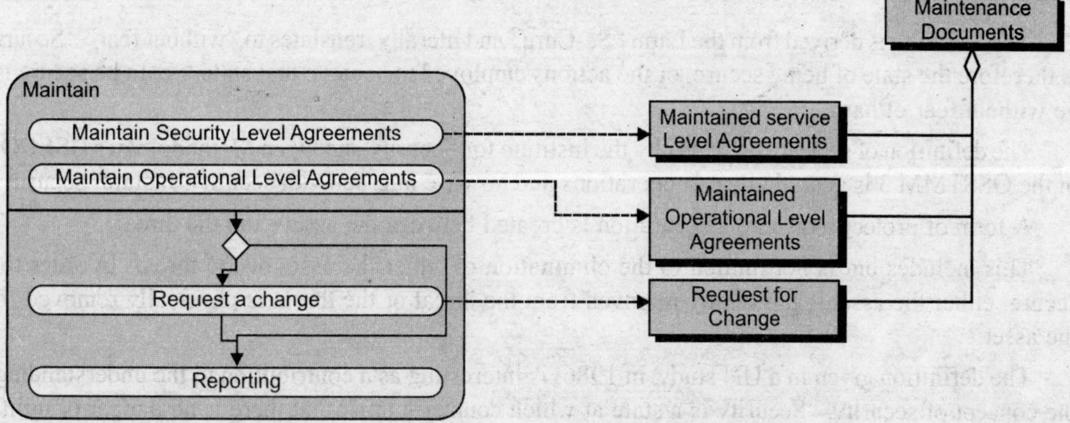


**Fig. 4.7:** Process-data model Maintenance Sub-process

The maintenance sub-process starts with the maintenance of the service level agreements and the maintenance of the operational level agreements. After these activities take place (in no particular order) and there is a request for a change the request for change activity will take place and after the request for change activity is concluded the reporting activity starts. If there is no request for a change then the reporting activity will start directly after the first two activities. The concepts in the meta-data model are created/ adjusted during the maintenance phase. For a list of the concepts and their definition take a look at table 4.10.

| **Table 4.10:** Concept and definition Plan sub-process Security management | |
|---|---|
| **Concept** | **Description** |
| EVALUATION | Evaluated/checked implementation. |
| MAINTENANCE DOCUMENTS | Agreements kept in proper condition. |
| MAINTAINED SERVICE LEVEL AGREEMENTS | Service Level Agreements (security paragraph) kept in proper condition. |

| | |
|---|---|
| MAINTAINED OPERATIONAL LEVEL AGREEMENTS | Operational Level Agreements kept in proper condition. |
| REQUEST FOR CHANGE | Form, or screen, used to record details of a request for a change to the SLA/OLA. |

## 4.2 SECURITY

Security is the degree of protection against danger, loss, and criminals.

Security has to be compared and contrasted with other related concepts: Safety, continuity, reliability. The key difference between security and reliability is that security must take into account the actions of people attempting to cause destruction.

### 4.2.1 Definitions

The word security is derived from the Latin "Se-Cura" and literally translates to "without fear". 'Security' is therefore the state of being secure, or the actions employed to achieve that state, i.e. to be secure is to be without fear of harm.

The definition of security provided by the Institute for Security and Open Methodologies (ISECOM) in the OSSTMM 3 is geared towards operations and how we interact with security. It states security is:

A form of protection where a separation is created between the assets and the threat.

This includes but is not limited to the elimination of either the asset or the threat. In order to be secure, either the asset is physically removed from the threat or the threat is physically removed from the asset.

The definition given in a UN study, in 1986, is interesting as a contribution to the understanding of the concept of security, "Security is a state at which countries think that there is no danger of military attack, political pressure, or economic coercion, so that they can develop and progress freely.

With respect to classified matter, the condition that prevents unauthorized persons from having to official that is safeguarded in the interests of .

Measures taken by a military unit, an activity or installation to protect itself against all acts designed to, or which may, impair its effectiveness.

### 4.2.2 Perceived Security Compared to Real Security

It is very often true that people's perception of security is not directly related to actual security.

For example, a fear of earthquakes is much more common than a fear of slipping on the bathroom floor; however, the latter kills far more people than the former.

The tool may be mistaken for the effect, for example when multiple computer security programs interfere with each other, the user assumes the computer is secure when actual security has vanished.

Another side of this is a phenomenon called security theatre where ineffective security measures such as screening of airline passengers based on static databases are introduced with little real increase in security or even, according to the critics of one such measure — Computer Assisted Passenger Prescreening System — with an actual decrease in real security.

Conversely, if it is perceived that there is security then there will be an increase in actual security, even if the perception of security is mistaken. Sometimes a sign may warn that video surveillance is covering an area, and even if there is no actual visual surveillance then some malicious agents will be deterred by the belief that there may be.

Also, often when there is actual security present in the area, such as video surveillance, an alarm system in a home, or an anti-theft system in a car such as a LoJack, signs advertising this security will increase its effectiveness, protecting the value of the secured vehicle or area itself.

Since some intruders will decide not to attempt to break into such areas or vehicles, there can actually be less damage to windows in addition to protection of valuable objects inside. Without such advertisement, a car-thief might, for example, approach a car, break the window, and then flee in response to an alarm being triggered. Either way, perhaps the car itself and the objects inside aren't stolen, but with perceived security even the windows of the car have a lower chance of being damaged, increasing the financial security of its owner(s).

However, the non-profit, security research group, ISECOM, has determined that such signs may actually increase the violence, daring, and desperation of an intruder. This claim shows that perceived security works mostly on the provider and is not security at all

It is important, however, for signs advertising security not to give clues as to how to subvert that security, for example in the case where a home burglar might be more likely to break into a certain home if he or she is able to learn beforehand which company makes its security system.

### 4.2.3 Categorising Security

There is an immense literature on the analysis and categorisation of security. Part of the reason for this is that, in most security systems, the "weakest link in the chain" is the most important. The situation is asymmetric since the defender must cover all points of attack while the attacker need only identify a single weak point upon which to concentrate.

**Table: 4.11:** Types of security

| IT realm | Physical realm | Political | Monetary |
|---|---|---|---|
| Application security | Airport security | Homeland security | Financial security |
| Computing security | Port security/Supply chain security | Human security | |
| Data security | Food security | International security | |
| Information security | Home security | National security | |
| Network security | Hospital security | Public security | |
| | Physical security | | |
| | Shopping centre security | | |
| | Infrastructure security | | |

Aviation security is a combination of measures and material and human resources intended to counter the unlawful interference with the aviation security.

Operations Security (OPSEC) is a compliment to other "traditional" security measures that evaluates the organization from an adversarial perspective.

### 4.2.4 Security Concepts

Certain concepts recur throughout different fields of security:

**Assurance** — assurance is the level of guarantee that a security system will behave as expected

**Countermeasure** — a countermeasure is a way to stop a threat from triggering a risk event

**Defense in depth** — never rely on one single security measure alone

**Exploit** — a vulnerability that has been triggered by a threat - a risk of 1.0 (100%)

**Risk** — a risk is a possible event which could cause a loss

**Threat** — a threat is a method of triggering a risk event that is dangerous

**Vulnerability** — a weakness in a target that can potentially be exploited by a threat

### 4.2.5 Security Management In Organizations

In the corporate world, various aspects of security were historically addressed separately - notably by distinct and often non-communicating departments for IT security, physical security, and fraud prevention. Today there is a greater recognition of the interconnected nature of security requirements, an approach variously known as holistic security, "all hazards" management, and other terms.

Inciting factors in the convergence of security disciplines include the development of digital video surveillance technologies and the digitization and networking of physical control systems. Greater interdisciplinary cooperation is further evidenced by the February 2005 creation of the Alliance for Enterprise Security Risk Management, a joint venture including leading associations in security (ASIS), information security (ISSA, the Information Systems Security Association), and IT audit (ISACA, the Information Systems Audit and Control Association).

## 4.3 COMPUTER SECURITY

**Computer security** is a branch of technology known as information security as applied to computers and networks. The objective of computer security includes protection of information and property from theft, corruption, or natural disaster, while allowing the information and property to remain accessible and productive to its intended users.

**Table: 4.12**

| Computer Security | Computer Insecurity | |
|---|---|---|
| Secure operating systems<br>Security architecture<br>Security by design<br>Secure coding | **Vulnerability** | Social engineering<br>Eavesdropping |
| | **Exploit** | Trojan<br>viruses and worms<br>Denial of service |
| | **Payload** | Backdoor<br>Rootkit<br>Keylogger |

### 4.3.1 Security by Design

The technologies of computer security are based on logic. As security is not necessarily the primary goal of most computer applications, designing a program with security in mind often imposes restrictions on that program's behavior.

There are several approaches to security in computing, sometimes a combination of approaches is valid:

- Trust all the software to abide by a security policy but the software is not trustworthy (this is computer insecurity).
- Trust all the software to abide by a security policy and the software is validated as trustworthy (by tedious branch and path analysis for example).
- Trust no software but enforce a security policy with mechanisms that are not trustworthy (again this is computer insecurity).
- Trust no software but enforce a security policy with trustworthy mechanisms.

Many systems have unintentionally resulted in the first possibility. Since approach two is expensive and non-deterministic, its use is very limited. Approaches one and three lead to failure. Because approach number four is often based on hardware mechanisms and avoids abstractions and a multiplicity of degrees of freedom, it is more practical. Combinations of approaches two and four are often used in a layered architecture with thin layers of two and thick layers of four.

There are various strategies and techniques used to design security systems. However there are few, if any, effective strategies to enhance security after design. One technique enforces the principle of least privilege to great extent, where an entity has only the privileges that are needed for its function. That way even if an attacker gains access to one part of the system, fine-grained security ensures that it is just as difficult for them to access the rest.

Furthermore, by breaking the system up into smaller components, the complexity of individual components is reduced, opening up the possibility of using techniques such as automated theorem proving to prove the correctness of crucial software subsystems. This enables a closed form solution to security that works well when only a single well-characterized property can be isolated as critical, and that property is also assessable to math. Not surprisingly, it is impractical for generalized correctness, which probably cannot even be defined, much less proven. Where formal correctness proofs are not possible, rigorous use of code review and unit testing represent a best-effort approach to make modules secure.

The design should use "defense in depth", where more than one subsystem needs to be violated to compromise the integrity of the system and the information it holds. Defense in depth works when the breaching of one security measure does not provide a platform to facilitate subverting another. Also, the cascading principle acknowledges that several low hurdles does not make a high hurdle. So cascading several weak mechanisms does not provide the safety of a single stronger mechanism.

Subsystems should default to secure settings, and wherever possible should be designed to "fail secure" rather than "fail insecure" .Ideally, a secure system should require a deliberate, conscious, knowledgeable and free decision on the part of legitimate authorities in order to make it insecure.

In addition, security should not be an all or nothing issue. The designers and operators of systems should assume that security breaches are inevitable. Full audit trails should be kept of system activity, so that when a security breach occurs, the mechanism and extent of the breach can be determined. Storing audit trails remotely, where they can only be appended to, can keep intruders from covering their tracks. Finally, full disclosure helps to ensure that when bugs are found the "window of vulnerability" is kept as short as possible.

### 4.3.2 Early History of Security by Design

The early Multics operating system was notable for its early emphasis on computer security by design, and Multics was possibly the very first operating system to be designed as a secure system from the ground up. In spite of this, Multics' security was broken, not once, but repeatedly. The strategy was known as 'penetrate and test' and has become widely known as a non-terminating process that fails to produce computer security. This led to further work on computer security that prefigured modern security engineering techniques producing closed form processes that terminate.

### 4.3.3 Security Architecture

Security Architecture can be defined as the design artifacts that describe how the security controls (security countermeasures) are positioned, and how they relate to the overall information technology architecture. These controls serve the purpose to maintain the system's quality attributes, among them confidentiality, integrity, availability, accountability and assurance." A security architecture is the plan that shows where security measures need to be placed. If the plan describes a specific solution then, prior to building such a plan, one would make a risk analysis. If the plan describes a generic high level design (reference architecture) then the plan should be based on a threat analysis.

### 4.3.4 Hardware Mechanisms that Protect Computers and Data

Hardware based or assisted computer security offers an alternative to software-only computer security. Devices such as dongles may be considered more secure due to the physical access required in order to be compromised.

While many software based security solutions encrypt the data to prevent data from being stolen, a malicious program or a hacker may corrupt the data in order to make it unrecoverable or unusable. Similarly, encrypted operating systems can be corrupted by a malicious program or a hacker, making the system unusable. Hardware-based security solutions can prevent read and write access to data and hence offers very strong protection against tampering and unauthorized access.

Working of hardware based security: A hardware device allows a user to login, logout and to set different privilege levels by doing manual actions. The device uses biometric technology to prevent malicious users from logging in, logging out, and changing privilege levels. The current state of a user of the device is read both by a computer and controllers in peripheral devices such as harddisks. Illegal access by a malicious user or a malicious program is interrupted based on the current state of a user by harddisk and DVD controllers making illegal access to data impossible. Hardware based access control is more secure than logging in and logging out using operating systems as operating systems are vulnerable to malicious attacks. Since software cannot manipulate the user privilege levels, it is impossible for a hacker or a malicious program to gain access to secure data protected by hardware or perform unauthorized privileged operations. The hardware protects the operating system image and file system privileges from being tampered. Therefore, a completely secure system can be created using a combination of hardware based security and secure system administration policies.

### 4.3.5 Applications

Computer security is critical in almost any technology-driven industry which operates on computer systems. Computer security can also be referred to as computer safety. The issues of computer based systems and addressing their countless vulnerabilities are an integral part of maintaining an operational industry.

### 4.3.6 Terminology

The following terms used in engineering secure systems are explained below.

1. **Authentication techniques** can be used to ensure that communication end-points are who they say they are.
2. **Automated theorem** proving and other verification tools can enable critical algorithms and code used in secure systems to be mathematically proven to meet their specifications.
3. **Capability and access control list** techniques can be used to ensure privilege separation and mandatory access control. The next sections discuss their use.
4. **Chain of trust techniques** can be used to attempt to ensure that all software loaded has been certified as authentic by the system's designers.
5. **Cryptographic techniques** can be used to defend data in transit between systems, reducing the probability that data exchanged between systems can be intercepted or modified.
6. **Firewalls** can provide some protection from online intrusion.
7. **Mandatory access control** can be used to ensure that privileged access is withdrawn when privileges are revoked. For example, deleting a user account should also stop any processes that are running with that user's privileges.
8. **Secure cryptoprocessors** can be used to leverage physical security techniques into protecting the security of the computer system. microkernels can be reliable against errors: eg EROS and Coyotos.

Some of the following items may belong to the computer insecurity:

1. **Access authorization** restricts access to a computer to group of users through the use of authentication systems. These systems can protect either the whole computer — such as through an interactive logon screen — or individual services, such as an FTP server. There are many methods for identifying and authenticating users, such as passwords, identification cards, and, more recently, smart cards and biometric systems.
2. **Anti-virus software** consists of computer programs that attempt to identify, thwart and eliminate computer viruses and other malicious software (malware).
3. **Application with known security flaws** should not be run. Either leave it turned off until it can be patched or otherwise fixed, or delete it and replace it with some other application. Publicly known flaws are the main entry used by worms to automatically break into a system and then spread to other systems connected to it. The security website Secunia provides a search tool for unpatched known flaws in popular products.

4. **Cryptographic techniques** involve transforming information, scrambling it so it becomes unreadable during transmission. The intended recipient can unscramble the message, but eavesdroppers cannot.

   Backups are a way of securing information; they are another copy of all the important computer files kept in another location. These files are kept on hard disks, CD-Rs, CD-RWs, and tapes. Suggested locations for backups are a fireproof, waterproof, and heat proof safe, or in a separate, offsite location than that in which the original files are contained. Some individuals and companies also keep their backups in safe deposit boxes inside bank vaults. There is also a fourth option, which involves using one of the file hosting services that backs up files over the Internet for both business and individuals.

5. **Backups** are also important for reasons other than security. Natural disasters, such as earthquakes, hurricanes, or tornadoes, may strike the building where the computer is located. The building can be on fire, or an explosion may occur. There needs to be a recent backup at an alternate secure location, in case of such kind of disaster. Further, it is recommended that the alternate location be placed where the same disaster would not affect both locations. Examples of alternate disaster recovery sites being compromised by the same disaster that affected the primary site include having had a primary site in World Trade Center I and the recovery site in 7 World Trade Center, both of which were destroyed in the 9/11 attack, and having one's primary site and recovery site in the same coastal region, which leads to both being vulnerable to hurricane damage (e.g. primary site in New Orleans and recovery site in Jefferson Parish, both of which were hit by Hurricane Katrina in 2005). The backup media should be moved between the geographic sites in a secure manner, in order to prevent them from being stolen.
6. **Encryption** is used to protect the message from the eyes of others. It can be done in several ways by switching the characters around, replacing characters with others, and even removing characters from the message. These have to be used in combination to make the encryption secure enough, that is to say, sufficiently difficult to crack. Public key encryption is a refined and practical way of doing encryption. It allows for example anyone to write a message for a list of recipients, and only those recipients will be able to read that message.
7. **Firewalls** are systems which help protect computers and computer networks from attack and subsequent intrusion by restricting the network traffic which can pass through them, based on a set of system administrator defined rules.
8. **Honey pots** are computers that are either intentionally or unintentionally left vulnerable to attack by crackers. They can be used to catch crackers or fix vulnerabilities.
9. **Intrusion-detection** systems can scan a network for people that are on the network but who should not be there or are doing things that they should not be doing, for example trying a lot of passwords to gain access to the network.
10. **Pinging:** The ping application can be used by potential crackers to find if an IP address is reachable. If a cracker finds a computer they can try a port scan to detect and attack services on that computer.
11. **Social engineering awareness** keeps employees aware of the dangers of social engineering and/or having a policy in place to prevent social engineering can reduce successful breaches of the network and servers.
12. **File Integrity Monitors** are tools used to detect changes in the integrity of systems and files.

## 4.4 INTERNET SECURITY

When a computer connects to a network and begins communicating with others, it is taking a risk. **Internet security** involves the protection of a computer's internet account and files from intrusion of an unknown user. Basic security measures involve protection by well selected passwords, change of file permissions and back up of computer's data.

Security concerns are in some ways peripheral to normal business working, but serve to highlight just how important it is that business users feel confident when using IT systems. Security will probably always be high on the IT agenda simply because cyber criminals know that a successful attack is very profitable. This means they will always strive to find new ways to circumvent IT security, and users will consequently need to be continually vigilant. Whenever decisions need to be made about how to enhance a system, security will need to be held uppermost among its requirements.

Internet security professionals should be fluent in the four major aspects:

1. Penetration testing
2. Intrusion Detection
3. Incidence Response
4. Legal / Audit Compliance

### 4.4.1 Anti-virus

Some apparently useful programs also contain features with hidden malicious intent. Such programs are known as Malware, Viruses, Trojans, Worms, Spyware and Bots.

1. **Malware** is the most general name for any malicious software designed for example to infiltrate, spy on or damage a computer or other programmable device or system of sufficient complexity, such as a home or office computer system, network, mobile phone, PDA, automated device or robot.
2. **Viruses** are programs which are able to replicate their structure or effect by integrating themselves or references to themselves, etc into existing files or structures on a penetrated computer. They usually also have a malicious or humorous payload designed to threaten or modify the actions or data of the host device or system without consent. For example by deleting, corrupting or otherwise hiding information from its owner.
3. **Trojans** (Trojan Horses are programs which may pretend to do one thing, but in reality steal information, alter it or cause other problems on a such as a computer or programmable device / system. Trojans can be hard to detect.
4. **Worms** are programs which are able to replicate themselves over a (possibly extensive) computer network, and also perform malicious acts that may ultimately affect a whole society / economy.
5. **Spyware** includes programs that surreptitiously monitor keystrokes, or other activity on a computer system and report that information to others without consent.
6. **Bots** are program which take over and use the resources of a computer system over a network without consent, and communicate those results to others who may control the Bots.

The above concepts overlap and they can obviously be combined. The terminology is evolving.

Antivirus programs and Internet security programs are useful in protecting a computer or programmable device / system from malware.

Such programs are used to detect and usually eliminate viruses. Anti-virus software can be purchased or downloaded via the internet. Care should be taken in selecting anti-virus software, as some programs are not as effective as others in finding and eliminating viruses or malware. Also, when downloading anti-virus software from the Internet, one should be cautious as some websites say they are providing protection from viruses with their software, but are really trying to install malware on your computer by disguising it as something else.

### 4.4.2 Anti-spyware

There are two major kinds of threats in relation to spyware:

1. Spyware collects and relays data from the compromised computer to a third-party.
2. Adware automatically plays, displays, or downloads advertisements. Some types of adware are also spyware and can be classified as privacy-invasive software. Adware often are integrated with other software.

### 4.4.3 Buffer Overflow Attacks

A buffer overflow is an attack that could be used by a hacker to get full system access through various methods. It is similar to "Brute Forcing" a computer in that it sends an immense attack to the victim computer until it cracks. Most internet security solutions today lack sufficient protection against these types of attacks.

## 4.5 PHYSICAL SECURITY

**Physical security** describes both measures that prevent or deter attackers from accessing a facility, resource, or information stored on physical media and guidance on how to design structures to resist various hostile acts. It can be as simple as a locked door or as elaborate as multiple layers of armed Security guards and Guardhouse placement.

Physical security, by no means, is a modern phenomenon. Physical security, as a field, exists in order to deter persons from entering a physical facility. Thus, as long as the need to defend physical facilities has existed, a need to provide for their security has also been needed. Historical examples of physical security include city walls, moats, booby traps, etc.

The key factor is the technology used for physical security has changed over time. While in past eras, there was no Passive Infrared (PIR) based technology, electronic access control systems, or Video Surveillance System (VSS) cameras, the essentially methodology of physical security has not altered over time.

### 4.5.1 Elements and Design

The field of security engineering has identified the following elements to physical security: explosion protection; obstacles, to frustrate trivial attackers and delay serious ones; alarms, security lighting, security guard patrols or closed-circuit television cameras, to make it likely that attacks will be noticed; and security response, to repel, catch or frustrate attackers when an attack is detected.

Fig. 4.8: Spikes atop a barrier wall

In a well designed system, these features must complement each other. There are at least four layers of physical security:

- Environmental design
- Mechanical and electronic access control
- Intrusion detection
- Video monitoring

The goal is to convince potential attackers that the likely costs of attack exceed the value of making the attack.

The initial layer of security for a campus, building, office, or physical space uses Crime Prevention Through Environmental Design to deter threats. Some of the most common examples are also the most basic — barbed wire, warning signs and fencing, concrete bollards, metal barriers, vehicle height-restrictors, site lighting and trenches.

The next layer is **mechanical** and includes gates, doors, and locks. Key control of the locks becomes a problem with large user populations and any user turnover. Keys quickly become unmanageable forcing the adoption of **electronic access control**. Electronic access control easily manages large user populations, controlling for user lifecycles times, dates, and individual access points. For example a user's access rights could allow access from 0700 to 1900 Monday through Friday and expires in 90 days.

Fig. 4.9: Electronic access control

An additional sub-layer of mechanical/electronic access control protection is reached by integrating a **key management system** to manage the possession and usage of mechanical keys to locks or property within a building or campus.

The third layer is **intrusion detection** systems or alarms. Intrusion detection monitors for attacks. It is less a preventative measure and more of a response measure, although some would argue that it is a deterrent. Intrusion detection has a high incidence of false alarms. In many jurisdictions, law enforcement will not respond to alarms from intrusion detection systems.

The last layer is **video monitoring** systems. Like intrusion detection, these are not much of a deterrent. Video monitoring systems are more useful for incident verification and historical analysis. For instance, if alarms are being generated and there is a camera in place, the camera could be viewed to verify the alarms. In instances when an attack has already occurred and a camera is in place at the point of attack, the recorded video can be reviewed. Although the term **closed-circuit television (CCTV)** is common, it is quickly becoming outdated as more video systems lose the closed circuit for signal transmission and are instead transmitting on computer networks. Advances in information technology are transforming video monitoring into video analysis. For instance, once an image is digitized it can become data that sophisticated algorithms can act upon. As the speed and accuracy of automated analysis increases, the video system could move from a monitoring system to an intrusion detection system or access control system. It is not a stretch to imagine a video camera inputting data to a processor that outputs to a door lock. Instead of using some kind of key, whether mechanical or electrical, a person's visage is the key.

**Fig. 4.10:** Closed-circuit television sign

Intertwined in these four layers are people. **Guards** have a role in all layers, in the first as patrols and at checkpoints. In the second to administer electronic access control. In the third to respond to alarms. The response force must be able to arrive on site in less time than it is expected that the attacker will require to breach the barriers. And in the fourth to monitor and analyze video. Users obviously have a role also by questioning and reporting suspicious people. Aiding in identifying people as known versus unknown are identification systems. Often photo ID badges are used and are frequently coupled to the electronic access control system. Visitors are often required to wear a visitor badge.

**Fig. 4.11:** Private factory guard

### 4.5.2 Examples of Physical Security

Instances of physical security in everyday life are numerous.

Many installations, serving a myriad of different purposes, have physical obstacles in place to deter intrusion. This can be high walls, barbed wire, glass mounted on top of walls, etc.

The presence of PIR-based motion detectors are common in many places, as a means of noting intrusion into a physical installation. Moreover, VSS/CCTV cameras are becoming increasingly common, as a means of identifying persons who intrude into physical locations.

ATMs (cash dispensers) are protected, not by making them invulnerable, but by spoiling the money inside when they are attacked. Money tainted with a dye could act as a flag to the money's unlawful acquisition.

Safes are rated in terms of the time in minutes which a skilled, well equipped safe-breaker is expected to require to open the safe. These ratings are developed by highly skilled safe breakers employed by insurance agencies, such as Underwriters Laboratories. In a properly designed system, either the time between inspections by a patrolling guard should be less than that time, or an alarm response force should be able to reach it in less than that time.

Hiding the resources, or hiding the fact that resources are valuable, is also often a good idea as it will reduce the exposure to opponents and will cause further delays during an attack, but should not be relied upon as a principal means of ensuring security (see security through obscurity and inside job).

Not all aspects of Physical Security need be high tech. Even something as simple as a thick or pointy bush can add a layer of physical security to some premises, especially in a residential setting. "Home Security Tips".

## 4.6 IDENTITY MANAGEMENT

Identity management or ID management is a broad administrative area that deals with identifying individuals in a system (such as a country, a network or an organization) and controlling the access to the resources in that system by placing restrictions on the established identities.

Identity management is multi-disciplinary and covers many dimensions such as:

- **Technical.** With identity management systems (identification, implementation, administration and termination of identities with access to information systems, buildings and data within an organization).
- **Legal.** Such as legislation for data protection.
- **Police.** For instance for dealing with identity theft.
- **Social and humanity.** Dealing with issues such as privacy.
- **Security.** With elements such as access control.
- **Organizations.**

### 4.6.1 History

Identity management or IDM is a term related to how humans are identified and authorized across computer networks. It covers issues such as how users are given an identity, the protection of that identity and the technologies supporting that protection such as network protocols, digital certificates, passwords and so on.

**Digital identity:** Personal identifying information (PII) selectively exposed over a network.

While the term management requires little explanation, the term identity is a more abstract concept that will always be difficult to define in a way that satisfies everyone. It is a concept that is fluid and contextual depending on a number of factors including culture.

Thus the term management is appended to "identity" to indicate that there is technological and best practices framework around a somewhat intractable philosophical concept. Digital identity can be interpreted as the codification of identity names and attributes of a physical instance in a way that facilitates processing. In each organisation there is normally a role or department that is responsible for managing the schema of digital identities of their staff and their own objects, these represented by object identities or object identifiers

### 4.6.2 Three Perspectives on IdM

In the real-world context of engineering online systems, identity management can involve three perspectives:

1. **The pure identity paradigm:** Creation, management and deletion of identities without regard to access or entitlements;
2. **The user access (log-on) paradigm:** For example: a smart card and its associated data used by a customer to log on to a service or services (a traditional view);
3. **The service paradigm:** A system that delivers personalized, role-based, online, on-demand, multimedia (content), presence-based services to users and their devices.

### 4.6.3 The Pure Identity Paradigm

A general model of identity can be constructed from a small set of axiomatic principles, for example that all identities in a given abstract name space are unique and distinctive, or that such identities bear a specific relationship to corresponding entities in the real world. An axiomatic model of this kind can be considered to express "pure identity" in the sense that the model is not constrained by the context in which it is applied. In general, an entity can have multiple identities, and each identity can consist of multiple attributes or identifiers, some of which are shared and some of which are unique within a given name space.

In most theoretical and all practical models of digital identity, a given identity object consists of a finite set of properties. These properties may be used to record information about the object, either for purposes external to the model itself or so as to assist the model operationally, for example in classification and retrieval. A "pure identity" model is strictly not concerned with the external semantics of these properties.

The most common departure from "pure identity" in practice occurs with properties intended to assure some aspect of identity, for example a digital signature or software token which the model may use internally to verify some aspect of the identity in satisfaction of an external purpose. To the extent that the model attempts to express these semantics internally, it is not a pure model.

Contrast this situation with properties which might be externally used for purposes of information security such as managing access or entitlement, but which are simply stored and retrieved, in other words not treated specially by the model. The absence of external semantics within the model qualifies it as a "pure identity" model.

Identity management, then, can be defined as a set of operations on a given identity model, or as a set of capabilities with reference to it. In practice, identity management is often used to express how identity information is to be provisioned and reconciled between multiple identity models.

### 4.6.4 The User Access Paradigm

Identity management in the user "log-on" perspective may involve an integrated system of business processes, policies and technologies that enable organizations to facilitate and control access by their users to critical online applications and resources — while protecting confidential personal and business information from unauthorized access. It represents a category of interrelated solutions which system administrators employ towards managing user authentication, Access rights and restrictions, account profiles, passwords, and other attributes supportive of the roles/profiles of user in relation to applications and/or systems. Organizations have traditionally been less concerned with how users can verify the identity of service providers. The emergence of phishing attacks demonstrated that this must be considered as an integral part of the user access paradigm, otherwise users can not know which services they access. Petname systems have been proposed as a general approach to providing service provider identity management solutions.

### 4.6.5 The Service Paradigm

In the service paradigm perspective, where organizations evolve their systems to the world of converged services, the scope of identity management becomes much larger, and its application more critical. The scope of identity management includes all the resources of the company deployed to deliver online services. These may include devices, network equipment, servers, portals, content, applications and/or products as well as a user's credentials, address books, preferences, entitlements and telephone numbers.

Today, many organizations face a major clean-up in their systems if they are to bring identity coherence into their influence. Such coherence has become a prerequisite for delivering unified services to very large numbers of users on demand — cheaply, with security and single-customer viewing facilities.

### 4.6.6 Emerging Fundamental Points

IdM provides significantly greater opportunities to online businesses beyond the process of authenticating and granting access to authorized users via cards, tokens and web access control systems.

- IdM provides the focus to deal with system-wide data quality and issues often encountered by fragmented databases and processes.
- IdM embraces what the user actually gets in terms of products and services and how and when they acquire them. Therefore, IdM applies to the products and services of an organization, such as health, media, insurance, travel and government services. It is also applicable to means by which these products and services are provisioned and assigned to (or removed from) "entitled" users.
- IdM can deliver single-customer views that include the presence and location of the customer, single products and services as well as single IT infrastructure and network views to the respective parties. Accordingly, IdM relates intrinsically to, security and privacy.

- IdM covers the machinery (system infrastructure components) that delivers such services because a system may assign the service of a user to: a particular network technology, content title, usage right, media server, mail server, soft switch, voice mailbox, product catalog set, security domain, billing system, etc.
- It is equally important for users to correctly identify and authenticate service providers as it is for service providers to identify and authenticate users. This aspect has largely been ignored during the early development of identity management, but will have to be taken seriously in the future.
- Critical factors in IdM projects include consideration of the online services of an organization (what the users log on to) and how they are managed from an internal and customer self-care perspective.

### 4.6.7 Issues

The management of identity raises a certain number of issues, such as privacy issues that may lead to the implementation of a surveillance society, or risk related to the stealing of identity (identity theft).

The advent of the social web, and in particular the important development of online social networking services, for which the management of their identities of their members represent a core element of these systems, also create a certain number of risks related to the disclosure of personal information, and in particular in losing an individual's privacy

## 4.7 ACCESS MANAGEMENT

### 4.7.1 Introduction

Access management is a simple concept. Every business has information that needs to be protected from unauthorized disclosure. To protect information, companies define policies that govern who can access specific classes of business and/or personal information. For example, if a manager seeks to access the salary of a subordinate, they should have authorization to do so, however, they should not be authorized to access the same information about a chief executive. That is, there is a policy that specifically governs the release of an employee's salary. Or is there? The answer is: "Probably not." What exists is a written policy related to disclosure of proprietary business information (and perhaps even a separate policy related to disclosure of employee personal information). Because human beings are skilled at generalizations, we expect someone in authority to be able to classify the request for salary information and make a decision.

Access Management software has a simple goal. It allows the human who previously acted as a guardian of sensitive information to be removed from the process without loss of access control. This sounds simple, but most businesses are struggling with the implementation of access management as they integrate and extend their applications. This is because machines cannot classify information or make access decisions unless they are explicitly programmed with algorithms to accomplish this. When you take the responsibility for access decisions away from human beings, it becomes necessary to insert software guards into your applications.

A costly problem lurks: The access policy used by software guards is often coded directly into the business application (typically requiring new database tables and/or directory infrastructure). When access policy or audit requirements change, application software must be modified, tested and redeployed.

Additionally, when access policy needs to be examined or applications audited for conformance a code review is required.

A service-oriented solution emerges: Access Management solutions, as defined by this paper, provide an alternative to the costly embedding of access policy. They allow application software guards to leverage services that enable access policy to be modified, tested and deployed dynamically without application code changes. This enables your developers to concentrate on providing business software. Access management solutions efficiently enable high performance access controls in distributed environments while allowing centralized management of access policy. An Access Management solution includes programming interfaces (APIs), policy management tools and auditing capabilities.

As part of your quest for an access management strategy, consider the following questions:

1. Who should be responsible for access policy?
2. What kind of access policy do you require?
3. What resources do you need to protect?
4. How do I plug in the access management solution?

This describes a systematic approach to managing the complexity associated with software access management. It outlines a service-oriented architecture that maintains a clean separation of concerns between application domain functionality and access management.

## 4.8 INTRUSION DETECTION SYSTEM

An **Intrusion detection system (IDS)** is software and/or hardware designed to detect unwanted attempts at accessing, manipulating, and/or disabling of computer systems, mainly through a network, such as the Internet. These attempts may take the form of attacks, as examples, by crackers, malware and/or disgruntled employees. An IDS cannot directly detect attacks within properly encrypted traffic.

An intrusion detection system is used to detect several types of malicious behaviors that can compromise the security and trust of a computer system. This includes network attacks against vulnerable services, data driven attacks on applications, host based attacks such as privilege escalation, unauthorized logins and access to sensitive files, and malware (viruses, trojan horses, and worms).

An IDS can be composed of several components: **Sensors** which generate security events, a **Console** to monitor events and alerts and control the sensors, and a central **Engine** that records events logged by the sensors in a database and uses a system of rules to generate alerts from security events received. There are several ways to categorize an IDS depending on the type and location of the sensors and the methodology used by the engine to generate alerts. In many simple IDS implementations all three components are combined in a single device or appliance.

### 4.8.1 IDS Terminology

**Alert/Alarm** — A signal suggesting a system has been or is being attacked.

**True attack stimulus** — An event that triggers an IDS to produce an alarm and react as though a real attack were in progress.

**False attack stimulus** — The event signaling an IDS to produce an alarm when no attack has taken place.

**False (False Positive)** — An alert or alarm that is triggered when no actual attack has taken place.

**False negative** — A failure of an IDS to detect an actual attack.

**Noise** — Data or interference that can trigger a false positive.

**Site policy** — Guidelines within an organization that control the rules and configurations of an IDS.

**Site policy awareness** — The ability an IDS has to dynamically change its rules and configurations in response to changing environmental activity.

**Confidence value** — A value an organization places on an IDS based on past performance and analysis to help determine its ability to effectively identify an attack.

**Alarm filtering** — The process of categorizing attack alerts produced from an IDS in order to distinguish false positives from actual attacks.

### 4.8.2 Types of Intrusion-Detection Systems

There are three main types of systems in which IDS can be used: **network, applications and hosts**.

In a **network-based** intrusion-detection system (NIDS), the sensors are located at choke points in network to be monitored, often in the demilitarized zone (DMZ) or at network borders. The sensor captures all network traffic and analyzes the content of individual packets for malicious traffic.

In **systems**, PIDS and APIDS are used to monitor the transport and protocols for illegal or inappropriate traffic or constructs of a language. For example forged SQL queries attempting to delete database records, virus in emails.

In a **host**-based system, the sensor usually consists of a software agent, which monitors all activity of the host on which it is installed. For example attempt to modify the master boot record, keylogger, file access.

**Various types**

- Network intrusion detection system (NIDS)
- Host-based intrusion detection system (HIDS)
- Protocol-based intrusion detection system (PIDS)
- Application protocol-based intrusion detection system (APIDS)
- Anomaly-based intrusion detection system
- Intrusion prevention system (IPS)
- Artificial immune system

Some of them are:

#### *4.8.2.1 Network Intrusion Detection System (NIDS)*

It is an independent platform which identifies intrusions by examining network traffic and monitors multiple hosts. Network Intrusion Detection Systems gain access to network traffic by connecting to a hub, network switch configured for port mirroring, or network tap. An example of a NIDS is Snort.

#### *4.8.2.2 Host-based Intrusion Detection System (HIDS)*

It consists of an agent on a host which identifies intrusions by analyzing system calls, application logs, file-system modifications (binaries, password files, capability/acl databases) and other host activities and state. An example of a HIDS is OSSEC.

#### 4.8.2.3 Protocol-based Intrusion Detection System (PIDS)

It consists of a system or agent that would typically sit at the front end of a server, monitoring and analyzing the communication protocol between a connected device (a user/PC or system) and the server. For a web server this would typically monitor the HTTPS protocol stream and understand the HTTP protocol relative to the web server/system it is trying to protect. Where HTTPS is in use then this system would need to reside in the "shim", or interface, between where HTTPS is un-encrypted and immediately prior to its entering the Web presentation layer.

#### 4.8.2.4 Application Protocol-based Intrusion Detection System (APIDS)

It consists of a system or agent that would typically sit within a group of servers, monitoring and analyzing the communication on application specific protocols. For example, in a web server with a database this would monitor the SQL protocol specific to the middleware/business logic as it transacts with the database.

#### 4.8.2.5 Hybrid Intrusion Detection System

It combines two or more approaches. Host agent data is combined with network information to form a comprehensive view of the network. An example of a Hybrid IDS is Prelude.

Intrusion detection systems can also be system-specific using custom tools and honeypots.

### 4.8.3 Passive System vs. Reactive System

In a **passive system**, the intrusion detection system (IDS) sensor detects a potential security breach, logs the information and signals an alert on the console and or owner. In a **reactive system**, also known as an intrusion prevention system (IPS), the IPS responds to the suspicious activity by resetting the connection or by reprogramming the firewall to block network traffic from the suspected malicious source. This can happen automatically or at the command of an operator.

Though they both relate to network security, an intrusion detection system (IDS) differs from a firewall in that a firewall looks outwardly for intrusions in order to stop them from happening. Firewalls limit access between networks to prevent intrusion and do not signal an attack from inside the network. An IDS evaluates a suspected intrusion once it has taken place and signals an alarm. An IDS also watches for attacks that originate from within a system. This is traditionally achieved by examining network communications, identifying heuristics and patterns (often known as signatures) of common computer attacks, and taking action to alert operators. A system which terminates connections is called an intrusion prevention system, and is another form of an application layer firewall.

The term IDPS is commonly used to refer to hybrid security systems that both "detect" and "prevent".

### 4.8.4 Statistical Anomaly and Signature based IDSes

All Intrusion Detection Systems use one of two detection techniques: statistical anomaly based and/or signature based.

1. **Statistical anomaly based IDS:** A statistical anomaly based IDS establishes a performance baseline based on normal network traffic evaluations. It will then sample current network traffic activity to this baseline in order to detect whether or not it is within baseline parameters. If the sampled traffic is outside baseline parameters an alarm will be triggered.

2. **Signature based IDS:** Network traffic is examined for pre-configured and predetermined attack patterns known as signatures. Many attacks today have distinct signatures. In good security practice, a collection of these signatures must be constantly updated to mitigate emerging threats.

### 4.8.5 Limitations

**Noise:** Noise can severely limit an Intrusion detection systems effectiveness. Bad packets generated from software bugs, corrupt DNS data, and local packets that escaped can create a significantly high false alarm rate.

**Too few attacks:** It is not uncommon for the number of real attacks to be far below the false alarm rate. Real attacks are often so far below the false alarm rate that they are often missed and ignored

**Signature updates:** Many attacks are geared for specific versions of software that are usually outdated. A constantly changing library of signatures is needed to mitigate threats. Outdated signature databases can leave the IDS vulnerable to new strategies

### 4.8.6 IDS Evasion Techniques

Intrusion detection system evasion techniques bypass detection by creating different states on the IDS and on the targeted computer. The adversary accomplishes this by manipulating either the attack itself or the network traffic that contains the attack.

### 4.8.7 Development

A preliminary concept of an IDS began with James P. Anderson and reviews of audit trails. An example of an audit trail would be a log of user access.

Fred Cohen noted in 1984 (see Intrusion Detection) that it is impossible to detect an intrusion in every case and that the resources needed to detect intrusions grows with the amount of usage.

Dorothy E. Denning, assisted by Peter Neumann, published a model of an IDS in 1986 that formed the basis for many systems today. Her model used statistics for anomaly detection, and resulted in an early IDS at SRI named the Intrusion detection expert system (IDES), which ran on Sun Workstations and could consider both user and network level data. IDES had a dual approach with a rule-based Expert System to detect known types of intrusions plus a statistical anomaly detection component based on profiles of users, host systems, and target systems. Lunt proposed adding an Artificial neural network as a third component. She said all three components could then report to a resolver. SRI followed IDES in 1993 with the Next-generation Intrusion Detection Expert System (NIDES).

The Multics intrusion detection and alerting system (MIDAS), an expert system using P-BEST and LISP, was developed in 1988 based on the work of Denning and Neumann. Haystack was also developed this year using statistics to reduce audit trails.

Wisdom & sense (W&S) was a statistics-based anomaly detector developed in 1989 at the Los Alamos National Laboratory. W&S created rules based on statistical analysis, and then used those rules for anomaly detection.

In 1990, the Time-based inductive machine (TIM) did anomaly detection using inductive learning of sequential user patterns in Common LISP on a VAX 3500 computer. The Network Security Monitor (NSM) performed masking on access matrices for anomaly detection on a Sun-3/50 workstation. The Information Security Officer's Assistant (ISOA) was a 1990 prototype that considered a variety of strategies including statistics, a profile checker, and an expert system. Computer Watch at AT&T Bell Labs used statistics and rules for audit data reduction and intrusion detection.

Then, in 1991, researchers at the University of California created a prototype Distributed intrusion detection system (DIDS), which was also an expert system. The Network anomaly detection and intrusion reporter (NADIR), also in 1991, was a prototype IDS developed at the Los Alamos National Laboratory's Integrated Computing Network (ICN), and was heavily influenced by the work of Denning and Lunt. NADIR used a statistics-based anomaly detector and an expert system.

The Lawrence Berkeley National Laboratory announced Bro in 1998 which used its own rule language for packet analysis from libpcap data. Network Flight Recorder (NFR)in 1999 also used libpcap. APE was developed as a packet sniffer, also using libpcap, in November, 1998, and was renamed Snort one month later.

The Audit data analysis and mining (ADAM) IDS in 2001 used tcpdump to build profiles of rules for classifications.

## 4.9 SECURITY INFORMATION MANAGEMENT

**Security information management (SIM)** is the industry-specific term in computer security referring to the collection of data (typically log files; e.g. eventlogs) into a central repository for trend analysis. SIM products generally comprise software agents running on the computers that are to be monitored, communicating with a centralized server acting as a "security console", sending it information about security-related events, which displays reports, charts, and graphs of that information, often in real time. The software agents can incorporate local filters, to reduce and manipulate the data that they send to the server. The security console is monitored by a human being, who reviews the consolidated information, and takes action in response to any alerts issued.

The data that are sent to the server, to be correlated and analyzed, are normalized by the software agents into a common form, usually XML. Those data are then aggregated, in order to reduce their overall size.

The terminology can easily be mistaken as a reference to the whole aspect of protecting one's infrastructure from any computer security breach. Due to historic reasons of terminology evolution; SIM refers to just the part of information security which consists of discovery of 'bad behavior' by using data collection techniques. The term commonly used to represent an entire security infrastructure that protects an environment is commonly called information security management (InfoSec).

Security information management is also referred to as or included in SEM (security event management) and SIEM (security information and event management).

Commercial SIEM products include Event Tracker by Prism Microsystems, Trigeo, ArcSight, SenSage, Cisco Security MARS, Snare and others.

Open Source SIEM products include OSSIM, and Prelude.

### 4.9.1 Definitions

The word security is derived from the Latin "Se-Cura" and literally translates to "without fear". 'Security' is therefore the state of being secure, or the actions employed to achieve that state, i.e. to be secure is to be without fear of harm.

The definition of security provided by the Institute for Security and Open Methodologies is geared towards operations and how we interact with security. It states security is:

**"A form of protection where a separation is created between the assets and the threat. This includes but is not limited to the elimination of either the asset or the threat. In order to be secure, either the asset is physically removed from the threat or the threat is physically removed from the asset."**

The definition given in a UN study, in 1986, is interesting as a contribution to the understanding of the concept of security, "Security is a state at which countries think that there is no danger of military attack, political pressure, or economic coercion, so that they can develop and progress freely.

With respect to classified matter, the condition that prevents unauthorized persons from having to official that is safeguarded in the interests of .

Measures taken by a military unit, an activity or installation to protect itself against all acts designed to, or which may, impair its effectiveness.

### 4.9.2 Security Concepts

Certain concepts recur throughout different fields of security:

— assurance is the level of guarantee that a security system will behave as expected

— a countermeasure is a way to stop a threat from triggering a risk event

— never rely on one single security measure alone

— a vulnerability that has been triggered by a threat — a risk of 1.0 (100%)

— a risk is a possible event which could cause a loss

— a threat is a method of triggering a risk event that is dangerous

— a weakness in a target that can potentially be exploited by a threat

### 4.9.3 Security Management in Organizations

In the corporate world, various aspects of security were historically addressed separately - notably by distinct and often non-communicating departments for IT security, physical security, and fraud prevention. Today there is a greater recognition of the interconnected nature of security requirements, an approach variously known as holistic security, "all hazards" management, and other terms.

Inciting factors in the convergence of security disciplines include the development of digital video surveillance technologies and the digitization and networking of physical control systems .Greater interdisciplinary cooperation is further evidenced by the February 2005 creation of the Alliance for Enterprise Security Risk Management, a joint venture including leading associations in security, information security (the Information Systems Security Association), and IT audit (the Information Systems Audit and Control Association).

# CHAPTER 5

# IT Ethics and Emerging Trends

**Information ethics** is the field that investigates the ethical issues arising from the development and application of information technologies. It provides a critical framework for considering moral issues concerning informational privacy, moral agency (e.g. whether artificial agents may be moral), new environmental issues (especially how agents should one behave in the infosphere), problems arising from the life-cycle (creation, collection, recording, distribution, processing, etc.) of information (especially ownership and copyright, digital divide). Information Ethics is related to the fields of computer ethics and the philosophy of information.

Dilemmas regarding the life of information are becoming increasingly important in a society that is defined as "the information society". Information transmission and literacy are essential concerns in establishing an ethical foundation that promotes fair, equitable, and responsible practices. Information ethics broadly examines issues related to ownership, access, privacy, security, and community.

Information technology affects fundamental rights involving copyright protection, intellectual freedom, accountability, and security.

Professional codes offer a basis for making ethical decisions and applying ethical solutions to situations involving information provision and use which reflect an organization's commitment to responsible information service. Evolving information formats and needs require continual reconsideration of ethical principles and how these codes are applied. Considerations regarding information ethics influence "personal decisions, professional practice, and public policy". Therefore, ethical analysis must provide a framework to take into consideration "many, diverse domains" regarding how information is distributed.

## 5.1 ETHICS OF TECHNOLOGY

**Ethics of technology** is a subfield of ethics addressing the ethical questions specific to the Technology Age. Some prominent works of philosopher Hans Jonas are devoted to ethics of technology. Technology itself is incapable of possessing moral or ethical qualities, since "technology" is merely tool making. Thus, "ethics of technology" refers instead to two basic subdivisions.

- The ethics involved in the development of new technology — whether it is always, never, or contextually right or wrong to invent and implement a technological innovation.

- The ethical questions that are exacerbated by the ways in which technology extends or curtails the power of individuals — how standard ethical questions are changed by the new powers.

In the former case, ethics of such things as computer security and computer viruses asks whether the very act of innovation is an ethically right or wrong act. Similarly, does a scientist have an ethical obligation to produce or fail to produce a nuclear weapon? What are the ethical questions surrounding the production of technologies that waste or conserve energy and resources? What are the ethical questions surrounding the production of new manufacturing processes that might inhibit employment, or might inflict suffering in the third world?

In the latter case, the ethics of technology quickly break down into the ethics of various human endeavors as they are altered by new technologies. For example, bioethics is now largely consumed with questions that have been exacerbated by the new life-preserving technologies, new cloning technologies, and new technologies for implantation. In law, the right of privacy is being continually attenuated by the emergence of new forms of surveillance and anonymity. The old ethical questions of privacy and free speech are given new shape and urgency in an Internet age. Such tracing devices as RFID, biometric analysis and identification, genetic screening, all take old ethical questions and amplify their import.

### 5.1.1 Cyber Ethics

Cyber ethics is distinct from cyber law. Laws are formal written directives that apply to everyone, interpreted by the judicial system, and enforced by the police. Ethics is a broad philosophical concept that goes beyond simple right and wrong, and looks towards "the good life".

### 5.1.2 Privacy

In the late 18th century, the invention of cameras spurred similar ethical debates as the internet does today. During a Harvard Law Review seminal in 1890, Warren and Brandeis defined privacy from an ethical and moral point of view to be "central to dignity and individuality and personhood. Privacy is also indispensable to a sense of autonomy - to 'a feeling that there is an area of an individual's life that is totally under his or her control, an area that is free from outside intrusion.' The deprivation of privacy can even endanger a person's health." (Warren & Brandeis, 1890). Over 100 years later, the internet and proliferation of private data through governments and ecommerce is a phenomenon which requires a new round of ethical debate involving a person's privacy.

Privacy can be decomposed to the limitation of others' access to an individual with "three elements of secrecy, anonymity, and solitude" (Gavison, 1984). Anonymity refers to the individual's right to protection from undesired attention. Solitude refers to the lack of physical proximity of an individual to others. Secrecy refers to the protection of personalized information from being freely distributed.

Individuals surrender private information when conducting transactions and registering for services. Ethical business practice protects the privacy of their customers by securing information which may contribute to the loss of secrecy, anonymity, and solitude. Credit card information, social security numbers, phone numbers, mothers' maiden names, addresses and phone numbers freely collected and shared over the internet may lead to a loss of Privacy.

Fraud and impersonation are some of the malicious activities that occur due to the direct or indirect abuse of private information. Identity theft is rising rapidly due to the availability of private information in the internet. For instance, seven million Americans have fallen victim to identity theft in 2002, making it the fastest growing crime in the United States (Latak, 2005). Public records search engines and databases are the main culprits contributing to the rise of cybercrime. Listed below are a few recommendations to restrict online databases from proliferating sensitive personnel information.

1. Exclude sensitive unique identifiers from database records such as social security numbers, birth dates, hometown and mothers' maiden names.
2. Exclude phone numbers that are normally unlisted.
3. Clear provision of a method which allows people to have their names removed from a database.
4. Banning the reverse social security number lookup services

### 5.1.3 Private Data Collection

Data warehouses are used today to collect and store huge amounts of personal data and consumer transactions. These facilities can preserve large volumes of consumer information for an indefinite amount of time. Some of the key architectures contributing to the erosion of privacy include databases, cookies and spyware.

Some may argue that data warehouses are supposed to stand alone and be protected. However, the fact is enough personal information can be gathered from corporate websites and social networking sites to initiate a reverse lookup. Therefore, is it not important to address some of the ethical issues regarding how protected data ends up in the public domain?

As a result, identity theft protection businesses are on the rise. Companies such as LifeLock and JPMorgan Chase have begun to capitalize on selling identity theft protection insurance.

### 5.1.4 Property

Ethical debate has long included the concept of property. This concept has created many clashes in the world of cyberethics. One philosophy of the internet is centered around the freedom of information. The controversy over ownership occurs when the property of information is infringed upon or uncertain.

### 5.1.5 Intellectual Property Rights

The ever-increasing speed of the internet and the emergence of compression technology, such as mp3 opened the doors to Peer-to-peer file sharing, a technology that allowed users to anonymously transfer files to each other, previously seen on programs such as Napster or now seen through communications protocol such as BitTorrent. Much of this however, was copyrighted music, illegal to transfer to other users. Whether it is ethical to transfer copyrighted media is another question.

Proponents of unrestricted file sharing point out how file sharing has given people broader and faster access to media, has increased exposure to new artists, and has reduced the costs of transferring media (including less environmental damage). Supporters of restrictions on file sharing argue that we must protect the income of our artists and other people who work to create our media. This argument is partially answered by pointing to the small proportion of money artists receive from the legitimate sale of media.

### 5.1.6 Security

Security has long been a topic of ethical debate. Is it better to protect the common good of the community or rather should we safeguard the rights of the individual? There is a continual dispute over the boundaries between the two and which compromises are right to make. As an ever increasing amount of people connect to the internet and more and more personal data is available online there is susceptibility to identity theft, cyber crimes and computer hacking.

### 5.1.7 Accuracy

Due to the ease of accessibility and sometimes collective nature of the internet we often come across issues of accuracy e.g. who is responsible for the authenticity and fidelity of the information available online? Ethically this includes debate over who should be allowed to contribute content and who should be held accountable if there are errors in the content or if it is false. This also brings up the question of how is the injured party, if any, to be made whole and under which jurisdiction does the offense lay?

### 5.1.8 Accessibility, Censorship and Filtering

Accessibility, censorship and filtering bring up many ethical issues that have several branches in cyberethics. Many questions have arisen which continue to challenge our understanding of privacy, security and our participation in society. Throughout the centuries mechanisms have been constructed in the name of protection and security. Today the applications are in the form of software that filters domains and content so that they may not be easily accessed or obtained without elaborate circumvention or on a personal and business level through free or content-control software. Internet censorship and filtering are used to control or suppress the publishing or accessing of information. The legal issues are similar to offline censorship and filtering. The same arguments that apply to offline censorship and filtering apply to online censorship and filtering; whether people are better off with free access to information or should be protected from what is considered by a governing body as harmful, indecent or illicit. The fear of access by minors drives much of the concern and many online advocate groups have sprung up to raise awareness and of controlling the accessibility of minors to the internet.

Censorship and filtering occurs on small to large scales, whether it be a company restricting their employees' access to cyberspace by blocking certain websites which are deemed as relevant only to personal usage and therefore damaging to productivity or on a larger scale where a government creates large firewalls which censor and filter access to certain information available online frequently from outside their country to their citizens and anyone within their borders.

### 5.1.9 Freedom of Information

Freedom of information, that is the freedom of speech as well as the freedom to seek, obtain and impart information brings up the question of who or what, has the jurisdiction in cyberspace. The right of freedom of information is commonly subject to limitations dependant upon the country, society and culture concerned.

### 5.1.10 Organizations Related to Cyberethics

The following organizations are of notable interest in the cyberethics debate:

- International Federation for Information Processing (IFIP) IFIP
- Association for Computer Machinery, Special Interest Group: Computers and Society (SIGCAS)
- Ethical and Professional Issues in Computing (EPIC) Electronic Privacy Information Center

- Electronic Frontier Foundation (EFF) Electronic Frontier Foundation
- International Center for Information Ethics (ICIE)
- Directions and Implications in Advanced Computing (DIAC)
- The Centre for Computing and Social Responsibility (CCSR)
- Cyber-Rights and Cyber-liberties

## 5.1.11 Codes of Ethics in Computing

Information Technology managers are required to establish a set of ethical standards common to their organization. There are many examples of ethical code currently published that can be tailored to fit any organization. Code of ethics is an instrument that establishes a common ethical framework for a large group of people. Four well known examples of Code of Ethics for IT professionals are listed below:

### *5.1.11.1 RFC 1087*

In January 1989, the Internet Architecture Board (IAB) in RFC 1087 defines an activity as unethical and unacceptable if it:

1. Seeks to gain unauthorized access to the resources of the Internet.
2. Disrupts the intended use of the Internet.
3. Wastes resources (people, capacity, computer) through such actions.
4. Destroys the integrity of computer-based information, or
5. Compromises the privacy of users (RFC 1087, 1989).

### *5.1.11.2 The Code of Fair Information Practices*

The Code of Fair Information Practices is based on five principles outlining the requirements for records keeping systems. This requirement was implemented in 1973 by the U.S. Department of Health, Education and Welfare.

1. There must be no personal data record-keeping systems whose very existence is secret.
2. There must be a way for a person to find out what information about the person is in a record and how it is used.
3. There must be a way for a person to prevent information about the person that was obtained for one purpose from being used or made available for other purposes without the person's consent.
4. There must be a way for a person to correct or amend a record of identifiable information about the person.
5. Any organization creating, maintaining, using, or disseminating records of identifiable personal data must assure the reliability of the data for their intended use and must take precautions to prevent misuses of the data (Harris, 2003).

### *5.1.11.3 Ten Commandments of Computer Ethics*

The ethical values as defined in 1992 by the Computer Ethics Institute; a nonprofit organization whose mission is to advance technology by ethical means, lists these rules as a guide to computer ethics:

1. You should not use a computer to harm other people.
2. You should not interfere with other people's computer work.
3. You should not snoop around in other people's computer files.
4. You should not use a computer to steal.
5. You should not use a computer to bear false witness.
6. You should not copy or use proprietary software for which you have not paid.
7. You should not use other people's computer resources without authorization or proper compensation.
8. You should not appropriate other people's intellectual output.
9. You should think about the social consequences of the program you are writing or the system you are designing.
10. You should always use a computer in ways that ensure consideration and respect for your fellow humans (Computer Ethics Institute, 1992).

## 5.2 INTELLECTUAL PROPERTY

**Intellectual property (IP)** is a number of distinct types of legal monopolies over creations of the mind, both artistic and commercial, and the corresponding fields of law. Under intellectual property law, owners are granted certain exclusive rights to a variety of intangible assets, such as musical, literary, and artistic works; ideas, discoveries and inventions; and words, phrases, symbols, and designs. Common types of intellectual property include copyrights, trademarks, patents, industrial design rights and trade secrets in some jurisdictions.

Intellectual property (IP) refers to creations of the mind: inventions, literary and artistic works, and symbols, names, images, and designs used in commerce.

Intellectual property is divided into two categories: Industrial property, which includes inventions (patents), trademarks, industrial designs, and geographic indications of source; and Copyright, which includes literary and artistic works such as novels, poems and plays, films, musical works, artistic works such as drawings, paintings, photographs and sculptures, and architectural designs. Rights related to copyright include those of performing artists in their performances, producers of phonograms in their recordings, and those of broadcasters in their radio and television programs

Industrial property legislation is part of the wider body of law known as intellectual property. The term intellectual property refers broadly to the creations of the human mind. Intellectual property rights protect the interests of creators by giving them property rights over their creations.

The Convention Establishing the World Intellectual Property Organization (1967) does not seek to define intellectual property, but gives the following list of the subject matter protected by intellectual property rights:

- literary, artistic and scientific works;
- performances of performing artists, phonograms, and broadcasts;
- inventions in all fields of human endeavor;
- scientific discoveries;

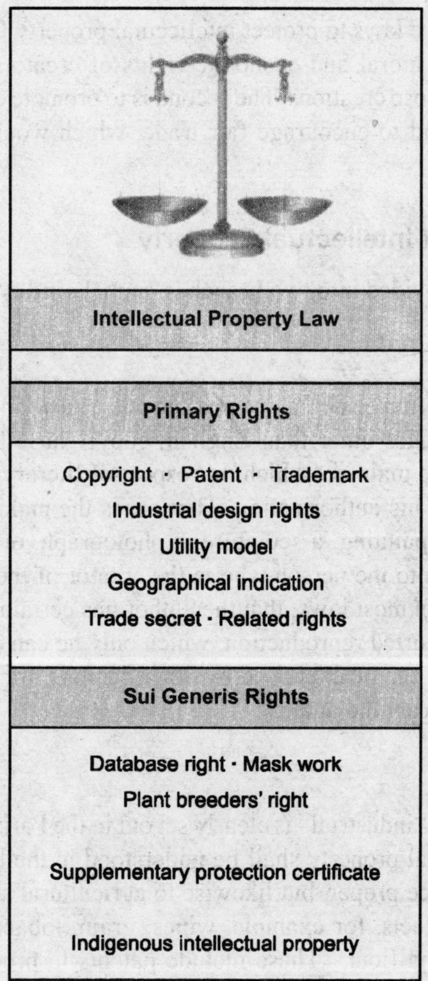


- industrial designs;
- trademarks, service marks, and commercial names and designations;
- protection against unfair competition;
- and "all other rights resulting from intellectual activity in the industrial, scientific, literary or artistic fields."

Intellectual property relates to items of information or knowledge, which can be incorporated in tangible objects at the same time in an unlimited number of copies at different locations anywhere in the world.

Intellectual property rights are also characterized by certain limitations, such as limited duration in the case of copyright and patents.

The importance of protecting intellectual property was first recognized in the Paris Convention for the Protection of Industrial Property in 1883 and the Berne Convention for the Protection of Literary and Artistic Works in 1886. Both treaties are administered by the World Intellectual Property Organization

(WIPO). Countries generally have laws to protect intellectual property for two main reasons. One is to give statutory expression to the moral and economic rights of creators in their creations and to the rights of the public in accessing those creations. The second is to promote creativity and the dissemination and application of its results, and to encourage fair trade, which would contribute to economic and social development.

### 5.2.1 The Two Branches of Intellectual Property

Intellectual property is usually divided into two branches, namely **industrial property** and **copyright**.

#### *5.2.1.1 Copyright*

Copyright relates to artistic creations, such as poems, novels, music, paintings, and cinematographic works. In most European languages other than English, copyright is known as author's rights. The expression copyright refers to the main act which, in respect of literary and artistic creations, may be made only by the author or with his authorization. That act is the making of copies of the literary or artistic work, such as a book, a painting, a sculpture, a photograph, or a motion picture. The second expression, author's rights refers to the person who is the creator of the artistic work, its author, thus underlining the fact, recognized in most laws, that the author has certain specific rights in his creation, such as the right to prevent a distorted reproduction, which only he can exercise, whereas other rights, such as the right to make copies, can be exercised by other persons, for example, a publisher who has obtained a license to this effect from the author.

#### *5.2.1.2 Industrial Property*

The broad application of the term "industrial" is clearly set out in the Paris Convention for the Protection of Industrial Property): "Industrial property shall be understood in the broadest sense and shall apply not only to industry and commerce proper, but likewise to agricultural and extractive industries and to all manufactured or natural products, for example, wines, grain, tobacco leaf, fruit, cattle, minerals, mineral waters, beer, flowers, and flour." These include patents to protect inventions; and industrial designs, which are aesthetic creations determining the appearance of industrial products. Industrial property also covers trademarks, service marks, layout-designs of integrated circuits, commercial names and designations, as well as geographical indications, and protection against unfair competition. In some of these, the aspect of intellectual creation, although existent, is less clearly defined. What counts here is that the object of industrial property typically consists of signs transmitting information, in particular to consumers, as regards products and services offered on the market. Protection is directed against unauthorized use of such signs likely to mislead consumers, and against misleading practices in general. Inventions may be defined in a non-legal sense as new solutions to technical problems. These new solutions are **ideas**, and are protected as such; protection of inventions under patent law does not require that the invention be represented in a physical embodiment. The protection accorded to inventors is, therefore, protection against any use of the invention without the authorization of the owner. Even a person who later makes the same invention independently, without copying or even being aware of the first inventor's work, must obtain authorization before he can exploit it.

Unlike protection of inventions, copyright law protects only the form of expression of ideas, not the ideas themselves. The creativity protected by copyright law is creativity in the choice and arrangement of words, musical notes, colors and shapes. So copyright law protects the owner of property rights against those who copy or otherwise take and use the form in which the original work was expressed by the author.

From this basic difference between inventions and literary and artistic works, it follows that the legal protection provided to each also differs. Since protection for inventions gives a monopoly right to exploit an idea, such protection is short in duration — usually about 20 years. The fact that the invention is protected must also be made known to the public. There must be an official notification that a specific, fully described invention is the property of a specific owner for a fixed number of years; in other words, the protected invention must be disclosed publicly in an official register.

Since the legal protection of literary and artistic works under copyright, by contrast, prevents only unauthorized use of the expressions of ideas, the duration of protection can be much longer than in the case of the protection of ideas themselves, without damage to the public interest. Also, the law can be — and in most countries is — simply declaratory, i.e., the law may state that the author of an original work has the right to prevent other persons from copying or otherwise using his work. So a created work is considered protected as soon as it exists, and a public register of copyright protected works is not necessary.

## 5.3 PRIVACY LAW

Privacy law is the area of law concerned with the protection and preservation of the privacy rights of individuals. Increasingly, governments and other public as well as private organizations collect vast amounts of personal information about individuals for a variety of purposes. The law of privacy regulates the type of information which may be collected and how this information may be used.

The scope of applicability of privacy laws is called expectation of privacy.

### 5.3.1 Classification of Privacy Laws

Privacy laws can be broadly classified into:

**General privacy laws** have an overall bearing on the personal information of individuals and affect the policies that govern many different areas of information.

**Specific privacy laws** are designed to regulate specific types of information. Some examples include:

- Health privacy laws
- Financial privacy laws
- Online privacy laws
- Communication privacy laws
- Information privacy laws
- Privacy in one's home

## 5.4 COMPUTER FORENSICS

**Computer forensics** is a branch of forensic science pertaining to legal evidence found in computers and digital storage mediums. Computer forensics is also known as digital forensics.

Data lost intentionally or accidentally can be recovered with the help of data recovery experts. Computer forensic is one such type where the cause for data loss is identified.

There are many definitions of computer forensics however generally, computer forensic refers to the detail investigation of the computers to carry out the required tasks. It performs the investigation of the maintained data of the computer to check out what exactly happened to the computer and who is responsible for it. The investigation process starts from the analysis of the ground situation and moves on further to the insides of the computer's operating system.

Computer forensic is a broader concept which is mainly related to the crimes happening in computer which is against law. Various laws have been imposed to check out the crimes but still they exist and are difficult to find the criminal due to lack of evidence. All these difficulties can be overcome with the help of computer forensics.

### What is Computer Forensics?

If you manage or administer information systems and networks, you should understand computer forensics. Forensics is the process of using scientific knowledge for collecting, analyzing, and presenting evidence to the courts. (The word forensics means "to bring to the court." ) Forensics deals primarily with the recovery and analysis of latent evidence. Latent evidence can take many forms, from fingerprints left on a window to DNA evidence recovered from blood stains to the files on a hard drive. Because computer forensics is a new discipline, there is little standardization and consistency across the courts and industry. As a result, it is not yet recognized as a formal "scientific" discipline. We define computer forensics as the discipline that combines elements of law and computer science to collect and analyze data from computer systems, networks, wireless communications, and storage devices in a way that is admissible as evidence in a court of law.

### Why is Computer Forensics Important?

Adding the ability to practice sound computer forensics will help you ensure the overall integrity and survivability of your network infrastructure. You can help your organization if you consider computer forensics as a new basic element in what is known as a "defense-in-depth", approach to network and computer security. For instance, understanding the legal and technical aspects of computer forensics will help you capture vital information if your network is compromised and will help you prosecute the case if the intruder is caught.

What happens if you ignore computer forensics or practice it badly? You risk destroying vital evidence or having forensic evidence ruled inadmissible in a court of law. Also, you or your organization may run afoul of new laws that mandate regulatory compliance and assign liability if certain types of data are not adequately protected. Recent legislation makes it possible to hold organizations liable in civil or criminal court if they fail to protect customer data. Computer forensics is also important because it can save your organization money. Many managers are allocating a greater portion of their information technology budgets for computer and network security. International Data Corporation (IDC) reported that the market for intrusion-detection and vulnerability-assessment software will reach 1.45 billion dollars in 2006. In increasing numbers, organizations are deploying network security devices such as intrusion detection systems (IDS), firewalls, proxies, and the like, which all report on the security status of networks. From a technical standpoint, the main goal of computer forensics is to identify, collect, preserve, and analyze data in a way that preserves the integrity of the evidence collected so it can be used effectively in a legal case. What are some typical aspects of a computer forensics investigation? First, those who investigate computers have to understand the kind of potential evidence they are looking for in order to structure their search. Crimes involving a computer can range across the spectrum of criminal activity, from child pornography to theft of personal data to destruction of intellectual property. Second, the investigator must pick the appropriate tools to use. Files may have been deleted, damaged, or encrypted, and the investigator must be familiar with an array of methods and software to prevent further damage in the recovery process. Two basic types of data are collected in computer forensics. Persistent data is the data that is stored on a local hard drive (or another medium) and is preserved when the computer is turned off. Volatile data is any data that is stored in memory, or exists in transit, that will be lost when the computer loses power or is turned off. Volatile data resides in registries, cache, and random access memory (RAM). Since volatile data is ephemeral, it is essential an investigator knows reliable ways to capture it. System administrators and security personnel must also have a basic understanding of how routine computer and network administrative tasks can affect both the forensic process (the potential admissibility of evidence at court) and the subsequent ability to recover data that may be critical to the identification and analysis of a security incident.

**Objective of Computer Forensic**

The main motto of computer forensic experts is not only to find the criminal but also to find out the evidence and the presentation of the evidence in a manner that leads to legal action of the culprit. The major reasons for criminal activity in computers are:

1. Unauthorized use of computers mainly stealing a username and password
2. Accessing the victims computer via the internet
3. Releasing a malicious computer program that is virus
4. Harassment and stalking in cyberspace
5. E-mail Fraud
6. Theft of company documents.

Computer forensic facilitates the organized and careful detection of computer related crime and abuse cases. The computer forensics expert should have a great deal of knowledge of the data recovery software as well as the hardware and should possess the qualification and knowledge required to carry out the task.

**Need for Computer Forensics**

The purpose of computer forensics is mainly due to the wide variety of computer crimes that take place. In the present technological advancements it is common for every organization to employ the services of the computer forensics experts. There are various computer crimes that occur on small scale as well as large scale. The loss caused is dependent upon the sensitivity of the computer data or the information for which the crime has been committed.

The computer forensics has become vital in the corporate world. There can be theft of the data from an organization in which case the organization may sustain heavy losses. For this purpose computer forensics are used as they help in tracking the criminal.

The need in the present age can be considered as much severe due to the internet advancements and the dependency on the internet. The people that gain access to the computer systems with out proper authorization should be dealt in. The network security is an important issue related to the computer world. The computer forensics is a threat against the wrong doers and the people with the negative mindsets.

The computer forensics is also efficient where in the data is stored in a single system for the backup. The data theft and the intentional damage of the data in a single system can also be minimized with the computer forensics. There are hardware and software that employ the security measures in order to track the changes and the updating of the data or the information. The user information is provided in the log files that can be effectively used to produce the evidence in case of any crime a legal manner.

The main purpose of the computer forensics is to produce evidence in the court that can lead to the punishment of the actual. The forensic science is actually the process of utilizing the scientific knowledge for the purpose of collection, analysis, and most importantly the presentation of the evidence in the court of law. The word forensic itself means to bring to the court.

The need or the importance of the computer forensics is to ensure the integrity of the computer system. The system with some small measures can avoid the cost of operating and maintaining the security. The subject provides in depth knowledge for the understanding of the legal as well as the technical aspects of computer crime. It is very much useful from a technical stand point, view.

The importance of computer forensics is evident in tracking the cases of the child pornography and email spanning. The computer forensics has been efficiently used to track down the terrorists from the various parts of the world. The terrorists using the internet as the medium of communication can be tracked down and their plans can be known.

There are many tools that can be used in combination with the computer forensics to find out the geographical information and the hide outs of the criminals. The IP address plays an important role to find out the geographical position of the terrorists. The security personnel deploy the effective measures using the computer forensics. The Intrusion Detecting Systems are used for that purpose.

**Computer Forensic Example**

- Recovery of over 1000 E-Mails off of a hard drive.
- A year and half after the individual left the company.
- After the hard drive had been formatted.
- After the machine was in use by another user for that year and a half
- "Best way to remove e-mail from a hard drive is to hit with a sledge hammer and throw it into a furnace." John Patzakis, President & Chief Legal Officer Guidance Software.

The field of computer forensics also has sub branches within it such as firewall forensics, network forensics, database forensics and mobile device forensics.

There are many reasons to employ the techniques of computer forensics:

- In legal cases, computer forensic techniques are frequently used to analyze computer systems belonging to defendants (in criminal cases) or litigants (in civil cases).
- To recover data in the event of a hardware or software failure.
- To analyze a computer system after a break-in, for example, to determine how the attacker gained access and what the attacker did.

- To gather evidence against an employee that an organization wishes to terminate.
- To gain information about how computer systems work for the purpose of debugging, performance optimization, or reverse-engineering.

Special measures should be taken when conducting a forensic investigation if it is desired for the results to be used in a court of law. One of the most important measures is to assure that the evidence has been accurately collected and that there is a clear chain of custody from the scene of the crime to the investigator — and ultimately to the court. In order to comply with the need to maintain the integrity of digital evidence, British examiners comply with the Association of Chief Police Officers (A.C.P.O.) guidelines. These are made up of four principles as follows:

**Principle 1:** No action taken by law enforcement agencies or their agents should change data held on a computer or storage media which may subsequently be relied upon in court.

**Principle 2:** In exceptional circumstances, where a person finds it necessary to access original data held on a computer or on storage media, that person must be competent to do so and be able to give evidence explaining the relevance and the implications of their actions.

**Principle 3:** An audit trail or other record of all processes applied to computer based electronic evidence should be created and preserved. An independent third party should be able to examine those processes and achieve the same result.

**Principle 4:** The person in charge of the investigation (the case officer) has overall responsibility for ensuring that the law and these principles are adhered to.

### 5.4.1 The Forensic Process

There are five basic steps to the computer forensics: Preparation (of the investigator, not the data)

1. Collection (the data)
2. Examination
3. Analysis
4. Reporting

The investigator must be properly trained to perform the specific kind of investigation that is at hand.

Tools that are used to generate reports for court should be validated. There are many tools to be used in the process. One should determine the proper tool to be used based on the case.

#### *5.4.1.1 Collecting Digital Evidence*

Digital evidence can be collected from many sources. Obvious sources include computers, cell phones, digital cameras, hard drives, CD-ROM, USB memory devices, and so on. Non-obvious sources include settings of digital thermometers, black boxes inside automobiles, RFID tags, and web pages (which must be preserved as they are subject to change).

Special care must be taken when handling computer evidence: most digital information is easily changed, and once changed it is usually impossible to detect that a change has taken place (or to revert the data back to its original state) unless other measures have been taken. For this reason it is common practice to calculate a cryptographic hash of an evidence file and to record that hash elsewhere, usually in an investigator's notebook, so that one can establish at a later point in time that the evidence has not been modified since the hash was calculated.

Other specific practices that have been adopted in the handling of digital evidence include:

- Imaging computer media using a write blocking tool to ensure that no data is added to the suspect device.
- Establish and maintain the chain of custody.
- Documenting everything that has been done.
- Only use tools and methods that have been tested and evaluated to validate their accuracy and reliability.

Some of the most valuable information obtained in the course of a forensic examination will come from the computer user. An interview with the user can yield valuable information about the system configuration, applications, encryption keys and methodology. Forensic analysis is much easier when analysts have the user's pass phrases to access encrypted files, containers, and network servers.

In an investigation in which the owner of the digital evidence has not given consent to have his or her media examined (as in some criminal cases) special care must be taken to ensure that the forensic specialist has the legal authority to seize, copy, and examine the data. Sometimes authority stems from a search warrant. As a general rule, one should not examine digital information unless one has the legal authority to do so. Amateur forensic examiners should keep this in mind before starting any unauthorized investigation.

#### 5.4.1.2 Live vs. Dead Analysis

Traditionally computer forensic investigations were performed on data at rest, for example, the content of hard drives. This can be thought of as a **dead analysis**. Investigators were told to shut down computer systems when they were impounded for fear that digital time-bombs might cause data to be erased.

In recent years there has increasingly been an emphasis on performing analysis on live systems. One reason is that many current attacks against computer systems leave no trace on the computer's hard drive; the attacker only exploits information in the computer's memory. Another reason is the growing use of cryptographic storage: it may be that the only copy of the keys to decrypt the storage are in the computer's memory, turning off the computer will cause that information to be lost.

#### 5.4.1.3 Imaging Electronic Media (Evidence)

The process of creating an exact duplicate of the original evidentiary media is often called **Imaging**. Using a stand-alone hard-drive duplicator or software imaging tools such as DCFLdd, IXimager or Guymager, the entire hard drive is completely duplicated. This is usually done at the sector level, making a bit-stream copy of every part of the user-accessible areas of the hard drive which can physically store data, rather than duplicating the file system. The original drive is then moved to secure storage to prevent tampering. During imaging, a write protection device or application is normally used to ensure that no information is introduced onto the evidentiary media during the forensic process.

The imaging process is verified by using the SHA-1 message digest algorithm (with a program such as sha1sum) or other still viable algorithms such as MD5. At critical points throughout the analysis, the media is verified again, known as "hashing", to ensure that the evidence is still in its original state.

In corporate environments seeking civil or internal charges, such steps are generally overlooked due to the time required to perform them. They are essential for evidence that is to be presented in a court room, however.

### 5.4.1.4 Collecting Volatile Data

If the machine is still active, any intelligence which can be gained by examining the applications currently open is recorded. If the machine is suspected of being used for illegal communications, such as terrorist traffic, not all of this information may be stored on the hard drive. If information stored solely in RAM is not recovered before powering down it may be lost. This results in the need to collect volatile data from the computer at the onset of the response.

Several Open Source tools are available to conduct an analysis of open ports, mapped drives (including through an active VPN connection), and open or mounted encrypted files (containers) on the live computer system. Utilizing open source tools and commercially available products, it is possible to obtain an image of these mapped drives and the open encrypted containers in an unencrypted format. Open Source tools for PCs include Knoppix and Helix. Commercial imaging tools include Access Data's Forensic Toolkit and Guidance Software's EnCase application.

The aforementioned Open Source tools can also scan RAM and Registry information to show recently accessed web-based email sites and the login/password combination used. Additionally these tools can also yield login/password for recently accessed local email applications including MS Outlook.

In the event that partitions with EFS are suspected to exist, the encryption keys to access the data can also be gathered during the collection process. With Microsoft's most recent addition, Vista, and Vista's use of Bit Locker and the Trusted Platform Module (TPM), it has become necessary in some instances to image the logical hard drive volumes before the computer is shut down.

RAM can be analyzed for prior content after power loss. Although as production methods become cleaner the impurities used to indicate a particular cell's charge prior to power loss are becoming less common. However, data held statically in an area of RAM for long periods of time are more likely to be detectable using these methods. The likelihood of such recovery increases as the originally applied voltages, operating temperatures and duration of data storage increases. Holding un powered RAM below - 60°C will help preserve the residual data by an order of magnitude, thus improving the chances of successful recovery. However, it can be impractical to do this during a field examination.

### 5.4.1.5 Analysis

All digital evidence must be analyzed to determine the type of information that is stored upon it. For this purpose, specialty tools are used that can display information in a format useful to investigators. Such forensic tools include: Access Data's FTK, Guidance Software's EnCase, Dr. Golden Richard III's file carving tool Scalpel, and Brian Carrier's Sleuth Kit. In many investigations, numerous other tools are used to analyze specific portions of information.

**Typical forensic analysis includes a manual review of material on the media, reviewing the Windows registry for suspect information, discovering and cracking passwords, keyword searches for topics related to the crime, and extracting e-mail and images for Reporting**

Once the analysis is complete, a report is generated. This report may be a written report, oral testimony, or some combination of the two.

### 5.4.2 Advantages Computer Forensics

Computer forensic is an elaborate topic and requires a vast amount of knowledge. Asit is a wide topic it has many advantages in it. There are even qualifications awarded by the council of computer forensics. Computer forensics professional should possess the knowledge of the hardware as well as the software tools that can be utilized for the purpose.

The main task or the advantage from the computer forensic is to catch the culprit or the criminal who is involved in the crime related to the computers. The information of the computer is advantageous in case where the involvement of hardware and software with which forensics expert is familiar. The basics of the computer design and architecture play a prominent role and the expert professional should have a great deal of knowledge about the fundamental software design and implementation.

This is quite often similar from one computer system to the other. Experience of one application, software, file system or the operating system can be applied to gain the results in the other aspects of the case. The computer crime exists in many forms.

Computer Forensics deals extensively to find the evidence in order to prove the crime and the culprit behind it in a court of law. The forensics provides the organization with a support and helps them recover their loss. If it is known that the data exists then the alternate formats of the same data or the information can also be recovered. The discovery of the data or the information that can provide vital clues in the prosecution of the criminal is itself a process.

A forensics expert always identifies many possibilities that to get a relevant evidence. In addition to all the benefits of utilizing the services of the computer forensics, the professional may also undertake the inspections of the location during on site premises. This may be required in the cases where the signs or clues of the physical movement are required. Some cases may also involve additional information regarding the earlier versions or the method of backups, formatted versions of data or information, which is either created or treated by the other application programs.

The application programs may have different formats also. Some of the application programs include the word processors, spreadsheets, email, timeline and scheduling applications and even the usage of graphical applications.

The important thing and the major advantage regarding the computer forensics is the preservation of the evidence that is collected during the process. The protection of evidence can be considered as critical. A computer forensics professional expert should ensure that computer system that is being dealt with is handled carefully. Since the subject is legalized and there are many laws hence the computer forensic professionals maintain a code of ethics.

The ethicality can be considered as an advantage of the forensics in computer systems. At last the computer forensics has emerged as important part in the disaster recovery management. Most of the organizations some time or the other employs the services of the computer forensics experts. The cost of operations is also lower in comparison with the security measures that are applied.

### 5.4.3 Disadvantages of Computer Forensics

Every thing that has an advantage obviously has some disadvantages as well. But the disadvantages in case of the computer forensics can be considered as the limitations of the subject. The major disadvantage of the computer forensics is the privacy concern. It may happen in some cases that the privacy of the client is compromised.

It is the duty of the computer forensics expert to maintain the high standards and the keep in mind the sensitivity of the case and maintain the privacy and secrecy of the data or the information of the client's interests. But in some circumstances it becomes almost impossible for the computer forensics professional to maintain the secrecy of the data or the information. This may happen if the information is necessary to prove the crime and should be produced as the evidence in the court of law in order to prove the crime.

There are other disadvantages as well regarding the computer forensics. It is also possible that some sensitive data or information that is important to the client may be lost in order to find the evidence. The forensics professional must maintain the concern that the data information or the possible evidence is not destroyed, damaged, or even otherwise be compromised by the procedures that are utilized for the purpose of investigating a computer system.

There are also the chances of introduction of some malicious programs in the computer system that may corrupt the data at a later stage of time. During the analysis process care should be taken that no possible computer virus is released or introduced in the computer system. IT is also possible that the hardware of the computer system is damaged physically.

The evidence that is physically extracted and the relevant evidence should be properly handled as well as protected from later damage that may either mechanical or electromagnetic in nature. The integrity of the data and the information that is acquired should be preserved. The custody of the data that is acquired as the evidence is the responsibility of the computer forensics team.

During the time case is solved; it may be required that the data or the information is stored in the court. In some cases it is also possible that the data is in dispute and neither of the disputing parties can use the data. Due to this reason the business operations may also be affected. The duty of the computer forensics expert is to ensure that justice is delivered as fast as possible so that the inconvenience and the subsequent loss to the organization can be avoided.

It is also important the information that is acquired during the forensic exploration is ethically and legally respected. More over despite some of the limitations of the Computer Forensics the subject is still perceived. Also the advantages and the benefits of the subject have wide applications in various situations. Measures should be taken and the care of the professional employed for the computer forensics is a must to avoid any subsequent damage to the computer system. It is also possible in cases that the operations cost may exceed. Steps should be taken to minimize the cost.

## 5.5 INTERNET ETHICS

In January 1989 the Internet Architecture Board (IAB) issued a statement of policy concerning Internet ethics. This document is referred to as RFC 1087 'Ethics and the Internet'.

An extract of RFC 1087 follows:

*The IAB strongly endorses the view of the Division Advisory Panel of the National Science Foundation Division of Network, Communications Research and Infrastructure which, in paraphrase, characterized as unethical and unacceptable any activity which purposely:*

- *Seeks to gain unauthorized access to the resources of the Internet.*
- *Disrupts the intended use of the Internet.*
- *Wastes resources (people, capacity, computer) through such actions.*

- *Destroys the integrity of computer-based information.*
- *Compromises the privacy of users.*

## 5.6 CYBER CRIME

Cyber crime is the latest and perhaps the most complicated problem in the cyber world. "Cyber crime may be said to be those species, of which, genus is the conventional crime, and where either the computer is an object or subject of the conduct constituting crime." "Any criminal activity that uses a computer either as an instrumentality, target or a means for perpetuating further crimes comes within the ambit of cyber crime"

**What is a Computer Crime?**

a. Criminals Can Operate Anonymously Over the Computer Networks.
b. Hackers Invade Privacy.
c. Hackers Destroy "Property" in the Form of Computer Files or Records.
d. Hackers Injure Other Computer Users by Destroying Information Systems.
e. Computer Pirates Steal Intellectual Property.

**Definition of Cyber Crime**

Defining cyber crimes, as "acts that are punishable by the Information Technology Act" would be unsuitable as the Indian Penal Code also covers many cyber crimes, such as email spoofing and cyber defamation, sending threatening emails etc. A simple yet sturdy definition of cyber crime would be "unlawful acts wherein the computer is either a tool or a target or both".

**Classification of Cyber Crimes**

*The Information Technology Act deals with the following cyber crimes along with others:*

- Tampering with computer source documents
- Hacking
- Publishing of information, which is obscene in electronic form
- Child Pornography
- Accessing protected system
- Breach of confidentiality and privacy

*Cyber crimes other than those mentioned under the IT Act*

- Cyber Stalking
- Cyber squatting
- Data Diddling
- Cyber Defamation
- Trojan Attack
- Forgery

- Financial crimes
- Internet time theft
- Virus/worm attack
- E-mail spoofing
- E-mail bombing
- Salami attack
- Web Jacking

A generalized definition of cyber crime may be " unlawful acts wherein the computer is either a tool or target or both". The computer may be used as a tool in the following kinds of activity- financial crimes, sale of illegal articles, pornography, online gambling, intellectual property crime, e-mail spoofing, forgery, cyber defamation, cyber stalking. The computer may however be target for unlawful acts in the following cases- unauthorized access to computer/ computer system/ computer networks, theft of information contained in the electronic form, e-mail bombing, data didling, salami attacks, logic bombs, Trojan attacks, internet time thefts, web jacking, theft of computer system, physically damaging the computer system.

### 5.6.1 Reasons For Cyber Crime

Hart in his work "The Concept of Law" has said 'human beings are vulnerable so rule of law is required to protect them'. Applying this to the cyberspace we may say that computers are vulnerable so rule of law is required to protect and safeguard them against cyber crime. The reasons for the vulnerability of computers may be said to be:

1. **Capacity to store data in comparatively small space:** The computer has unique characteristic of storing data in a very small space. This affords to remove or derive information either through physical or virtual medium makes it much more easier.
2. **Easy to access:** The problem encountered in guarding a computer system from unauthorised access is that there is every possibility of breach not due to human error but due to the complex technology. By secretly implanted logic bomb, key loggers that can steal access codes, advanced voice recorders; retina imagers etc. that can fool biometric systems and bypass firewalls can be utilized to get past many a security system.
3. **Complex:** The computers work on operating systems and these operating systems in turn are composed of millions of codes. Human mind is fallible and it is not possible that there might not be a lapse at any stage. The cyber criminals take advantage of these lacunas and penetrate into the computer system.
4. **Negligence:** Negligence is very closely connected with human conduct. It is therefore very probable that while protecting the computer system there might be any negligence, which in turn provides a cyber criminal to gain access and control over the computer system.
5. **Loss of evidence:** Loss of evidence is a very common & obvious problem as all the data are routinely destroyed. Further collection of data outside the territorial extent also paralyses this system of crime investigation.

### 5.6.2 Cyber Criminals

The cyber criminals constitute of various groups/category. This division may be justified on the basis of the object that they have in their mind. The following are the category of cyber criminals-

1. **Children and adolescents between the age group of 6–18 years:** The simple reason for this type of delinquent behaviour pattern in children is seen mostly due to the inquisitiveness to know and explore the things. Other cognate reason may be to prove themselves to be outstanding amongst other children in their group.
2. **Organised hackers:** These kinds of hackers are mostly organised together to fulfil certain objective. The reason may be to fulfil their political bias, fundamentalism, etc. The Pakistanis are said to be one of the best quality hackers in the world. They mainly target the Indian government sites with the purpose to fulfil their political objectives. Further the NASA as well as the Microsoft sites is always under attack by the hackers.
3. **Professional hackers/crackers:** Their work is motivated by the color of money. These kinds of hackers are mostly employed to hack the site of the rivals and get credible, reliable and valuable information.
4. **Discontented employees:** This group include those people who have been either sacked by their employer or are dissatisfied with their employer. To avenge they normally hack the system of their employee.

### 5.6.3 Mode And Manner of Committing Cyber Crime

1. **Unauthorized access to computer systems or networks/Hacking:** This kind of offence is normally referred as hacking in the generic sense. However the framers of the information technology act 2000 have no where used this term so to avoid any confusion we would not interchangeably use the word hacking for 'unauthorized access' as the latter has wide connotation.
2. **Theft of information contained in electronic form:** This includes information stored in computer hard disks, removable storage media etc. Theft may be either by appropriating the data physically or by tampering them through the virtual medium.
3. **Email bombing:** This kind of activity refers to sending large numbers of mail to the victim, which may be an individual or a company or even mail servers there by ultimately resulting into crashing.
4. **Data diddling:** This kind of an attack involves altering raw data just before a computer processes it and then changing it back after the processing is completed. The electricity board faced similar problem of data diddling while the department was being computerised.
5. **Salami attacks:** This kind of crime is normally prevalent in the financial institutions or for the purpose of committing financial crimes. An important feature of this type of offence is that the alteration is so small that it would normally go unnoticed. E.g. the Ziegler case wherein a logic bomb was introduced in the bank's system, which deducted 10 cents from every account and deposited it in a particular account.
6. **Denial of Service attack:** The computer of the victim is flooded with more requests than it can handle which cause it to crash. Distributed Denial of Service (DDoS) attack is also a type of denial of service attack, in which the offenders are wide in number and widespread. E.g. Amazon, Yahoo.

7. **Virus/worm attacks:** Viruses are programs that attach themselves to a computer or a file and then circulate themselves to other files and to other computers on a network. They usually affect the data on a computer, either by altering or deleting it. Worms, unlike viruses do not need the host to attach themselves to. They merely make functional copies of themselves and do this repeatedly till they eat up all the available space on a computer's memory. E.g. love bug virus, which affected at least 5 % of the computers of the globe. The losses were accounted to be $ 10 million. The world's most famous worm was the Internet worm let loose on the Internet by Robert Morris sometime in 1988. Almost brought development of Internet to a complete halt.
8. **Logic bombs:** These are event dependent programs. This implies that these programs are created to do something only when a certain event (known as a trigger event) occurs. E.g. even some viruses may be termed logic bombs because they lie dormant all through the year and become active only on a particular date (like the Chernobyl virus).
9. **Trojan attacks:** This term has its origin in the word 'Trojan horse'. In software field this means an unauthorized programme, which passively gains control over another's system by representing itself as an authorised programme. The most common form of installing a Trojan is through e-mail.
10. **Internet time thefts:** Normally in these kinds of thefts the Internet surfing hours of the victim are used up by another person. This is done by gaining access to the login ID and the password. E.g. Colonel Bajwa's case- the Internet hours were used up by any other person. This was perhaps one of the first reported cases related to cyber crime in India.
11. **Web jacking:** This term is derived from the term hi jacking. In these kinds of offences the hacker gains access and control over the web site of another. He may even mutilate or change the information on the site. This may be done for fulfilling political objectives or for money. E.g. recently the site of MIT (Ministry of Information Technology) was hacked by the Pakistani hackers and some obscene matter was placed therein. Further the site of Bombay crime branch was also web jacked. Another case of web jacking is that of the 'gold fish' case. In this case the site was hacked and the information pertaining to gold fish was changed. Thus web jacking is a process where by control over the site of another is made backed by some consideration for it.

### 5.6.4 Classification

The subject of cyber crime may be broadly classified under the following three groups. They are:

1. **Against Individuals**
   a. the person &
   b. the property of an individual
2. **Against Organization**
   a. Government
   b. Firm, Company, Group of Individuals.
3. **Against Society at large**

**4. Against Individual Property**

a. Computer vandalism.

b. Transmitting virus.

c. Netrespass

d. Unauthorized control/access over computer system.

e. Intellectual Property crimes

f. Internet time thefts

**5. Against Organization**

a. Unauthorized control/access over computer system

b. Possession of unauthorized information.

c. Cyber terrorism against the government organization.

d. Distribution of pirated software etc.

**6. Against Society at large**

a. Pornography (basically child pornography).

b. Polluting the youth through indecent exposure.

c. Trafficking

d. Financial crimes

e. Sale of illegal articles

f. Online gambling

g. Forgery

The above mentioned offences may discussed in brief as follows:

1. **Harassment via e-mails:** Harassment through e-mails is not a new concept. It is very similar to harassing through letters.
2. **Cyber-stalking:** The Oxford dictionary defines stalking as "pursuing stealthily". Cyber stalking involves following a person's movements across the Internet by posting messages (sometimes threatening) on the bulletin boards frequented by the victim, entering the chat-rooms frequented by the victim, constantly bombarding the victim with emails etc.
3. **Dissemination of obscene material/ Indecent exposure/ Pornography (basically child pornography) / Polluting through indecent exposure.**
4. **Defamation:** It is an act of imputing any person with intent to lower the person in the estimation of the right-thinking members of society generally or to cause him to be shunned or avoided or to expose him to hatred, contempt or ridicule. Cyber defamation is not different from conventional defamation except the involvement of a virtual medium. E.g. the mail account of *Rohit* was hacked and some mails were sent from his account to some of his batch mates.
5. **Unauthorized control/access over computer system:** This activity is commonly referred to as hacking. The Indian law has however given a different connotation to the term hacking, so we will not use the term "unauthorized access" interchangeably with the term "hacking" to prevent confusion as the term used in the Act of 2000 is much wider than hacking.

6. **E-mail spoofing:** A spoofed e-mail may be said to be one, which misrepresents its origin. It shows it's origin to be different from which actually it originates.
7. **Computer vandalism:** Vandalism means deliberately destroying or damaging property of another. Thus computer vandalism may include within its purview any kind of physical harm done to the computer of any person. These acts may take the form of the theft of a computer, some part of a computer or a peripheral attached to the computer or by physically damaging a computer or its peripherals.
8. **Transmitting virus/worms.**
9. **Intellectual Property crimes / Distribution of pirated software:** Intellectual property consists of a bundle of rights. Any unlawful act by which the owner is deprived completely or partially of his rights is an offence. The common form of IPR violation may be said to be software piracy, copyright infringement, trademark and service mark violation, theft of computer source code, etc.

   The *Hyderabad Court* has in a land mark judgement has convicted three people and sentenced them to six months imprisonment and fine of 50,000 each for unauthorized copying and sell of pirated software.
10. **Cyber terrorism against the government organization:** At this juncture a necessity may be felt that what is the need to distinguish between cyber terrorism and cyber crime. Both are criminal acts. However there is a compelling need to distinguish between both these crimes. A cyber crime is generally a domestic issue, which may have international consequences, however cyber terrorism is a global concern, which has domestic as well as international consequences. The common form of these terrorist attacks on the Internet is by distributed denial of service attacks, hate websites and hate emails, attacks on sensitive computer networks, etc. Technology savvy terrorists are using 512-bit encryption, which is next to impossible to decrypt.

    Cyber terrorism may be defined to be "*the premeditated use of disruptive activities, or the threat thereof, in cyber space, with the intention to further social, ideological, religious, political or similar objectives, or to intimidate any person in furtherance of such objectives.*"

    Another definition may be attempted to cover within its ambit every act of cyber terrorism.

    *A terrorist means a person who indulges in wanton killing of persons or in violence or in disruption of services or means of communications essential to the community or in damaging property with the view to—*

    (1) putting the public or any section of the public in fear; or

    (2) affecting adversely the harmony between different religious, racial, language or regional groups or castes or communities; or

    (3) coercing or overawing the government established by law; or

    (4) endangering the sovereignty and integrity of the nation and a cyber terrorist is the person who uses the computer system as a means or ends to achieve the above objectives. Every act done in pursuance thereof is an act of cyber terrorism.

11. **Trafficking:** Trafficking may assume different forms. It may be trafficking in drugs, human beings, arms weapons etc. These forms of trafficking are going unchecked because they are carried on under pseudonyms. A racket was busted in Chennai where drugs were being sold under the pseudonym of honey.
12. **Fraud & Cheating:** Online fraud and cheating is one of the most lucrative businesses that are growing today in the cyber space. It may assume different forms. Some of the cases of online fraud and cheating that have come to light are those pertaining to credit card crimes, contractual crimes, offering jobs, etc

### 5.6.5 Prevention Of Cyber Crime

Prevention is always better than cure. It is always better to take certain precaution while operating the net. 5P mantra for online security: Precaution, Prevention, Protection, Preservation and Perseverance. A netizen should keep in mind the following things:

1. to prevent cyber stalking avoid disclosing any information pertaining to oneself. This is as good as disclosing your identity to strangers in public place.
2. always avoid sending any photograph online particularly to strangers and chat friends as there have been incidents of misuse of the photographs.
3. always use latest and up date anti virus software to guard against virus attacks.
4. always keep back up volumes so that one may not suffer data loss in case of virus contamination
5. never send your credit card number to any site that is not secured, to guard against frauds.
6. always keep a watch on the sites that your children are accessing to prevent any kind of harassment or depravation in children.
7. it is better to use a security programme that gives control over the cookies and send information back to the site as leaving the cookies unguarded might prove fatal.
8. web site owners should watch traffic and check any irregularity on the site. Putting host-based intrusion detection devices on servers may do this.
9. use of firewalls may be beneficial.
10. web servers running public sites must be physically separate protected from internal corporate network.

## 5.7 TOP IT TRENDS IN INDIA

The local Indian market will come into its own for technology outsourcing. India is already the largest local market in Asia Pacific after Australia and Japan and the booming Indian economy will mean there is significantly more technology outsourcing to be done by local Indian companies in 2007.

"A one per cent growth in the national GDP will translate into a 20–22 per cent growth in the domestic IT market," says Alok Shende, director ICT practice (India), Frost and Sullivan. Utkarsh Palnitkar, partner, Ernst & Young (E&Y) concurs: "There will a double digit growth for the $8 billion domestic market."

"This will be especially true of the government, financial services and telecom sectors — estimated size of $2.5–3 billion for contracts of up to $25 million each," pitches in Sidharth Pai, Partner, TPI.

The BPO industry will continue to move up the value chain. "Outsourcing is set to go up from low value intermediates / APIs to late stage intermediates/ APIs/ formulation side," says Palinitkar.

Also 2007 will see the bid market, that is Fortune 1400 and below companies outsourcing to India. "The Fortune 1400 and below companies will now jump onto the outsourcing market," shares Shende.

Even consolidation is set to increase as firms look at improving topline based on matching of synergies. Favouring the European Union due to continuation of favourable valuations for more M&As to take place vis-à-vis United States, Palnitkar says: "Inorganic avenues of growth are being seriously looked at by domestic companies to take advantages of the flattening of the world."

While the reason for acquisition could be pipeline, relationship-building or technological competence for IT India Inc where the top five still contribute to a major chunk of the industry's revenues, "the consolidation will be among the top 10 players to consolidate their market share," says Shende.

India Inc will once again be in the news for winning the big ticket contracts. "In 2006 the frequency had come down as companies go through a 4–5 year cycle for reviewing their contracts and 2007 there will be announcements for major international deals taking place with India Inc winning a few," says Shende.

**MEGA-TREND #1** is the acquiring of scale. The Indian economy, Indian companies and Indian markets were mostly small or tiny. Remember that the Ambani family wealth seven years ago was about Rs 5,000 crore (Rs 50 billion) — the same as Jignesh Shah's today. Don't know about him? He is a first-generation entrepreneur who is not yet 40.

The telecom market was 5 million connections 15 years ago; now it is over 180 million, and the fastest growing in the world. The fourth-largest phone company in India is now being valued at $20 billion. Or take commercial space: all of India's cities used to have office space totalling 40 million square feet. Now we are adding that much as new commercial space every year.

The total Indian car market was half a million vehicles in 2000; by 2010, a single company will be turning out twice that number, and India will be a small car manufacturing hub for the world. Companies, when they hired, used to do so in the hundreds; now the big ones do it in the tens of thousands.

**MEGA-TREND #2** is the spread of connectivity and awareness. In John Naisbitt's original identification of mega-trends, back in 1982, he called it networking.

Imagine the difference between a country that has 5 million phones and another with 180 million; between a country with 10 million TV sets and one with 120 million; between a country whose trucks move at 25 km per hour on the highways (counting the time taken for stops), and 50 km per hour.

Think of the consequences as Country No. 1 morphs into Country No. 2: better supply chain management, just in time delivery, and therefore scale of production if you can start at dawn and give delivery 500 km away by dusk (tomorrow it may be 800 km).

Think different awareness levels and therefore a different quality of decision-making; and think speed of response because you can reach someone on a mobile phone anytime anywhere. In short, think productivity gains — which is what the growth story is all about.

**MEGA-TREND #3** is the growth of the middle class — talked about and anticipated for 20 years, but finally acquiring true scale. In 2001-02, there were 61 million Indians belonging to families that earned more than Rs 2 lakh (Rs 200,000) a year; by last year (2005-06), that number had crossed 100 million.

In 2009–10, the National Council for Applied Economic Research forecasts it will be 173 million. Marry that with growing urbanisation, and it is a safe guess that well over a third of all Lok Sabha constituencies will have a sizeable middle class and urban voter base. Think, then, of the many changes this might bring about. The obvious point is about growth of consumption, but we can go beyond that.

**MEGA-TREND #4** has to do with the growing problems of growth. There is the environment: the increasing pollution of air (all those additional cars), the dropping of the groundwater table, and the failure to renew resources (like forests).

There is the energy question: do we really think the world oil market will not go haywire if we treble our consumption? The fact is that we are locked into a pattern of increasingly energy-intensive, resource-gobbling production and consumption from which there is probably no escape any more because everyone wants the western middle-class dream.

As surely as night follows day, then, there will be consequences. As someone said, other than weapons of mass destruction, the only thing that can extinguish human life is environmental change.

The third problem of growth is disparity, which is almost certain to increase (think all the way from executive jets and Bentleys to luxury watches and multi-crore apartments). How will this play in a democratic system, if others don't have food to eat and are committing suicide?

Consider then how politicians are trying to mediate the tensions: reservations of seats and jobs, cesses of various kinds to finance big spending programmes. If the rich have thought they can secede into gated residential communities and offices in corporate parks, hang on because outside reality will intrude.

**MEGA-TREND #5** has to do with India's increasing openness to the world. The number of US visas issued in India doubled in 2006, to over 800,000 — more than in any other country, barring Mexico. More Indian students are studying in other countries than those of any other nationality, barring perhaps China. Neither of these was remotely true 15 years ago.

The foreign trade component of India's GDP (if you include trade in both goods and services, like software) is now about 55 per cent — nearly three times what it used to be. Foreign institutional investors own about 25 per cent of India's listed stock. And Indian firms were buying three overseas companies a week, through 2006.

A country that is open to the world reacts in fundamentally different ways from a closed system (of the kind that India used to be).

There is greater self-confidence, faster acceptance of new influences and ideas, a willingness to accept global benchmarking, and a speedier response to changing circumstance. It is simply a more adaptive and therefore a more efficient system. Translate that to mean more productivity growth.

**MEGA-TREND #6** the continuing dominance of youth. Something like half of India is under 25, and it will remain that way for some time. This is usually spun around into the economic fact that a higher percentage of people will be in the working age till the mid-twenty-first century, but that is only one facet.

Youngsters are different from oldies in a hundred ways, and anyone can make a long list of the differences. How this will affect Indian society cannot really be predicted, except to say that it will be more mobile (think more migrants), and more volatile (stronger responses to frustrations— one manifestation being the spread of extremist Left ideology in some 60 districts).

It will adapt faster to new trends, and marketers will be encouraged to focus on low-cost products and services because youngsters usually have less money. It will probably mean that the two-parent home (for nurturing children) will remain the predominant norm for long, and that there will be a strong saving habit because families will be planning (among other things) for their children's educational future.

Four of these six mega-trends have almost entirely positive implications; one is clearly negative, and the last can cut both ways. There could be other negative trends too, like the steady collapse of governance and the country's politics shooting off the tracks.

## 5.8 WHAT IS E-COMMERCE?

Electronic commerce or e-commerce refers to a wide range of online business activities for products and services. It also pertains to "any form of business transaction in which the parties interact electronically rather than by physical exchanges or direct physical contact." E-commerce is usually associated with buying and selling over the Internet, or conducting any transaction involving the transfer of ownership or rights to use goods or services through a computer-mediated network. Though popular, this definition is not comprehensive enough to capture recent developments in this new and revolutionary business phenomenon. A more complete definition is: E-commerce is the use of electronic communications and digital information processing technology in business transactions to create, transform, and redefine relationships for value creation between or among organizations, and between organizations and individuals

Three primary processes are enhanced in e-business:

1. **Production processes**, which include procurement, ordering and replenishment of stocks; processing of payments; electronic links with suppliers; and production control processes, among others;
2. **Customer-focused processes**, which include promotional and marketing efforts, selling over the Internet, processing of customers' purchase orders and payments, and customer support, among others; and
3. **Internal management processes**, which include employee services, training, internal information-sharing, video-conferencing, and recruiting. Electronic applications enhance information flow between production and sales forces to improve sales force productivity. Workgroup communications and electronic publishing of internal business information are likewise made more efficient.

**Electronic Commerce**, commonly known as (electronic marketing) **e-commerce** or **eCommerce**, consists of the buying and selling of products or services over electronic systems such as the Internet and other computer networks. The amount of trade conducted electronically has grown extraordinarily with widespread Internet usage. The use of commerce is conducted in this way, spurring and drawing on innovations in electronic funds transfer, supply chain management, Internet marketing, online transaction processing, electronic data interchange (EDI), inventory management systems, and automated data collection systems. Modern electronic commerce typically uses the World Wide Web at least at some point in the transaction's lifecycle, although it can encompass a wider range of technologies such as e-mail as well.

A large percentage of electronic commerce is conducted entirely electronically for virtual items such as access to premium content on a website, but most electronic commerce involves the transportation of physical items in some way. Online retailers are sometimes known as e-tailers and online retail is sometimes known as **e-tail**. Almost all big retailers have electronic commerce presence on the World Wide Web.

Electronic commerce that is conducted between businesses is referred to as business-to-business or B2B. B2B can be open to all interested parties (e.g. commodity exchange) or limited to specific, pre-qualified participants (private electronic market). Electronic commerce that is conducted between businesses and consumers, on the other hand, is referred to as business-to-consumer or B2C. This is the type of electronic commerce conducted by companies such as Amazon.com.

Electronic commerce is generally considered to be the sales aspect of e-business. It also consists of the exchange of data to facilitate the financing and payment aspects of the business transactions.

### 5.8.1 Types of E-Commerce

In simple words, E-Commerce is doing the work of commerce electronically. Now, it is not that we have E-Commerce between certain groups only; rather we have E-Commerce that can be between many groups. Therefore, we do not have only one type of the E-Commerce, but we have many types of the E-Commerce. Our E-Commerce can be between business and business, or between business and consumers, or can be between business and employees, and can be many more.

Following are the different kinds of the E-Commerce of Creative Web Store:

**B2E — Business to Employee**

**C2B — Consumer to Business**

**B2B — Business to Business**

**B2C — Business to Consumer**

**C2C — Consumer to Consumer**

#### *5.8.1.1 B2B — Business to Business*

B2B is the selling between companies, wholesale rather than retail. But it means more than that. Efficient use of capital demands small inventories, which entails anticipating demand, and so maintaining detailed information flows between all parties involved in today's complex manufacturing processes. B2B involves widening the circle of suppliers (for safety and competition), and of centralizing control (for records and discounts).

B2B ecommerce is an important part of any online business. Leaving aside the simple transfer of funds — covered here — many businesses need some combination of:

- creditworthiness assessment.
- guarantee of quality and delivery of goods (escrow services).

- safeguards against fraud.
- fast collection of funds, with ability to vary the collection period.
- reporting: approval of sale, invoicing, delivery, payment.
- procedures to handle disputes.

Information of all types — corporate, technical, identity-building — has to be interchanged across the scattered divisions of large companies, and new ideas fostered, assessed and disseminated. Speed is vital, as are improved communication, collaboration, and customer understanding. All these requirements can be handled by IT, and software has been developed to meet the challenge — customer relationship management, enterprise resource planning, online auction, supply chain management, etc. Little of it is off-the-shelf, but is devised as systems to be extended and built round individual company requirements.

### 5.8.1.2 B2C — Business to Consumer

B2C (Business to Consumer): Refers to a business communicating with or selling to an individual rather than a company.

Doing business online no longer requires a huge investment by retailers, thanks to developments in template based online stores which are based on packaged applications that are delivered over the internet.

As nearly all online stores will require the same functions: catalogues, order baskets, payment processing, content management and member management, it makes sense for those components to be created once and shared by all stores, with each store effectively 'renting' its own copy of the applications.

The one area where it's important for online stores to differentiate is their look and feel, and natural retailers feel very strongly about their business branding. So the ability to create a unique 'skin' for each site is an important part of a template-based e-store offering.

Using the latest internet application technology, individual sites can be created within minutes the retailer selecting a template and supplying graphics such as logos. Typically, retailers will pay only a modest monthly rental charge – and retailers require no specialist hardware or software, other t internet access.

Anyone who wants to sell products and services over the internet, or who wants customers to be able to research their purchases on the internet, should consider an online store.

These days, a web site should be a standard part of the promotional and advertising mix for business, along with other tools such as Yellow Pages, newspaper advertising and signage.

**Advantages of B2C e-commerce**

B2C e-commerce has the following advantages:

* Shopping can be faster and more convenient.
* Offerings and prices can change instantaneously.
* Call centers can be integrated with the website.
* Broadband telecommunications will enhance the buying experience.

**Challenges faced by B2C e-commerce**

The two main challenges faced by B2C e-commerce are building traffic and sustaining customer loyalty. Due to the winner-take-all nature of the B2C structure, many smaller firms find it difficult to enter a market and remain competitive. In addition, online shoppers are very price-sensitive and are easily lured away, so acquiring and keeping new customers is difficult.

### *5.8.1.3 B2E — Business to Employee*

B2E (Business to Employee) E-Commerce generally refers to the requisitioning of supplies by employees for use in their jobs, but this really has grown to encompass much more. For example, B2E makes it very easy for an employee to requisition a new toner cartridge and printer paper - the order is entirely electronic, and supervisors are asked to approved the requisition in the event that the total order exceeds preset limits for that particular employee. However, B2E has grown into technologies that allow the employee to access their employee records to update address information, shift investments in the 401K plan, or maintain their internal resume. Many companies have found that B2E technologies have dramatically reduced the administrative burdens with the human resources department. Admittedly, maintaining employee information has little to do with commerce, but this term has grown to encapsulate this activity into the B2E definition.

### *5.8.1.4 C2B — Consumer to Business*

A consumer posts his project with a set budget online and within hours companies review the consumer's requirements and bid on the project. The consumer reviews the bids and selects the company that will complete the project. Elance empowers consumers around the world by providing the meeting ground and platform for such transactions

C2B is a rather peculiar Internet phenomenon. An example of C2B e-commerce could be the following. A student wants to fly from London to New York, but has only £200 ($320) in the bank to pay for this round trip. They put up an ad in an Internet C2B site, seeking airlines that are willing to offer the transatlantic round trip for £200 or less.

Many analysts state that C2B and C2C e-commerce will thrive in the near future. It is a challenging task, however, to construct these e-commerce systems because of their diverse nature. The existing EC construction tools, which usually focus on B2B and B2C e-commerce schemes, were designed for constructing specific e-commerce systems, making them unsuitable for developing consumer-initiated e-commerce systems.

### *5.8.1.5 C2C — Consumer to Consumer*

The introduction of the new economy has helped to create a very individualistic and independent society. Consumers are no longer totally reliant on corporations and are increasingly looking to conduct their own business transactions.

There are many sites offering free classifieds, auctions, and forums where individuals can buy and sell thanks to online payment systems like PayPal where people can send and receive money online with ease. eBay's auction service is a great example of where person-to-person transactions take place everyday since 1995.

Companies using internal networks to offer their employees products and services online — not necessarily online on the Web — are engaging in B2E (Business-to-Employee) ecommerce.

G2G (Government-to-Government), G2E (Government-to-Employee), G2B (Government-to-Business), B2G (Business-to-Government), G2C (Government-to-Citizen), C2G (Citizen-to-Government) are other forms of ecommerce that involve transactions with the government — from procurement to filing taxes to business registrations to renewing licenses. There are other categories of ecommerce out there, but they tend to be superfluous.

Other examples of Consumer-to-Consumer applications are service and employment websites such as Monster.com, Seek.com.au and CareerOne.com.au. These websites provide a valuable service to consumers looking for jobs. Employers can advertise on these websites and potential employees can contact their organization for an interview.

Web-based communication organizations are one final example of a C2C operation. Sites such as Sastashopping.com ICQ.com and MSN.com act as a communications medium for peer-to-peer deliberations. Although there is no commercial benefit to the website, they do provide the facilities for Consumer-to-Consumer exchange.

Consumer-to-Consumer applications are a growing area of eCommerce. As online business expands, peer-to-peer transactions will continue to grow in popularity and the industry will become highly profitable.

### 5.8.2 Business Applications

Some common applications related to electronic commerce are the following:

- Email
- Enterprise content management
- Instant messaging
- Newsgroups
- Online shopping and order tracking
- Online banking
- Online office suites
- Domestic and international payment systems
- Shopping cart software
- Teleconferencing
- Electronic tickets

## 5.9 EDI — ELECTRONIC DATA INTERCHANGE

### 5.9.1 What is EDI?

Electronic data interchange(EDI) is the inter-organisational exchange of business documents in structured, machine processable form. Electronic data Interchange can be used to electronically transmit documents such as purchase orders, invoices, shipping bills, receiving advices and other standard business correspondence between trading partners. EDI can also be used to transmit financial information and payments in electronic form. Payments carried out over EDI are usually referred to as Electronic Funds Transfer (EFT). EDI should not be viewed as simply a way of replacing paper documents and traditional methods of transmission such as mail, phone or in-person delivery with electronic transmission. But it should be seen not as an "end" but as a means to streamline procedures and improving efficiency and productivity.

Computers have speeded up the production of invoices, purchase orders, receiving tickets and the like. When these documents are produced by high speed printers, however, they still must be bursted, inserted and distributed (usually mailed) and copies must be filed by the originating organisation. The originals must be physically transported to the addresse, opened, carried to the appropriate individual within the addresse organization and processed, which actually means manually keying the data into an MIS system.

In EDI, in the place of traditional methods for the transmission of for e.g. a purchase order between a buyer and a seller, data is entered into the buyer's computer system, the same data is electronically sent into the seller's computer without the need for rekeying or reentry. This is normally referred to as application-to-application EDI. When EDI is fully integrated with application programs, not only does data flow electronically between trading partners without the need for rekeying, but data also flows electronically between internal applications of each of the trading partners.

The use of EDI eliminates many of these problems associated with traditional information flow, as listed below:

— The delays associated with handling, filing and transportation of paper documents are eliminated.

— Since data is keyed in only once the chances of error are reduced.

— Time required to re-enter data is saved.

— As data is not re-entered at each step in the process, labour costs can be reduced.

— Because time delays are reduced, there is more certainty in information flow. The other advantage in the use of EDI is that it generates a functional acknowledgment whenever an EDI message is received and it is electronically transmitted to the sender. This states that the message has been received. Therefore the core concept of EDI is that data is transferred electronically in machine processable form. EDI is often applied in the following situations when there are

— A large number of repetitive standard actions

— Very tight operating margins

— Strong competition requiring significant productivity improvements.

— Operational time constraints.

**Electronic Data Interchange (EDI)** refers to the structured transmission of data between organizations by electronic means. It is used to transfer electronic documents from one computer system to another (ie) from one trading partner to another trading partner. It is more than mere E-mail; for instance, organizations might replace bills of lading and even checks with appropriate EDI messages. It also refers specifically to a family of standards, including the X12 series. However, EDI also exhibits its pre-Internet roots, and the standards tend to focus on ASCII (American Standard Code for Information Interchange)-formatted single messages rather than the whole sequence of conditions and exchanges that make up an inter-organization business process.

The National Institute of Standards and Technology in a 1996 publication defines Electronic Data Interchange as "the computer-to-computer interchange of strictly formatted messages that represent documents other than monetary instruments. EDI implies a sequence of messages between two parties, either of whom may serve as originator or recipient. The formatted data representing the documents may be transmitted from originator to recipient via telecommunications or physically transported on electronic storage media.". It goes on further to say that "In EDI, the usual processing of received messages is by computer only. Human intervention in the processing of a received message is typically intended only for error conditions, for quality review, and for special situations. For example, the transmission of binary or textual data is not EDI as defined here unless the data are treated as one or more data elements of an EDI message and are not normally intended for human interpretation as part of online data processing."

EDI can be formally defined as 'The transfer of structured data, by agreed message standards, from one computer system to another without human intervention'. Most other definitions used are variations on this theme. Even in this era of technologies such as XML web services, the Internet and the World Wide Web, EDI is still the data format used by the vast majority of electronic commerce transactions in the world.

### 5.9.2 EDI Software

**EDI software** consists of computer instructions that translate the information from company-specific format to the structured EDI format, and then communicates the EDI message. EDI software also receives the message and translates from standard format to company specific format. Thus the major functions of the EDI software are data conversion, data formatting and message communication.

EDI software is available for mainframes, mini computers, and micro computers. The requirements for implementing EDI include a computer of any type, a communication modem and appropriate software.

In addition a major requirement is that software should be capable of handling and controlling any incoming or outgoing EDI message to any number or combination of trading partners.

Such software is generally called EDI converter or translator and is totally independent of the computer applications that pass data to it or receive data from it.

**EDI solutions can be broadly configured into four categories:**

1. Stand-alone EDI converter software on PC which generate data with the help of data entry forms or screens.
2. Front-end of EDI gateway - connects EDI PC to the existing in-house computer and helps import/export flat-files into/from the application software.
3. EDI software co-hosting on in-house mainframe - Application program interface with EDI using API or FPI (File Programme Interface or File Bridge).
4. Using the EDI conversion and communication facility provided by third party Value Added Networks (VANs).

### 5.9.3 Benefits of EDI

- Faster payment process by eliminating mail time and data entry.
- Shorter ordering cycles by increasing the speed of each transaction.

- Increased employee efficiency by automating process.
- Lowered chance of input errors by eliminating manual entry.
- Stronger business relationship.

## 5.10 SMART CARD

### 5.10.1 What is a Smart Card?

A **smart card**, **chip card**, or **integrated circuit card (ICC)**, is any pocket-sized card with embedded integrated circuits which can process data. This implies that it can receive input which is processed — by way of the ICC applications — and delivered as an output. There are two broad categories of ICCs. Memory cards contain only non-volatile memory storage components, and perhaps some specific security logic. Microprocessor cards contain volatile memory and microprocessor components. The card is made of plastic, generally PVC, but sometimes ABS. The card may embed a hologram to avoid counterfeiting. Using smartcards is also a form of strong security authentication for single sign-on within large companies and organizations.

A Smart Card is a plastic card the size of a credit card with an integrated circuit built into it. This integrated circuit may consist only of EEPROM in the case of a memory card, or it may also contain ROM, RAM and even a CPU.

Most smart cards have been designed with the look and feel of a credit or debit card, but can function on at least three levels (credit - debit - personal information). Smart cards include a microchip as the central processing unit, random access memory (RAM) and data storage of around 10 MB.

A smart card is a mini-computer without the display screen and keyboard. Smart cards contain a microchip with an integrated circuit capable of processing and storing thousands of bytes of electronic data. Due to the portability and size of smart cards they are seen as the next generation of data exchange.

Smart cards contain an operating system just like personal computers. Smart cards can store and process information and are fully interactive. Advanced smart cards also contain a file structure with secret keys and encryption algorithms. Due to the encrypted file system, data can be stored in separated files with full security.

Organizations are steadily migrating toward this technology. The days are numbered for a single mainframe used for computing every directive. Today, the delegation of tasks is being transferred to small, but dedicated smart cards. Their usefulness may soon exceed that of the standard computer for a variety of applications due, in part, to their portability and ease of use.

The smart card is an electronic recording device. Information in the microchip can instantaneously verify the cardholder's identity and any privileges to which the cardholder may be entitled. Information such as withdrawals, sales, and bills can be processed immediately and if/when necessary; those records can be transmitted to a central computer for file updating.

Smart cards are secure, compact and intelligent data carriers. Smart cards should be regarded as specialized computers capable of processing, storing and safeguarding thousands of bytes of data. Smart cards have electrical contacts and a thin metallic plate just above center line on one side of the card. Beneath this dime-sized plate is an integrated circuit (IC) chip containing a central processing unit (CPU), random access memory (RAM) and non-volatile data storage. Data stored in the smart card's microchip can be accessed only through the chip operating system (COS), providing a high level of data security. This security takes the form of passwords allowing a user to access parts of the IC chip's memory or encryption/decryption measures which translate the bytes stored in memory into useful information.

Smart cards typically hold 2,000 to 8,000 electronic bytes of data (the equivalent of several pages of data). Because those bytes can be electronically coded, the effective storage capacity of each card is significantly increased. Magnetic-stripe cards, such as those issued by banks and credit card companies, lack the security of microchips but remain inexpensive due to their status as a single-purpose card. Smart cards can be a carrier of multiple records for multiple purposes. Once those purposes are maximized, the smart card is often viewed as superior and, ultimately, less expensive. The distributed processing possible with smart cards reduces the need for ever-larger mainframe computers and the expense of local and long-distance phone circuits required to maintain an on-line connection to a central computer.

Smart cards are defined by the ISO 7816 standards.

A "smart card" is also characterized as follows:

- Dimensions are normally credit card size. The ID-1 of ISO/IEC 7810 standard defines them as 85.60 × 53.98 mm. Another popular size is ID-000 which is 25 × 15 mm (commonly used in SIM cards). Both are 0.76 mm thick.
- Contains a security system with tamper-resistant properties (e.g. a secure cryptoprocessor, secure file system, human-readable features) and is capable of providing security services (e.g. confidentiality of information in the memory).
- Asset managed by way of a central administration system which interchanges information and configuration settings with the card through the security system. The latter includes card hotlisting, updates for application data.
- Card data is transferred to the central administration system through card reading devices, such as ticket readers, ATMs etc.

### 5.10.2 Benefits

Smart cards can be used for identification, authentication, and data storage.

Smart cards provide a means of effecting business transactions in a flexible, secure, standard way with minimal human intervention. Smart card can provide strong authentication for single sign-on or enterprise single sign-on to computers, laptops, data with encryption, enterprise resource planning platforms such as SAP, etc.

### 5.10.3 Smart Card Usage

The uses of smart cards are as versatile as any mini-computer. At a hospital emergency room, for example, the card could identify the person's health-insurance carrier and transfer all necessary information from the microchip to an admittance sheet. Tests, treatment, billing and prescriptions could be processed more quickly using the card. Major clinical findings could be added to the medical information section within the microchip.

In the U.S., smart cards are utilized in GSM mobile telephones, in DirecTV and EchoStar satellite receivers, and in the American Express Blue card.

### 5.10.4 Smart Card Operating Systems

Smart cards designed for specific applications may run proprietary operating systems. Smart cards designed with the capability to run multiple applications usually run MULTOS or Java Card.

**Table 5.1**

| Card | EEPROM Storage | Features |
|---|---|---|
| SLE4418 | 1KB | Write protect |
| SLE4428 | 1KB | Write protect, 2 byte security code |
| SLE4432 | 256B | 32B write-once memory |
| SLE4436 | 221b | 24 bit ROM, 40 bit PROM |
| SLE4442 | 256B | 3 byte security code, 32B write-once memory |
| ACOS1–1k | 1KB | Triple DES, Authentication, 8 byte PIN |
| ACOS1–8k | 8KB | Triple DES, Authentication, 8 byte PIN |

### 5.10.5 How does a Smart Card Reader work?

Smart Card Readers are also known as card programmers (because they can write to a card), card terminals, card acceptance device (CAD) or an interface device (IFD). There is a slight difference between the card reader and the terminal. The term 'reader' is generally used to describe a unit that interfaces with a PC for the majority of its processing requirements. In contrast, a 'terminal' is a self-contained processing device.

Smart cards are portable data cards that must communicate with another device to gain access to a display device or a network. Cards can be plugged into a reader, commonly referred to as a card terminal, or they can operate using radio frequencies (RF).

When the smart card and the card reader come into contact, each identifies itself to the other by sending and receiving information. If the messages exchanged do not match, no further processing takes place. So, unlike ordinary bank cards, smart cards can defend themselves against unauthorized users and uses in innovative security measures.

### 5.10.6 Communicating with a Smart Card Reader

The reader provides a path for your application to send and receive commands from the card. There are many types of readers available, such as serial, PCCard, and standard keyboard models. Unfortunately, the ISO group was unable to provide a standard for communicating with the readers so there is no one-size-fits-all approach to smart card communication.

**Each manufacturer provides a different protocol for communication with the reader.**

- First you have to communicate with the reader.
- Second, the reader communicates with the card, acting as the intermediary before sending the data to the card.
- Third, communication with a smart card is based on the APDU format. The card will process the data and return it to the reader, which will then return the data to its originating source.

**The following classes are used for communicating with the reader:**

- ISO command classes for communicating with 7816 protocol
- Classes for communicating with the reader
- Classes for converting data to a manufacturer-specific format
- An application for testing and using the cards for an intended and specific purpose.

Readers come in many forms, factors and capabilities. The easiest way to describe a reader is by the method of its interface to a PC. Smart card readers are available that interface to RS232 serial ports, USB ports, PCMCIA slots, floppy disk slots, parallel ports, infrared IRDA ports and keyboards and keyboard wedge readers. Card readers are used to read data from - and write data to - the smart card. Readers can easily be integrated into a PC utilizing Windows 98/Me, 2000, or XP platforms. However, some computer systems already come equipped with a built-in smart card reader. Some card readers come with advanced security features such as secure PIN entry, secure display and an integrated fingerprint scanners for the next-generation of multi-layer security and three-factor authentication.

Another difference in reader types is on-board intelligence and capabilities. An extensive price and performance difference exists between an industrial strength reader that supports a wide variety of card protocols and the less expensive win-card reader that only works with microprocessor cards and performs all processing of the data in the PC.

The options in terminal choices are just as varied. Most units have their own operating systems and development tools. They typically support other functions such as magnetic-stripe reading, modem functions and transaction printing.

To process a smart card the computer has to be equipped with a smart card reader possessing the following mandatory features:

- **Smart Card Interface Standard:** ISO 7816 is an international standard that describes the interface requirements for contact-type smart cards. These standards have multiple parts. For instance, part 1, 2 and 3 are applicable to card readers. Part 1 defines the physical characteristics of the card. Part 2 defines dimension and location of smart card chip contacts. Part 3 defines the electronic signals and transmission protocols of the card. Card readers may be referred to as conforming to ISO 7816 1/2/3, or in its simplified term, ISO 7816.
- **Driver:** This refers to the software used by the operating system (OS) of a PC for managing a smart card and applicable card reader. To read a smart ID card, the driver of the card reader must be PC/SC compliant which is supported by most card reader products currently available. It should be noted that different OS would require different drivers. In acquiring card readers, the compatibility between the driver and the OS has to be determined and ensured.

### 5.10.7 Desirable Features in a Smart Card Reader

Card Contact Types refers to how the contact between a card reader and a smart card is physically made. There are two primary types of contact: landing contact and friction contact (also known as sliding or wiping). For card readers featuring friction contact, the contact part is fixed. The contact wipes on the card surface and the chip when a card is inserted.

Smart card readers are also used as smart card programmers to configure and personalize integrated circuit cards. These programmers not only read data, but also put data into the card memory. This means that not only CPU based smart cards, but also simple memory cards can be programmed using a smart card reader. Of course the card reader must support the appropriate protocol such as the asynchronous T = 0, T = 1 or synchronous I2C protocols.

It won't take long before smart card readers become an integral part of every computer - and, subsequently, the lives of computer users. Computer systems with keyboards that have smart card reader/writer integration are also available.

Smart card readers are also accessible in the form of USB dongle. USB dongles are frequently used with GSM phones, which contain a SIM smart card. Additionally, phone numbers can be edited on a PC using the USB smart card dongle.

### 5.10.8 How does a Smart Card Programmer work?

A smart card is a mini computer which requires programming to run. A smart card doesn't contain an interface-like display or keyboard, so smart card readers are used to read or update the data to\from smart cards. Smart cards contain an operating system which provides a platform to run applications.

Smart card operating systems can be divided into two categories.

The first kind of operating system is based on the Disk Drive approach. This operating system contains an active memory manager which can load any file or application in the card on demand. The Card Operating System allows for active file allocation and management (JAVA Card OS is an example of this approach).

The advantage of Disk Drive based operating system is that the substitution cost for cards is less expensive, but the start-up costs are higher. This card requires a lager amount of free memory to cope with future application uploads. Due to the heavy use of expensive semiconductors, the cost is higher for these cards. The security infrastructure costs are also higher due to the multiple points of entry to card system functions.

The second approach treats the card as a secure device where, files and permissions to these files are all set by the admin. The only access to the cards is through the operating system. There is no other way to access the file structure. Data can be accessed as per the permissions set by the user. These operating systems can then run your applications. Commands can be passed to the card via the card reader and then the desired application can be accessed through the smart card.

One of the most commonly used smart card operating systems is JavaCard. It provides standard API to load and run java applets directly on a standard ISO 7816 compliant card. JavaCards enable secure and chip-independent execution of various applications.

The following requirement needs to be addressed before starting application development on smart cards:

- Smart card reader
- Software to communicate with the reader
- Software to communicate with the smart card
- Smart cards and smart card hardware

Before we address smart card programming, we have to be able to communicate with the reader. Because there are many different cards, there are many different readers. So proper interface implementation should be used for communication.

Once the above setup is complete, programming and application upload can begin utilizing the smart card. JavaCard allows applications to be loaded on demand.

In the early years of smart card development, each software application representing a product on a card was written for a specific card with a specific operating system, which in turn was specific to a hardware application. Sometimes a direct application was also installed without an operating system to make the card very specific to that application. However, the evolution of multiple application operating systems brought about a new era. JavaCard is an open, multi-application operating system for smart cards. Any person can develop applications using Java programming language. The java programs can run independently on the card and can be run on any ISO 7816 compliant smart cards. This way applications from various vendors can be combined, yet remain separate from each other.

The ISO 7816 standard was developed to define the mechanical and electrical characteristics along with the protocol for communication with the card. Unfortunately, the ISO group was unable to baseline a standard for communicating with the reader. So, in order to communicate with the smart card it is required to first understand the commands supported by the card. Then these commands need to be encapsulated into ISO standard commands.

Now, let's take a look of the APIs which allow us to send commands from an application to a reader. The reader communicates with the card where the actual processing takes place. From a technical standpoint, the key is a smart card API. This is a layer of software that allows an application to communicate with smart cards and readers from more than one manufacturer. The API allows the programmers or users the ability to select smart cards from multiple vendors. Running an application on multiple smart cards encourages competition among card vendors and the benefits of that competition include greater quality and lower prices.

The smart card programming API provides an application layer between the smart card and the application interface. The unit of exchange with a smart card is the called as Application Protocol Data Unit (APDU) packet. Communication with the card and the reader is performed using APDUs. An APDU can be considered a data packet that contains a complete instruction for the card or a complete response from a card.

The following are some of the classes provided for transporting APDUs and their function:

- Response
- Command
- ISOCommand
- ISOCardReader interface
- ISOCardReader

Sun has developed the Java Electronic Commerce Framework (JECF), an extension to the core Java platform that allows developers to easily and rapidly develop electronic commerce applications. JECF provides several classes that easily support communication with smart cards. It can be downloaded free of charge from Sun's website and can be used easily by a smart card programmer.

The smart card application development process includes following steps:

- **User requirements:** What does the user want to accomplish?
- **Software requirements:** Map user requirements to software requirements.
- **Architectural design:** Design the architecture of the solution.
- **Code Generation:** Create code as per the architecture.

- **Emulation:** Use emulators to test the code on virtual card.
- **In-card Emulation:** Run the code on actual card using card reader.
- **Verification and Validation:** It involves the testing.
- **Final testing and maintenance.**

### 5.10.9 What is Smart Card Software?

A smart card contains an integrated circuit (IC) chip containing a central processing unit (CPU), random access memory (RAM) and non-volatile data storage. Data stored in the smart card's microchip can be accessed only through the chip operating system (COS). Smart cards provide a secure, portable platform for "any time, anywhere" computing that can contain and manipulate substantial amounts of data, especially an individual's personal digital identity.

Smart cards are a type of mini computer with an operating system capable of running a variety of applications. JavaCard is a multi-application smart card operating system which provides an API with a set of standard classes through which common java applets can be loaded and executed on the smart card. Java's portability allows smart cards to become a general-purpose computing platform while creating a potentially huge market for application software and development. Due to the increasing demand for smart card applications, businesses and service providers are constantly looking for innovations and applications for available services that could utilize smart card technology.

There are various business interests who provide custom software for smart cards. Smart cards can bring security, convenience and ease-of-use to millions worldwide. With a growing market and technological advances, smart cards can be placed in a wide and growing range of applications from mobile telephony, CRM, rewards programs, as well as the development of next-generation applications and services. Smart cards are playing a growing role in application fields like electronic cash, bill pay, purchase, as well as security and access control.

Contemporary services provided by smart card solutions include:

- RFID Tags
- Fleet control and management
- Student and campus management
- Electronic cash (Mondex)
- Transportation charge applications
- Automatic fare collection applications
- Security and access management
- Financial services
- Affinity programs
- Cellular phones
- Set-top boxes
- Secure network access
- Communications applications
- Government programs

- Information security
- Physical access
- Transportation
- Consumer reward/redemption tracking
- Health card
- All-purpose student ID card

Other applications of smart cards and JavaCard technology include: mobile communication, mass transit, driving licensing, electronic toll collection, healthcare, information technology, etc...

### 5.10.10 History

The automated chip card was invented by German rocket scientist Helmut Gröttrup and his colleague Jürgen Dethloff in 1968; the patent was finally approved in 1982. The first mass use of the cards was for payment in French pay phones, starting in 1983.

Roland Moreno actually patented his first concept of the memory card in 1974. In 1977, Michel Ugon from Honeywell Bull invented the first microprocessor smart card. In 1978, Bull patented the SPOM (Self Programmable One-chip Microcomputer) that defines the necessary architecture to auto-program the chip. Three years later, the very first "CP8" based on this patent was produced by Motorola. At that time, Bull had 1200 patents related to smart cards. In 2001, Bull sold its CP8 Division together with all its patents to Schlumberger. Subsequently, Schlumberger combined its smart card department and CP8 and created Axalto. In 2006, Axalto and Gemplus, at the time the world's no.2 and no.1 smart card manufacturers, merged and became Gemalto.

Figure 5.1 shows A smart card, combining credit card and debit card properties. The 3 by 5 mm security chip embedded in the card is shown enlarged in the inset. The contact pads on the card enables electronic access to the chip.

Fig. 5.1

The second use was with the integration of microchips into all French debit cards (Carte Bleue) completed in 1992. When paying in France with a Carte Bleue, one inserts the card into the merchant's terminal, then types the PIN, before the transaction is accepted. Only very limited transactions (such as paying small autoroute tolls) are accepted without PIN.

Smart-card-based electronic purse systems (in which value is stored on the card chip, not in an externally recorded account, so that machines accepting the card need no network connectivity) were tried throughout Europe from the mid-1990s, most notably in Germany (Geldkarte), Austria (Quick), Belgium (Proton), France (Moneo), the Netherlands (Chipknip and Chipper), Switzerland ("Cash"), Norway ("Mondex"), Sweden ("Cash"), Finland ("Avant"), UK ("Mondex"), Denmark ("Danmønt") and Portugal ("Porta-moedas Multibanco").

The major boom in smart card use came in the 1990s, with the introduction of the smart-card-based SIM used in GSM mobile phone equipment in Europe. With the ubiquity of mobile phones in Europe, smart cards have become very common.

The international payment brands MasterCard, Visa, and Europay agreed in 1993 to work together to develop the specifications for the use of smart cards in payment cards used as either a debit or a credit card. The first version of the EMV system was released in 1994. In 1998 a stable release of the specifications was available. EMVco, the company responsible for the long-term maintenance of the system, upgraded the specification in 2000 and most recently in 2004. The goal of EMVco is to assure the various financial institutions and retailers that the specifications retain backward compatibility with the 1998 version.

With the exception of countries such as the United States of America there has been significant progress in the deployment of EMV-compliant point of sale equipment and the issuance of debit and or credit cards adhering the EMV specifications. Typically, a country's national payment association, in coordination with MasterCard International, Visa International, American Express and JCB, develop detailed implementation plans assuring a coordinated effort by the various stakeholders involved.

The backers of EMV claim it is a paradigm shift in the way one looks at payment systems. In countries where banks do not currently offer a single card capable of supporting multiple account types, there may be merit to this statement. Though some banks in these countries are considering issuing one card that will serve as both a debit card and as a credit card, the business justification for this is still quite elusive. Within EMV a concept called Application Selection defines how the consumer selects which means of payment to employ for that purchase at the point of sale.

For the banks interested in introducing smart cards the only quantifiable benefit is the ability to forecast a significant reduction in fraud, in particular counterfeit, lost and stolen. The current level of fraud a country is experiencing, coupled with whether that country's laws assign the risk of fraud to the consumer or the bank, determines if there is a business case for the financial institutions. Some critics claim that the savings are far less than the cost of implementing EMV, and thus many believe that the USA payments industry will opt to wait out the current EMV life cycle in order to implement new, contactless technology.

Smart cards with contactless interfaces are becoming increasingly popular for payment and ticketing applications such as mass transit. Visa and MasterCard have agreed to an easy-to-implement version currently being deployed (2004-2006) in the USA. Across the globe, contactless fare collection systems are being implemented to drive efficiencies in public transit. The various standards emerging are local in focus and are not compatible, though the MIFARE Standard card from Philips has a considerable market share in the US and Europe.

Smart cards are also being introduced in personal identification and entitlement schemes at regional, national, and international levels. Citizen cards, drivers' licenses, and patient card schemes are becoming more prevalent; For example in Malaysia, the compulsory national ID scheme MyKad includes 8 different applications and is rolled out for 18 million users. Contactless smart cards are being integrated into ICAO biometric passports to enhance security for international travel.

## 5.10.11 Contact Smart Card

Contact smart cards have a contact area, comprising several gold-plated contact pads, that is about 1 cm square. When inserted into a reader, the chip makes contact with electrical connectors that can read information from the chip and write information back. The ISO/IEC 7816 and ISO/IEC 7810 series of standards define:

- the physical shape
- the positions and shapes of the electrical connectors
- the electrical characteristics
- the communications protocols, that includes the format of the commands sent to the card and the responses returned by the card.
- robustness of the card
- the functionality

The cards do not contain batteries; energy is supplied by the card reader.

## 5.10.12 Electrical Signals Description

**Fig. 5.2:** A smart card pinout

**VCC :** Power supply input

**RST :** Either used itself (reset signal supplied from the interface device) or in combination with an internal reset control circuit (optional use by the card). If internal reset is implemented, the voltage supply on Vcc is mandatory.

**CLK :** Clocking or timing signal (optional use by the card).

**GND :** Ground (reference voltage).

**VPP :** Programming voltage input (deprecated / optional use by the card).

**I/O :** Input or Output for serial data to the integrated circuit inside the card.

**NOTE:** The use of the two remaining contacts will be defined in the appropriate application standards.

### 5.10.13 Reader

Contact smart card readers are used as a communications medium between the smart card and a host, e.g. a computer, a point of sale terminal, or a mobile telephone.

Since the chips in the financial cards are the same as those used for mobile phone Subscriber Identity Module (SIM) cards, just programmed differently and embedded in a different shaped piece of PVC, the chip manufacturers are building to the more demanding GSM/3G standards. So, for instance, although EMV allows a chip card to draw 50 mA from its terminal, cards are normally well inside the telephone industry's 6mA limit. This is allowing financial card terminals to become smaller and cheaper, and moves are afoot to equip every home PC with a card reader and software to make internet shopping more secure.

### 5.10.14 Contactless Smart Card

A second type is the contactless smart card, in which the chip communicates with the card reader through RFID induction technology (at data rates of 106 to 848 kbit/s). These cards require only close proximity to an antenna to complete transaction. They are often used when transactions must be processed quickly or hands-free, such as on mass transit systems, where smart cards can be used without even removing them from a wallet.

The standard for contactless smart card communications is ISO/IEC 14443. It defines two types of contactless cards ("A" and "B"), allows for communications at distances up to 10 cm. There had been proposals for ISO/IEC 14443 types C, D, E, F and G that have been rejected by the International Organization for Standardization. An alternative standard for contactless smart cards is ISO 15693, which allows communications at distances up to 50 cm.

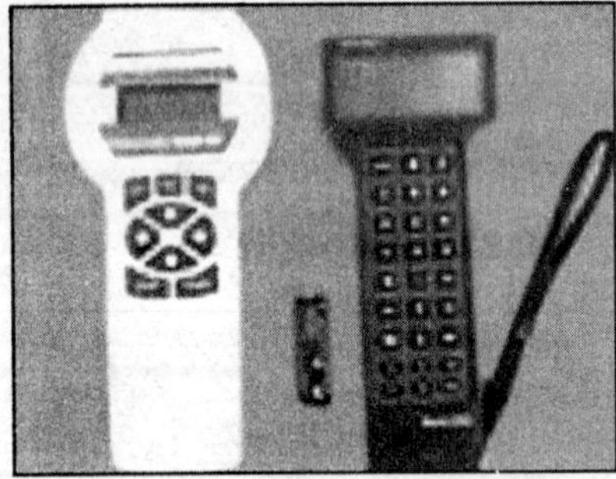

Fig. 5.3: Novosibirsk (Russia). Transport fare collection terminal CFT

Fig. 5.4: Smartcard being used to pay for public transportation in the Helsinki area.

Fig. 5.5: Compass Card being used to pay for public transportation in the San Diego area.

A related contactless technology is RFID (radio frequency identification). In certain cases, it can be used for applications similar to those of contactless smart cards, such as for electronic toll collection. RFID devices usually do not include writeable memory or microcontroller processing capability as contactless smart cards often do.

There are dual-interface cards that implement contactless and contact interfaces on a single card with some shared storage and processing. An example is Porto's multi-application transport card, called Andante, that uses a chip in contact and contactless (ISO/IEC 14443 Type B). Like smart cards with contacts, contactless cards do not have a battery. Instead, they use a built-in inductor to capture some of the incident radio-frequency interrogation signal, rectify it, and use it to power the card's electronics.

## 5.10.15 Cryptographic Smart Cards

Cryptographic smart cards are often used for single sign-on. Most advanced smart cards are equipped with specialized cryptographic hardware that let you use algorithms such as RSA and DSA on board. Today's cryptographic smart cards are also able to generate key pairs on board, to avoid the risk of having more than one copy of the key (since by design there usually isn't a way to extract private keys from a smart card).

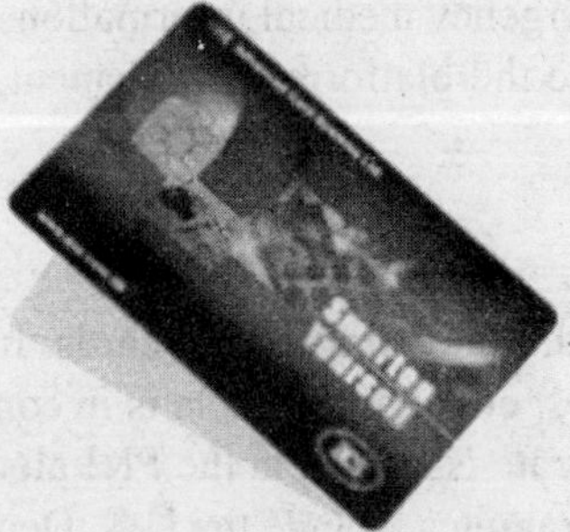

**Fig. 5.6:** A cryptographic smart card for PKI application

Such smart cards are mainly used for digital signature and secure identification, (see applications section).

The most common way to access cryptographic smart card functions on a computer is to use a PKCS#11 library provided by the vendor. On Microsoft Windows platforms the CSP API is also adopted.

The most widely used cryptographic algorithms in smart cards (excluding the GSM so-called "crypto algorithm") are 3DES (Triple DES) and RSA. The key set is usually loaded (DES) or generated (RSA) on the card at the personalization stage.

## 5.10.16 Applications

### *5.10.16.1 Computer Security*

The Mozilla Firefox web browser can use smart cards to store certificates for use in secure web browsing. Some disk encryption systems, such as FreeOTFE or TrueCrypt, can use smart cards to securely hold encryption keys, and also to add another layer of encryption to critical parts of the secured disk.

Smartcards are also used for single sign-on to log on to computers

Smartcards support functionality has been added to Windows Live Passports

#### 5.10.16.2 Financial

The applications of smart cards include their use as credit or ATM cards, in a fuel card, SIMs for mobile phones, authorization cards for pay television, pre-pay utilities in household, high-security identification and access-control cards, and public transport and public phone payment cards.

Smart cards may also be used as electronic wallets. The smart card chip can be loaded with funds which can be spent in parking meters and vending machines or at various merchants. Cryptographic protocols protect the exchange of money between the smart card and the accepting machine. There is no connection to the issuing bank necessary, so the holder of the card can use it regardless of him being the owner.

#### 5.10.16.3 Health Care (Medical)

Smart health cards can improve the security and privacy of patient information, provide the secure carrier for portable medical records, reduce health care fraud, support new processes for portable medical records, provide secure access to emergency medical information, enable compliance with government initiatives and mandates, and provide the platform to implement other applications as needed by the health care organization.

#### 5.10.16.4 Identification

A quickly growing application is in digital identification cards. In this application, the cards are used for authentication of identity. The most common example is in conjunction with a PKI. The smart card will store an encrypted digital certificate issued from the PKI along with any other relevant or needed information about the card holder. Examples include the U.S. Department of Defense (DoD) Common Access Card (CAC), and the use of various smart cards by many governments as identification cards for their citizens. When combined with biometrics, smart cards can provide two- or three-factor authentication. Smart cards are not always a privacy-enhancing technology, for the subject carries possibly incriminating information about him all the time. By employing contactless smart cards, that can be read without having to remove the card from the wallet or even the garment it is in, one can add even more authentication value to the human carrier of the cards.

The first smart card driver's license system in the world was issued in 1995 in Mendoza, a province of Argentina. Mendoza has a high level of road accidents, driving offenses, and a poor record of recovering outstanding fines. The smart licenses keep an up-to-date record of driving offenses and unpaid fines. They also store personal information, license type and number, and a photograph of the holder. Emergency medical information like blood type, allergies, and biometrics (fingerprints) can be stored on the chip if the cardholder wishes. The Argentina government anticipates that this new system will help to recover more than $10 million per year in fines.

Gujarat was the first state in India to introduce the smart card license system in 1999. To date the Gujarat Government has issued 5 million smart card driving licenses to its people. This card is basically a plastic card having ISO/IEC 7810 certification and integrated circuit, capable of storing and verifying information according to its programming.

## 5.11 EXPERT SYSTEM

An expert system is a computer program that simulates the judgement and behavior of a human or an organization that has expert knowledge and experience in a particular field. Typically, such a system contains a knowledge base containing accumulated experience and a set of rules for applying the knowledge base to each particular situation that is described to the program. Sophisticated expert systems can be enhanced with additions to the knowledge base or to the set of rules.

Among the best-known expert systems have been those that play chess and that assist in medical diagnosis.

A computer application that performs a task that would otherwise be performed by a human expert. For example, there are expert systems that can diagnose human illnesses, make financial forecasts, and schedule routes for delivery vehicles. Some expert systems are designed to take the place of human experts, while others are designed to aid them.

Expert systems are part of a general category of computer applications known as artificial intelligence . To design an expert system, one needs a knowledge engineer, an individual who studies how human experts make decisions and translates the rules into terms that a computer can understand.

An **expert system** is software that attempts to provide an answer to a problem, or clarify uncertainties where normally one or more human experts would need to be consulted. Expert systems are most common in a specific problem domain, and is a traditional application and/or subfield of artificial intelligence. A wide variety of methods can be used to simulate the performance of the expert however common to most of all are 1) the creation of a so-called "knowledgebase" which uses some knowledge representation formalism to capture the Subject Matter Expert's (SME) knowledge and 2) a process of gathering that knowledge from the SME and codifying it according to the formalism, which is called knowledge engineering. Expert systems may or may not have learning components but a third common element is that once the system is developed it is proven by being placed in the same real world problem solving situation as the human SME, typically as an aid to human workers or a supplement to some information system.

### 5.11.1 Expert Systems Topics

#### *5.11.1.1 Chaining*

There are two main methods of reasoning when using inference rules: backward chaining and forward chaining. Forward chaining starts with the data available and uses the inference rules to conclude more data until a desired goal is reached. An inference engine using forward chaining searches the inference rules until it finds one in which the if clause is known to be true. It then concludes the then clause and adds this information to its data. It would continue to do this until a goal is reached. Because the data available determines which inference rules are used, this method is also called data driven.

Backward chaining starts with a list of goals and works backwards to see if there is data which will allow it to conclude any of these goals. An inference engine using backward chaining would search the inference rules until it finds one which has a then clause that matches a desired goal. If the if clause of that inference rule is not known to be true, then it is added to the list of goals. For example, suppose a rule base contains

1. If Fritz is green then Fritz is a frog.
2. If Fritz is a frog then Fritz hops.

Suppose a goal is to conclude that Fritz hops. The rule base would be searched and rule (2) would be selected because its conclusion (the then clause) matches the goal. It is not known that Fritz is a frog, so this "if" statement is added to the goal list. The rule base is again searched and this time rule (1) is selected because its then clause matches the new goal just added to the list. This time, the if clause (Fritz is green) is known to be true and the goal that Fritz hops is concluded. Because the list of goals determines which rules are selected and used, this method is called goal driven.

#### 5.11.1.2 Certainty Factors

One advantage of expert systems over traditional methods of programming is that they allow the use of "confidences", also known as certainty factors. A human, when reasoning, does not always conclude things with 100% confidence: he might venture, "If Fritz is green, then he is probably a frog" (after all, he might be a chameleon). This type of reasoning can be imitated by using numeric values called confidences. For example, if it is known that Fritz is green, it might be concluded with 0.85 confidence that he is a frog; or, if it is known that he is a frog, it might be concluded with 0.95 confidence that he hops. These numbers are similar in nature to probabilities, but they are not the same: they are meant to imitate the confidences humans use in reasoning rather than to follow the mathematical definitions used in calculating probabilities.

### 5.11.2 Expert System Architecture

The following general points about expert systems and their architecture have been illustrated.

1. The sequence of steps taken to reach a conclusion is dynamically synthesized with each new case. It is not explicitly programmed when the system is built.
2. Expert systems can process multiple values for any problem parameter. This permits more than one line of reasoning to be pursued and the results of incomplete (not fully determined) reasoning to be presented.
3. Problem solving is accomplished by applying specific knowledge rather than specific technique. This is a key idea in expert systems technology. It reflects the belief that human experts do not process their knowledge differently from others, but they do possess different knowledge. With this philosophy, when one finds that their expert system does not produce the desired results, work begins to expand the knowledge base, not to re-program the procedures.

There are various expert systems in which a rulebase and an inference engine cooperate to simulate the reasoning process that a human expert pursues in analyzing a problem and arriving at a conclusion. In these systems, in order to simulate the human reasoning process, a vast amount of knowledge needed to be stored in the knowledge base. Generally, the knowledge base of such an expert system consisted of a relatively large number of "if then" type of statements that were interrelated in a manner that, in theory at least, resembled the sequence of mental steps that were involved in the human reasoning process.

Because of the need for large storage capacities and related programs to store the rulebase, most expert systems have, in the past, been run only on large information handling systems. Recently, the storage capacity of personal computers has increased to a point where it is becoming possible to consider running some types of simple expert systems on personal computers.

In some applications of expert systems, the nature of the application and the amount of stored information necessary to simulate the human reasoning process for that application is just too vast to store in the active memory of a computer. In other applications of expert systems, the nature of the application is such that not all of the information is always needed in the reasoning process. An example of this latter type application would be the use of an expert system to diagnose a data processing system comprising many separate components, some of which are optional. When that type of expert system employs a single integrated rulebase to diagnose the minimum system configuration of the data processing system, much of the rulebase is not required since many of the components which are optional units of the system will not be present in the system. Nevertheless, earlier expert systems require the entire rulebase to be stored since all the rules were, in effect, chained or linked together by the structure of the rulebase.

When the rulebase is segmented, preferably into contextual segments or units, it is then possible to eliminate portions of the Rulebase containing data or knowledge that is not needed in a particular application. The segmenting of the rulebase also allows the expert system to be run with systems or on systems having much smaller memory capacities than was possible with earlier arrangements since each segment of the rulebase can be paged into and out of the system as needed. The segmenting of the rulebase into contextual segments requires that the expert system manage various intersegment relationships as segments are paged into and out of memory during execution of the program. Since the system permits a rulebase segment to be called and executed at any time during the processing of the first rulebase, provision must be made to store the data that has been accumulated up to that point so that at some time later in the process, when the system returns to the first segment, it can proceed from the last point or rule node that was processed. Also, provision must be made so that data that has been collected by the system up to that point can be passed to the second segment of the rulebase after it has been paged into the system and data collected during the processing of the second segment can be passed to the first segment when the system returns to complete processing that segment.

The user interface and the procedure interface are two important functions in the information collection process.

### 5.11.3 End User

The end-user usually sees an expert system through an interactive dialog, an example of which follows:

**Q.** Do you know which restaurant you want to go to?

Ans. No

**Q.** Is there any kind of food you would particularly like?

Ans. No

**Q.** Do you like spicy food?

Ans. No

**Q.** Do you usually drink wine with meals?

Ans. Yes

**Q.** When you drink wine, is it French wine?

Ans. Yes

As can be seen from this dialog, the system is leading the user through a set of questions, the purpose of which is to determine a suitable set of restaurants to recommend. This dialog begins with the system asking if the user already knows the restaurant choice (a common feature of expert systems) and immediately illustrates a characteristic of expert systems; users may choose not to respond to any question. In expert systems, dialogs are not pre-planned. There is no fixed control structure. Dialogs are synthesized from the current information and the contents of the knowledge base. Because of this, not being able to supply the answer to a particular question does not stop the consultation.

### 5.11.4 Explanation System

Another major distinction between expert systems and traditional systems is illustrated by the following answer given by the system when the user answers a question with another question, "Why", as occurred in the above example. The answer is:

*A. I am trying to determine the type of restaurant to suggest. So far Chinese is not a likely choice. It is possible that French is a likely choice. I know that if the diner is a wine drinker, and the preferred wine is French, then there is strong evidence that the restaurant choice should include French.*

It is very difficult to implement a general explanation system (answering questions like "Why" and "How") in a traditional computer program. An expert system can generate an explanation by retracing the steps of its reasoning. The response of the expert system to the question WHY is an exposure of the underlying knowledge structure. It is a rule; a set of antecedent conditions which, if true, allow the assertion of a consequent. The rule references values, and tests them against various constraints or asserts constraints onto them. This, in fact, is a significant part of the knowledge structure. There are values, which may be associated with some organizing entity. For example, the individual diner is an entity with various attributes (values) including whether they drink wine and the kind of wine. There are also rules, which associate the currently known values of some attributes with assertions that can be made about other attributes. It is the orderly processing of these rules that dictates the dialog itself.

### 5.11.5 Expert Systems Versus Problem-solving Systems

The principal distinction between expert systems and traditional problem solving programs is the way in which the problem related expertise is coded. In traditional applications, problem expertise is encoded in both program and data structures. In the expert system approach all of the problem related expertise is encoded in data structures only; no problem-specific information is encoded in the program structure. This organization has several benefits.

An example may help contrast the traditional problem solving program with the expert system approach. The example is the problem of tax advice. In the traditional approach data structures describe the taxpayer and tax tables, and a program in which there are statements representing an expert tax consultant's knowledge, such as statements which relate information about the taxpayer to tax table choices. It is this representation of the tax expert's knowledge that is difficult for the tax expert to understand or modify.

In the expert system approach, the information about taxpayers and tax computations is again found in data structures, but now the knowledge describing the relationships between them is encoded in data structures as well. The programs of an expert system are independent of the problem domain (taxes) and serve to process the data structures without regard to the nature of the problem area they describe. For example, there are programs to acquire the described data values through user interaction, programs to represent and process special organizations of description, and programs to process the declarations that represent semantic relationships within the problem domain and an algorithm to control the processing sequence and focus.

The general architecture of an expert system involves two principal components: a problem dependent set of data declarations called the knowledge base or rule base, and a problem independent (although highly data structure dependent) program which is called the inference engine.

### 5.11.6 Individuals Involved with Expert Systems

There are generally three individuals having an interaction with expert systems. Primary among these is the end-user; the individual who uses the system for its problem solving assistance. In the building and maintenance of the system there are two other roles: thc problem domain expert who builds and supplies the knowledge base providing the domain expertise, and a knowledge engineer who assists the experts in determining the representation of their knowledge, enters this knowledge into an explanation module and who defines the inference technique required to obtain useful problem solving activity. Usually, the knowledge engineer will represent the problem solving activity in the form of rules which is referred to as a rule-based expert system. When these rules are created from the domain expertise, the knowledge base stores the rules of the expert system.

### 5.11.7 Inference Rule

An understanding of the "inference rule" concept is important to understand expert systems. An inference rule is a statement that has two parts, an if clause and a then clause. This rule is what gives expert systems the ability to find solutions to diagnostic and prescriptive problems. An example of an inference rule is:

If the restaurant choice includes French, and the occasion is romantic,

Then the restaurant choice is definitely Paul Bocuse.

An expert system's rulebase is made up of many such inference rules. They are entered as separate rules and it is the inference engine that uses them together to draw conclusions. Because each rule is a unit, rules may be deleted or added without affecting other rules (though it should affect which conclusions are reached). One advantage of inference rules over traditional programming is that inference rules use reasoning which more closely resemble human reasoning.

Thus, when a conclusion is drawn, it is possible to understand how this conclusion was reached. Furthermore, because the expert system uses knowledge in a form similar to the expert, it may be easier to retrieve this information from the expert.

### 5.11.8 Procedure Node Interface

The function of the procedure node interface is to receive information from the procedures coordinator and create the appropriate procedure call. The ability to call a procedure and receive information from that procedure can be viewed as simply a generalization of input from the external world. While in some earlier expert systems external information has been obtained, that information was obtained only in a predetermined manner so only certain information could actually be acquired. This expert system, disclosed in the cross-referenced application, through the knowledge base, is permitted to invoke any procedure allowed on its host system. This makes the expert system useful in a much wider class of knowledge domains than if it had no external access or only limited external access.

In the area of machine diagnostics using expert systems, particularly self-diagnostic applications, it is not possible to conclude the current state of "health" of a machine without some information. The best source of information is the machine itself, for it contains much detailed information that could not reasonably be provided by the operator.

The knowledge that is represented in the system appears in the rulebase. In the rulebase described in the cross-referenced applications, there are basically four different types of objects, with associated information present.

1. **Classes** — these are questions asked to the user.
2. **Parameters** — a parameter is a place holder for a character string which may be a variable that can be inserted into a class question at the point in the question where the parameter is positioned.
3. **Procedures** — these are definitions of calls to external procedures.
4. **Rule Nodes:** The inferencing in the system is done by a tree structure which indicates the rules or logic which mimics human reasoning. The nodes of these trees are called rule nodes. There are several different types of rule nodes.

The rulebase comprises a forest of many trees. The top node of the tree is called the goal node, in that it contains the conclusion. Each tree in the forest has a different goal node. The leaves of the tree are also referred to as rule nodes, or one of the types of rule nodes. A leaf may be an evidence node, an external node, or a reference node.

An evidence node functions to obtain information from the operator by asking a specific question. In responding to a question presented by an evidence node, the operator is generally instructed to answer "yes" or "no" represented by numeric values 1 and 0 or provide a value of between 0 and 1, represented by a "maybe."

Questions which require a response from the operator other than yes or no or a value between 0 and 1 are handled in a different manner.

A leaf that is an external node indicates that data will be used which was obtained from a procedure call.

A reference node functions to refer to another tree or subtree.

A tree may also contain intermediate or minor nodes between the goal node and the leaf node. An intermediate node can represent logical operations like And or Or.

The inference logic has two functions. It selects a tree to trace and then it traces that tree. Once a tree has been selected, that tree is traced, depth-first, left to right.

The word "tracing" refers to the action the system takes as it traverses the tree, asking classes (questions), calling procedures, and calculating confidences as it proceeds.

As explained in the cross-referenced applications, the selection of a tree depends on the ordering of the trees. The original ordering of the trees is the order in which they appear in the rule base. This order can be changed, however, by assigning an evidence node an attribute "initial" which is described in detail in these applications. The first action taken is to obtain values for all evidence nodes which have been assigned an "initial" attribute. Using only the answers to these initial evidences, the rules are ordered so that the most likely to succeed is evaluated first. The trees can be further re-ordered since they are constantly being updated as a selected tree is being traced.

It has been found that the type of information that is solicited by the system from the user by means of questions or classes should be tailored to the level of knowledge of the user. In many applications, the group of prospective uses is nicely defined and the knowledge level can be estimated so that the questions can be presented at a level which corresponds generally to the average user. However, in other applications, knowledge of the specific domain of the expert system might vary considerably among the group of prospective users.

One application where this is particularly true involves the use of an expert system, operating in a self-diagnostic mode on a personal computer to assist the operator of the personal computer to diagnose the cause of a fault or error in either the hardware or software. In general, asking the operator for information is the most straightforward way for the expert system to gather information assuming, of course, that the information is or should be within the operator's understanding. For example, in diagnosing a personal computer, the expert system must know the major functional components of the system. It could ask the operator, for instance, if the display is a monochrome or color display. The operator should, in all probability, be able to provide the correct answer 100% of the time. The expert system could, on the other hand, cause a test unit to be run to determine the type of display. The accuracy of the data collected by either approach in this instance probably would not be that different so the knowledge engineer could employ either approach without affecting the accuracy of the diagnosis. However, in many instances, because of the nature of the information being solicited, it is better to obtain the information from the system rather than asking the operator, because the accuracy of the data supplied by the operator is so low that the system could not effectively process it to a meaningful conclusion.

In many situations the information is already in the system, in a form of which permits the correct answer to a question to be obtained through a process of inductive or deductive reasoning. The data previously collected by the system could be answers provided by the user to less complex questions that were asked for a different reason or results returned from test units that were previously run.

### 5.11.9 User Interface

The function of the user interface is to present questions and information to the user and supply the user's responses to the inference engine.

Any values entered by the user must be received and interpreted by the user interface. Some responses are restricted to a set of possible legal answers, others are not. The user interface checks all responses to insure that they are of the correct data type. Any responses that are restricted to a legal set of answers are compared against these legal answers. Whenever the user enters an illegal answer, the user interface informs the user that his answer was invalid and prompts him to correct it.

### 5.11.10 Application of Expert Systems

Expert systems are designed and created to facilitate tasks in the fields of accounting, medicine, process control, financial service, production, human resources etc. Indeed, the foundation of a successful expert system depends on a series of technical procedures and development that may be designed by certain technicians and related experts.

A good example of application of expert systems in banking area is expert systems for mortgages. Loan departments are interested in expert systems for mortgages because of the growing cost of labour which makes the handling and acceptance of relatively small loans less profitable. They also see in the application of expert systems a possibility for standardised, efficient handling of mortgage loan, and appreciate that for the acceptance of mortgages there are hard and fast rules which do not always exist with other types of loans.

While expert systems have distinguished themselves in AI research in finding practical application, their application has been limited. Expert systems are notoriously narrow in their domain of knowledge — as an amusing example, a researcher used the "skin disease" expert system to diagnose his rustbucket car as likely to have developed measles — and the systems were thus prone to making errors that humans would easily spot. Additionally, once some of the mystique had worn off, most programmers realized that simple expert systems were essentially just slightly more elaborate versions of the decision logic they had already been using. Therefore, some of the techniques of expert systems can now be found in most complex programs without any fuss about them.

An example, and a good demonstration of the limitations of, an expert system used by many people is the Microsoft Windows operating system troubleshooting software located in the "help" section in the taskbar menu. Obtaining expert/technical operating system support is often difficult for individuals not closely involved with the development of the operating system. Microsoft has designed their expert system to provide solutions, advice, and suggestions to common errors encountered throughout using the operating systems.

Another 1970s and 1980s application of expert systems — which we today would simply call AI — was in computer games. For example, the computer baseball games Earl Weaver Baseball and Tony La Russa Baseball each had highly detailed simulations of the game strategies of those two baseball managers. When a human played the game against the computer, the computer queried the Earl Weaver or Tony La Russa Expert System for a decision on what strategy to follow. Even those choices where some randomness was part of the natural system (such as when to throw a surprise pitch-out to try to trick a runner trying to steal a base) were decided based on probabilities supplied by Weaver or La Russa. Today we would simply say that "the game's AI provided the opposing manager's strategy."

### 5.11.11 Advantages and Disadvantages

**Advantages:**

- Provides consistent answers for repetitive decisions, processes and tasks
- Holds and maintains significant levels of information
- Encourages organizations to clarify the logic of their decision-making
- Never "forgets" to ask a question, as a human might
- Can work round the clock
- Can be used by the user more frequently
- A multi-user expert system can serve more users at a time

**Disadvantages:**

- Lacks common sense needed in some decision making
- Cannot make creative responses as human expert would in unusual circumstances
- Domain experts not always able to explain their logic and reasoning
- Errors may occur in the knowledge base, and lead to wrong decisions
- Cannot adapt to changing environments, unless knowledge base is changed

### 5.11.12 Types of Problems Solved by Expert Systems

Expert systems are most valuable to organizations that have a high-level of know-how experience and expertise that cannot be easily transferred to other members. They are designed to carry the intelligence and information found in the intellect of experts and provide this knowledge to other members of the organization for problem-solving purposes.

Typically, the problems to be solved are of the sort that would normally be tackled by a medical or other professional. Real experts in the problem domain (which will typically be very narrow, for instance "diagnosing skin conditions in human teenagers") are asked to provide "rules of thumb" on how they evaluate the problems, either explicitly with the aid of experienced systems developers, or sometimes implicitly, by getting such experts to evaluate test cases and using computer programs to examine the test data and (in a strictly limited manner) derive rules from that. Generally, expert systems are used for problems for which there is no single "correct" solution which can be encoded in a conventional algorithm — one would not write an expert system to find shortest paths through graphs, or sort data, as there are simply easier ways to do these tasks.

Simple systems use simple true/false logic to evaluate data. More sophisticated systems are capable of performing at least some evaluation, taking into account real-world uncertainties, using such methods as fuzzy logic. Such sophistication is difficult to develop and still highly imperfect.

### 5.11.13 Expert Systems Shells or Inference Engine

A shell is a complete development environment for building and maintaining knowledge-based applications. It provides a step-by-step methodology, and ideally a user-friendly interface such as a graphical interface, for a knowledge engineer that allows the domain experts themselves to be directly involved in structuring and encoding the knowledge. Many commercial shells are available, one example being eGanges which aims to remove the need for a knowledge engineer.

### 5.11.14 Expert Systems and Artificial Intelligence

**Expert systems** are computer programs that are derived from a branch of computer science research called **Artificial Intelligence (AI)**. AI's scientific goal is to understand intelligence by building computer programs that exhibit intelligent behavior. It is concerned with the concepts and methods of symbolic inference, or reasoning, by a computer, and how the knowledge used to make those inferences will be represented inside the machine.

Of course, the term intelligence covers many cognitive skills, including the ability to solve problems, learn, and understand language; AI addresses all of those. But most progress to date in AI has been made in the area of problem solving — concepts and methods for building programs that reason about problems rather than calculate a solution.

AI programs that achieve expert-level competence in solving problems in task areas by bringing to bear a body of knowledge about specific tasks are called knowledge-based or expert systems. Often, the term expert systems is reserved for programs whose knowledge base contains the knowledge used by human experts, in contrast to knowledge gathered from textbooks or non-experts. More often than not, the two terms, expert systems (ES) and knowledge-based systems (KBS), are used synonymously. Taken together, they represent the most widespread type of AI application. The area of human intellectual endeavor to be captured in an expert system is called the task domain. Task refers to some goal-oriented, problem-solving activity. Domain refers to the area within which the task is being performed. Typical tasks are diagnosis, planning, scheduling, configuration and design.

Building an expert system is known as knowledge engineering and its practitioners are called knowledge engineers. The knowledge engineer must make sure that the computer has all the knowledge needed to solve a problem. The knowledge engineer must choose one or more forms in which to represent the required knowledge as symbol patterns in the memory of the computer — that is, he (or she) must choose a knowledge representation. He must also ensure that the computer can use the knowledge efficiently by selecting from a handful of reasoning methods. The practice of knowledge engineering is described later. We first describe the components of expert systems.

### 5.11.15 The Building Blocks of Expert Systems

Every expert system consists of two principal parts: the knowledge base; and the reasoning, or inference, engine. *The knowledge base* of expert systems contains both factual and heuristic knowledge. *Factual knowledge* is that knowledge of the task domain that is widely shared, typically found in textbooks or journals, and commonly agreed upon by those knowledgeable in the particular field.

*Heuristic knowledge* is the less rigorous, more experiential, more judgmental knowledge of performance. In contrast to factual knowledge, heuristic knowledge is rarely discussed, and is largely individualistic. It is the knowledge of good practice, good judgment, and plausible reasoning in the field. It is the knowledge that underlies the "art of good guessing."

*Knowledge representation* formalizes and organizes the knowledge. One widely used representation is the *production rule*, or simply rule. A rule consists of an IF part and a THEN part (also called a *condition* and an *action*). The IF part lists a set of conditions in some logical combination. The piece of knowledge represented by the production rule is relevant to the line of reasoning being developed if the IF part of the rule is satisfied; consequently, the THEN part can be concluded, or its problem-solving action taken. Expert systems whose knowledge is represented in rule form are called *rule-based systems*.

Another widely used representation, called the unit (also known as *frame*, *schema*, or *list structure*) is based upon a more passive view of knowledge. The unit is an assemblage of associated symbolic knowledge about an entity to be represented. Typically, a unit consists of a list of properties of the entity and associated values for those properties.

Since every task domain consists of many entities that stand in various relations, the properties can also be used to specify relations, and the values of these properties are the names of other units that are linked according to the relations. One unit can also represent knowledge that is a "special case" of another unit, or some units can be "parts of" another unit.

The *problem-solving model*, or *paradigm*, organizes and controls the steps taken to solve the problem. One common but powerful paradigm involves chaining of IF-THEN rules to form a line of reasoning. If the chaining starts from a set of conditions and moves toward some conclusion, the method is called *forward chaining*. If the conclusion is known (for example, a goal to be achieved) but the path to that conclusion is not known, then reasoning backwards is called for, and the method is *backward chaining*. These problem-solving methods are built into program modules called *inference engines* or *inference procedures* that manipulate and use knowledge in the knowledge base to form a line of reasoning.

The knowledge base an expert uses is what he learned at school, from colleagues, and from years of experience. Presumably the more experience he has, the larger his store of knowledge. Knowledge allows him to interpret the information in his databases to advantage in diagnosis, design, and analysis.

Though an expert system consists primarily of a knowledge base and an inference engine, a couple of other features are worth mentioning: reasoning with uncertainty, and explanation of the line of reasoning.

Knowledge is almost always incomplete and uncertain. To deal with uncertain knowledge, a rule may have associated with it a *confidence factor* or a weight. The set of methods for using uncertain knowledge in combination with uncertain data in the reasoning process is called *reasoning with uncertainty*. An important subclass of methods for reasoning with uncertainty is called "fuzzy logic," and the systems that use them are known as "fuzzy systems."

Because an expert system uses uncertain or heuristic knowledge (as we humans do) its credibility is often in question (as is the case with humans). When an answer to a problem is questionable, we tend to want to know the rationale. If the rationale seems plausible, we tend to believe the answer. So it is with expert systems. Most expert systems have the ability to answer questions of the form: "Why is the answer X?" Explanations can be generated by tracing the line of reasoning used by the inference engine (Feigenbaum, McCorduck et al. 1988).

The most important ingredient in any expert system is knowledge. The power of expert systems resides in the specific, high-quality knowledge they contain about task domains. AI researchers will continue to explore and add to the current repertoire of knowledge representation and reasoning methods. But in knowledge resides the power. Because of the importance of knowledge in expert systems and because the current knowledge acquisition method is slow and tedious, much of the future of expert systems depends on breaking the knowledge acquisition bottleneck and in codifying and representing a large knowledge infrastructure.

### 5.11.16 Knowledge Engineering

Knowledge engineering is the art of designing and building expert systems, and knowledge engineers are its practitioners. Gerald M. Weinberg said of programming in *The Psychology of Programming*: "'Programming,' — like 'loving,' — is a single word that encompasses an infinitude of activities" (Weinberg 1971). Knowledge engineering is the same, perhaps more so. We stated earlier that knowledge engineering is an applied part of the science of artificial intelligence which, in turn, is a part of computer science. Theoretically, then, a knowledge engineer is a computer scientist who knows how to design and implement programs that incorporate artificial intelligence techniques. The nature of knowledge engineering is changing, however, and a new breed of knowledge engineers is emerging. We'll discuss the evolving nature of knowledge engineering later.

Today there are two ways to build an expert system. They can be built from scratch, or built using a piece of development software known as a "tool" or a "shell." Before we discuss these tools, let's briefly discuss what knowledge engineers do. Though different styles and methods of knowledge engineering exist, the basic approach is the same: a knowledge engineer interviews and observes a human expert or a group of experts and learns what the experts know, and how they reason with their knowledge. The engineer then translates the knowledge into a computer-usable language, and designs an inference engine, a reasoning structure, that uses the knowledge appropriately. He also determines how to integrate the use of uncertain knowledge in the reasoning process, and what kinds of explanation would be useful to the end user.

Next, the inference engine and facilities for representing knowledge and for explaining are programmed, and the domain knowledge is entered into the program piece by piece. It may be that the inference engine is not just right; the form of knowledge representation is awkward for the kind of knowledge needed for the task; and the expert might decide the pieces of knowledge are wrong. All these are discovered and modified as the expert system gradually gains competence.

The discovery and cumulation of techniques of machine reasoning and knowledge representation is generally the work of artificial intelligence research. The discovery and cumulation of knowledge of a task domain is the province of domain experts. Domain knowledge consists of both formal, textbook knowledge, and experiential knowledge — the expertise of the experts.

### 5.11.17 Tools, Shells, and Skeletons

Compared to the wide variation in domain knowledge, only a small number of AI methods are known that are useful in expert systems. That is, currently there are only a handful of ways in which to represent knowledge, or to make inferences, or to generate explanations. Thus, systems can be built that contain these useful methods without any domain-specific knowledge. Such systems are known as *skeletal systems, shells*, or *simply AI tools*.

Building expert systems by using shells offers significant advantages. A system can be built to perform a unique task by entering into a shell all the necessary knowledge about a task domain. The inference engine that applies the knowledge to the task at hand is built into the shell. If the program is not very complicated and if an expert has had some training in the use of a shell, the expert can enter the knowledge himself.

Many commercial shells are available today, ranging in size from shells on PCs, to shells on workstations, to shells on large mainframe computers. They range in price from hundreds to tens of thousands of dollars, and range in complexity from simple, forward-chained, rule-based systems requiring two days of training to those so complex that only highly trained knowledge engineers can use them to advantage. They range from general-purpose shells to shells custom-tailored to a class of tasks, such as financial planning or real-time process control.

Although shells simplify programming, in general they don't help with knowledge acquisition. Knowledge acquisition refers to the task of endowing expert systems with knowledge, a task currently performed by knowledge engineers. The choice of reasoning method, or a shell, is important, but it isn't as important as the accumulation of high-quality knowledge. The power of an expert system lies in its store of knowledge about the task domain — the more knowledge a system is given, the more competent it becomes.

### 5.11.18 Bricks and Mortar

The fundamental working hypothesis of AI is that intelligent behavior can be precisely described as symbol manipulation and can be modeled with the symbol processing capabilities of the computer.

In the late 1950s, special programming languages were invented that facilitate symbol manipulation. The most prominent is called LISP (LISt Processing). Because of its simple elegance and flexibility, most AI research programs are written in LISP, but commercial applications have moved away from LISP.

In the early 1970s another AI programming language was invented in France. It is called PROLOG (PROgramming in LOGic). LISP has its roots in one area of mathematics (lambda calculus), PROLOG in another (first-order predicate calculus).

PROLOG consists of English-like statements which are facts (assertions), rules (of inference), and questions. Here is an inference rule: "If object-x is part-of object-y then a component-of object-y is object-x."

Programs written in PROLOG have behavior similar to rule-based systems written in LISP. PROLOG, however, did not immediately become a language of choice for AI programmers. In the early 1980s it was given impetus with the announcement by the Japanese that they would use a logic programming language for the Fifth Generation Computing Systems (FGCS) Project. A variety of logic-based programming languages have since arisen, and the term prolog has become generic.

### 5.11.19 The Applications of Expert Systems

The spectrum of applications of expert systems technology to industrial and commercial problems is so wide as to defy easy characterization. The applications find their way into most areas of knowledge work. They are as varied as helping salespersons sell modular factory-built homes to helping NASA plan the maintenance of a space shuttle in preparation for its next flight.

Applications tend to cluster into seven major classes.

#### *5.11.19.1 Diagnosis and Troubleshooting of Devices and Systems of All Kinds*

This class comprises systems that deduce faults and suggest corrective actions for a malfunctioning device or process. Medical diagnosis was one of the first knowledge areas to which ES technology was applied (for example, see Shortliffe 1976), but diagnosis of engineered systems quickly surpassed medical diagnosis. There are probably more diagnostic applications of ES than any other type. The diagnostic problem can be stated in the abstract as: given the evidence presenting itself, what is the underlying problem/reason/cause?

#### *5.11.19.2 Planning and Scheduling*

Systems that fall into this class analyze a set of one or more potentially complex and interacting goals in order to determine a set of actions to achieve those goals, and/or provide a detailed temporal ordering of those actions, taking into account personnel, materiel, and other constraints. This class has great commercial potential, which has been recognized. Examples involve airline scheduling of flights, personnel, and gates; manufacturing job-shop scheduling; and manufacturing process planning.

#### *5.11.19.3 Configuration of Manufactured Objects from Subassemblies*

Configuration, whereby a solution to a problem is synthesized from a given set of elements related by a set of constraints, is historically one of the most important of expert system applications. Configuration applications were pioneered by computer companies as a means of facilitating the manufacture of semi-custom minicomputers (McDermott 1981). The technique has found its way into use in many different industries, for example, modular home building, manufacturing, and other problems involving complex engineering design and manufacturing.

#### *5.11.19.4 Financial Decision Making*

The financial services industry has been a vigorous user of expert system techniques. Advisory programs have been created to assist bankers in determining whether to make loans to businesses and individuals. Insurance companies have used expert systems to assess the risk presented by the customer and to determine a price for the insurance. A typical application in the financial markets is in foreign exchange trading.

#### *5.11.19.5 Knowledge Publishing*

This is a relatively new, but also potentially explosive area. The primary function of the expert system is to deliver knowledge that is relevant to the user's problem, in the context of the user's problem. The two most widely distributed expert systems in the world are in this category. The first is an advisor which counsels a user on appropriate grammatical usage in a text. The second is a tax advisor that accompanies a tax preparation program and advises the user on tax strategy, tactics, and individual tax policy.

#### *5.11.19.6 Process Monitoring and Control*

Systems falling in this class analyze real-time data from physical devices with the goal of noticing anomalies, predicting trends, and controlling for both optimality and failure correction. Examples of real-time systems that actively monitor processes can be found in the steel making and oil refining industries.

#### *5.11.19.7 Design and Manufacturing*

These systems assist in the design of physical devices and processes, ranging from high-level conceptual design of abstract entities all the way to factory floor configuration of manufacturing processes.

### 5.11.20 Benefits To End Users

Primarily, the benefits of ESs to end users include:

A speed-up of human professional or semi-professional work — typically by a factor of ten and sometimes by a factor of a hundred or more.

Within companies, major internal cost savings. For small systems, savings are sometimes in the tens or hundreds of thousands of dollars; but for large systems, often in the tens of millions of dollars and as high as hundreds of millions of dollars. These cost savings are a result of quality improvement, a major motivation for employing expert system technology. Improved quality of decision making. In some cases, the quality or correctness of decisions evaluated after the fact show a ten-fold improvement.

Preservation of scarce expertise. ESs are used to preserve scarce know-how in organizations, to capture the expertise of individuals who are retiring, and to preserve corporate know-how so that it can be widely distributed to other factories, offices or plants of the company. Introduction of new products. A good example of a new product is a pathology advisor sold to clinical pathologists in hospitals to assist in the diagnosis of diseased tissue.

# Question Bank

## UNIT-1

1. Define the factors to be considered in designing of IT organizations.
2. What are the methods to identify customer's requirement?
3. Define the various elements of the IT System.
4. Explain the various objectives of infrastructure management.
5. Define the following terms:
   - Network Activities.
   - System management.
   - Technical activities, in concern with infrastructure management.
6. Give a brief summary of the Internet & its related terms.
7. What are the various types of storage devices? Explain each in detail.
8. What are analog computers? Give at least two examples of analog computers.
9. Explain the purpose of the: Control Unit, Memory Unit, Arithmetic logic unit in computer.
10. Explain various types of computers.
11. Explain in brief the various generations in computer technology.
12. Write a short note on Fifth generation of computer. What makes it different from Fourth generation computer?
13. Explain the difference between main memory and secondary storage.
14. Explain at least 4 input and 4 output devices.
15. What is IT infrastructure management? Explain in detail.
16. What are the various components of IT System?
17. Define the following terms:
    - Computer Network.
    - Network Topology.

18. Write short note on IT infrastructure Library.
19. Differentiate between:
    - Differentiate between the Input and output devices.
    - Differentiate between RAM and ROM.
    - Differentiate between Secondary memory and cache memory.
    - Differentiate between Hardware and software.
    - Differentiate between system software and application software.
    - Differentiate between primary memory and secondary memory.
    - Differentiate between static RAM and dynamic RAM.
    - Differentiate between compiler and interpreter.
    - Differentiate between high level language and low level language.
20. How can you perform the following:
    (a) Determine the customer's requirements.
    (b) Identify system components to manage.
21. Define the characteristics of client.
22. What is service desk?

## UNIT-2

1. Define service support process.
2. Describe various disciplines associated with service support process.
3. What is the importance of configuration management?
4. Describe the objectives of incident management.
5. Explain the various benefits associated with incident management.
6. What is IT service continuity management?
7. Explain the various benefits of IT financial management.
8. Explain the process flow diagram of IT service continuity management.
9. Why do we require IT financial management?
10. What is service delivery process? Define its various disciplines.
11. Define the basic goal of SLM (service level management) with the process objectives.
12. Draw the process flow diagram of SLM.
13. Define service level plan.
14. With the help of diagram explain the process involved in capacity management.
15. Illustrate the basic concept of availability management and how it is related to other process of what is Computer Forensics.

18. What are the three pillars of service quality measurement?
19. Explain activities related with capacity management.
20. Describe the benefits obtain from capacity management.
21. What are the basic problem associated with capacity management?

## UNIT-3

1. Define service support process.
2. Describe various disciplines associated with service support process.
3. What is the importance of configuration management?
4. Define problem management. What are its various benefits?
5. Describe change management. What are its various process?
6. Write a short on release management. What are its various benefits?
7. Explain incident management.
8. Explain various components of data storage and show its hierarchy.
9. What are the various characteristics of data storage?
10. What do you mean by disaster recovery?
11. Define database protection.
12. Explain bare machine recovery.

## UNIT-4

1. What are the different approaches to access management? Explain each of them.
2. Define intrusion detection. Explain the different types of intrusion detection systems.
3. How can you say that data backup is important for a business? What are the different types of backup? Explain them .
4. What is the purpose of release management.
5. What do you mean by information security? What is the role of identity management in information security?
6. How can you find out the footprints left by an intruder on your computer system?
7. Explain the difference between active and passive system in instruction detection system.
8. Define the working and types of firewall.
9. What is identity management?
10. What is IDM and how is it beneficial for the society ?
11. What are the possible problems in security?
12. Define security management process.

## UNIT-5

1. Define E-Commerece. What are the types of E-Commerece?
2. Explain in brief E-Business and its benefits.
3. What is the significance of using Smart Cards?
4. Write short notes on mobile communication.
5. Explain EDI in detail. What are its advantages?
6. What is Intellectual Property. What are the two branches of Intellectual Property?
7. Describe the classification of privacy law.
8. What is the importance of computer forensic?
9. Define computer forensic. What are its advantages & disadvantages?
10. What are the reasons for cyber crimes?
11. Explain Cyber crime ,its classification & prevention of cyber crimes.
12. What do you mean by Expert system?
13. Describe various applications of Expert system.